The Watcher
on the Cast-Iron Balcony

by the same author

The Watcher
on the Cast-Iron Balcony

AN AUSTRALIAN AUTOBIOGRAPHY

Hal Porter

faber and faber

First published in 1963
by Faber and Faber Limited
3 Queen Square London W.C.1
First published in this edition 1967
Reprinted 1971
Reissued in association with
Oxford University Press, 1984
Reprinted in this edition, 1986

Printed in Australia by
The Dominion Press-Hedges & Bell

ISBN 0 571 08179 7

© *Hal Porter 1963*

For
that best of friends
KENNETH SLESSOR

In a half-century of living I have seen two corpses, two only. I do not know if this total is conventional or unconventional for an Australian of my age.

The first corpse is that of a woman of forty. I see its locked and denying face through a lens of tears, and hear, beyond the useless hullabaloo of my début in grief, its unbelievable silence prophesying unbelievable silence for me. It is not until twenty-eight years later that I see, through eyes this time dry and polished as glass, my second corpse, which is that of a seventy-three-year-old man. Tears? No tears, not any, none at all. The silence of this corpse is as credible as my own silence is to be, and no excuse for not lighting another cigarette. I light it, tearless, while the bereaved others scatter their anguish in laments like handbills. I am tearless because twenty-eight years have taught that it is not the dead one should weep for but the living.

Once upon a time, it seems, but in reality on or about the day King Edward VII died, these two corpses have been young, agile and lustful enough to mortise themselves together to make me. Since the dead wear no ears that hear and have no tongues to inform, there can now be no answer, should the question be asked, as to where the mating takes place, how zestfully or grotesquely, under which ceiling, on which kapok mattress—no answer anywhere, ever.

In time, the woman, Mother, is six months large with me, and Dr. Crippen is hanged. In time, and missing Edwardian babyhood by nine months, I am born. I am born a good boy, good but not innocent, this two-sided endowment laying me wide open to assaults of evil not only from without but also from within. I am a Thursday's child with far to go, brought forth under the sign of Aquarius, and with a cleft palate. This is skilfully sewn up. In which hospital? When I am how few months old? By whom now dead or nearing death? No one, I think, no one living now knows. Thus secretly mended,

9

and secretly carrying, as it were, my first lie tattooed on the roof of the mouth that is to sound out so many later lies, I grow. I am exactly one week old when the first aeroplane ever to do so flies over my birthplace. On aesthetic grounds or for superstitious reasons I am unvaccinated; I am superstitiously and fashionably uncircumcised, plump, blue-eyed and white-haired. I have a silver rattle, Hindu, in the shape of a rococo elephant hung on a bone ring. I crawl. The *Titanic* sinks. I stand. The Archduke is assassinated at Sarajevo, and I walk at last into my own memories.

These earliest memories are of Kensington, a Melbourne suburb, and one less elegant than that in which I am born between the tray-flat waters of Albert Park Lake and the furrowed and wind-harrowed waters of Port Phillip Bay. The memories are centred in a house then 36 Bellair Street, Kensington. Of this house and of what takes place within it until I am six, I alone can tell. That is, perhaps, why I must tell. No one but I will know if a lie be told, therefore I must try for the truth which is the blood and breath and nerves of the elaborate and unimportant facts.

At the age of six I physically leave Kensington and 36 Bellair Street for ever, lightly picking up and taking with me Kensington and 36 Bellair Street. Until this very point in time a baggage of memories has travelled with me.

The moment of unpacking at hand I am astounded by the size and complexity of this child's luggage. Even now, a middle-aged man, I cannot unpack all: I have not yet the skill to unlade what a happy egocentric little boy skilfully jammed into invisible nothing.

Let me immediately reveal, in my largely visual recollections of this pre-six era, that my father and my mother are not visually alive to me as the young woman and young man they then are. I cannot see them. I remember the face of Father's gold pocket-watch, and the hair-line crack across its enamel, but not his; I remember exactly the pearls and rubies in Mother's crescent brooch but not her eyes. Except for Mother's singing, I cannot hear them; a mere little litter of words blows down the galleries of time, some of it aesthetically haunting, more of it unforgettably trite. I do remember his fatherliness and her motherliness, essences informed by their youth and vitality and simplicity in which I have every trust. Fatherliness, motherliness, youth, vitality and simplicity I would not now trust for a moment. Each can destroy. Each helps destroy my parents; each helps them lay waste about them. But, however omniscient the child, he dares not, particularly if he be first born, further blind the parents he has already blinded with his existence by showing that he knows they are dupes not only of himself but of nature. So, my parents, imagining their physical selves as clearly seen as they think they see themselves in looking-glasses, move with blind instinct about me and always towards me and my imperious ego. They play the fool for me. They put on voices. They spend money on rubbish, toys for their toy. They cannot know that they themselves are clouds only, symbolic blurs meaning certainty and warmth and happiness, slaves without faces in a small universe where everything else is exquisitely clear.

The detail!

The colour!

Except in dreams, neither detail nor colour has ever since been so detailed or coloured; the fine edge of seeing for the first time too early wears blunt. But the first seeing is so sure that nothing smudges it. Take Bellair Street.

Bellair Street, built about 1870, is a withdrawn street overhung by great plane-trees and is on the way to nowhere else. It is only several blocks long and, so far as houses are concerned, one-sided. This is because it is the last street, three-quarters of the way down, of several streets lying horizontally along the eastern slope of a ridge crowned with Norfolk Island pines, non-conformist churches of brick the colour of cannas or gravy-beef, and a state school of brick the colour of brick. The slope makes it necessary to ascend from the front gate of 36 along a path of encaustic tiles, next by eight wooden steps on to a front veranda which is therefore a long balcony balustraded with elaborately convoluted cast-iron railings. From this balconic veranda I look over the plane-trees towards a miles-off miles-long horizon composed of the trees of the Zoo, Prince's Park, Royal Park and the Melbourne University. There are the towers and domes of the University and the Exhibition Buildings, and countless nameless spires.

This prospect is less colonial Australian than eighteenth-century English in quality: billowy green trees, misty towers, even a shallow winding stream that starts and ends in obscurity like a painter's device. Southern Hemisphere clouds pile themselves up, up above, and take on Englishy oil-landscape tones, or steel-engraving shafts of biblical light strike down, or incandescent Mississippis of lightning. Between this romantic or dramatic background and the watcher at the cast-iron lace of the balustrade innumerable more sordid elements are disposed: paltry municipal parks like seedy displays of parsley; endless terraces of houses; endless perspectives of ignoble streets and, strange as palaces, many three-storeyed stucco hotels whose baroque façades topped with urns and krateres protrude here and there above an agitation of humbler roofs of slate or terra-cotta but largely of unpainted corrugated iron. Sometimes, brilliant and perfectly executed hailstorms load the gulches of the roofs with white. Sometimes, a sunset behind Kensington ridge is reflected in sumless distant windows like spots of golden oil. I seem to be often watching, now and again with Mother a shape behind my shoulder, but most often alone. This watching, this down-gazing, this faraway staring, is an exercise in solitude and non-involvement. Perhaps my relish for aloneness, that deep and quenching draught, a content I have at times wrestled ferociously with circumstances to pluck from the hubbub of gregariousness, explains why no human beings appear in memories of that fanned out landscape. Disdain and self-sufficiency have sponged them off. This landscape, transfixed and unpeopled, untouchable and mute and mine, is my first glimpse of a world I am to see far too much and yet not nearly enough of and into. Let my eyes, so sated and so deprived, turn from the scene and peer at closer matters.

Behind the watcher's back lies a more restricted world, tangible, cluttered, comfortable, a world from which I can pick up sections and smash them to smithereens. I am too much of a good boy to do this. It is, moreover, a sensual world I like more than my view but love less although it contains more love than I shall ever need or ever need to seek.

My parents are generous with their natural love, and exact no more from me than the barest minimum of sensible behaviour in gratitude for not eating me in a *fricassée* or giving me to the old-clothes-man. This lop-sided bargain, of whatever advantage to them then and none now, is of lasting advantage to me. It has fattened my confidence to the point where I can be treacherous to their conception of privacy. Had I been less loved, I could not drag them from their graves without warning, for the dead cannot wash behind their ears before appearing in public.

Behind the watcher's back, one each side of the wooden front door painted and grained to resemble some other wasp-coloured wood, lie the front bedroom (right) and the front room (left).

I am child of an era and a class in which adults are one tribe and children another, each with its separate rights and duties, freedoms and restrictions, expected gentlenesses and condoned barbarities, each with its special reticences and sacred areas. One area taboo to children is the front room. I am, of course, sometimes permitted to enter the congested sanctuary, a magnanimity that leaves me now, so far as I know, the one creature living who knows what was within. Its contents and their stylized arrangement are equally an aspect of the Australian lower middle class of the Great War years and my mother, an indictment of suburban vulgarity and my mother, and an indictment, too, of my father, marking him down as an indubitable Australian, one of a nation of men willing to live in a feminized house. My mother says, as Australian women say to this day, *my* dinner service, *my* doormats, *my* umbrella-stand, *my* pickle-fork.

Outside the door of *her* front room, Japanese wind-bells

hang from the passage ceiling, a dangle on threads of triangular and rectangular slices of glass from which air in motion splashes delicious scraps of sound. Thirty years later, in a brothel street by a canal in Osaka, I hear wind-bells through the giggles of drunkards and the sound of the samisen and, there, under paper lanterns large as oil-drums, see again the front room and its ritual garnishings.

There is the richly fringed saddlebag and Utrecht velvet suite. On its mainly magenta sofa leans a magenta velvet cushion on which three padded white velvet arum lilies poke out their yellow velvet phalli. A be-bobbled mantel-drape of magenta plush skirts the chimney-shelf burdened with Mary Gregories. There are an eight-sided occasional table on which an antlered buck of fake bronze attitudinizes sniffily, two gipsy tables, a bamboo music canterbury, a Renardi upright grand of Italian walnut before which sits a tri-legged revolving piano-stool. A dog-ended nickel fender and a yard-long set of nickel fire-irons, never used, weekly burnished, the shovel pierced almost to filigree, occupy the hearth. It is a room that bruises sound; in its air that suffers an inflammation the hoofs of horses passing on the asphalt roadway come wooden and weary to the ear.

On the other hand, the front bedroom, the parental one, is filled with a luminosity that seems to swing and sway like a bird-cage, white with a tinge of jade. Through this the hoof-beats click sharply and swiftly as though the roadway of Bellair Street is ivory, and the hoofs of carved ivory. This pretty-pretty evocation suggests that Mother has taste after all. It is scarcely so. It is what can be afforded of what offers when a young woman from the country becomes a suburban bride.

Nottingham lace curtains, whereon a self-conscious liaison of bracts of white fern and pendent bunches of white muscatels occurs, hang at the window, their scalloped edges skimming the leek-green linoleum blotched with white chrysanthemums. In the centre of one wall, and rigidly at right angles to it, a Venetian double bed of white enamel columns banded and curlicued with nickel asserts an importance as of a sacrificial altar or an operating-theatre table. On each side of the bed, dead parallel to the dead-straight hems of the dead-white quilt, lies a shaggy white mohair mat. A fourfold Japanese screen, reeds and cranes embroidered in greenish gold on linen, conceals a cabinet that contains the chamber-pot into which, sometimes, from my own next-door bedroom, I half-asleep hear, dispassionately yet with some interest, my father or my mother urinating. Sometimes, one later than the other, I hear them both. For some atavistic reason or because of some information obtained in the womb, it is easy to recognize who is engaged. It is only during this brief period of their and my lives that such opportunities to use my untainted animal hearing happen. Very little later, the ability to distinguish without hesitation or mistake whether, for example, Mother, unseen in the next room, is talking while lying down or talking while standing or talking while moving about or talking while sitting and brushing her hair, is an ability I lose. A child is forced to abandon purely animal faculties such as this one.

Now that the eye and the ear of the watcher have been brought closer enough to these humans who made my body it seems that Mother is revealed, in the furnishings of the front bedroom, as guilty of an intention to an inhuman scheme of Austral-*japonoiserie* until the eye swivels to the walnut duchesse dressing-table with its central swing-mirror and hinged side-mirrors, its many brass-handled drawers and bracketed shelves. On this piece of furniture, set out on doilies or crocheted runners, are evidences of humanity. Here lies the last of Mother's girlish vanity, although not the last of her girlishness. Here are the tag-ends of courting devices. Here are many objects soon to disappear, not because the fashion for them changes or Mother's vanity grows less but because, as the number of my brothers and sisters increases disproportionately to my father's income, time strikes them from her hands to replace them with more brutal weapons: the vaginal syringe, the breast-pump, the preserving-pan, the vegetable garden hoe, the sewing-machine nibbling stitches into boys' galatea blouses and flannel under-shirts, into girls' corduroy velvet dresses, serge skirts and pink cotton sunbonnets. Here, for a little longer, and to me for ever, lie tortoise-shell-backed brushes and tortoise-shell combs, curling-tongs, hair-curlers, hairpins, hairnets, and those soft sausages of hair-padding Mother calls rats. Here hangs the embroidered hair-tidy plump with combings; here hang three horse-tail-like switches of her own made-up hair. Here are all the other humble artifices she needs to construct a woman of the conventional shape of coiffure, smell and colour to appear, without diffidence, publicly as young wife and mother. Here are the hock-bottle-green flask of eau-de-Cologne, the atomizer, the two circular boxes of Swansdown Adhesive Powder, White and *Rosée*, the prism of French nail-polish, the disc of dry rouge, the cake of Castile soap in its china dish decorated with moss roses.

Because, already scrubbed, combed and decorated, I am often made to sit on the white Dante chair while my parents finish decorating themselves, my memories of the bedroom are detailed and accompanied by memories of those gesticulations that immediately preface outings: Mother's hands and arms soaring with sure and accidentally graceful movements to skewer on her hat with foot-long hatpins knobbed with enamelled flowers, imitation cairngorms, pear-shaped *Ballet Russe* pearls or *ersatz* cameos; Father trimming his nails with a mother-of-pearl-handled penknife; Mother buttoning her kid gloves; Father fixing through its special vertical buttonhole in his waistcoat either the gold watchchain from which hangs a sovereign or his silver chain which bears a shark's tooth rooted in agate. Gestures of going out—how indicative it is of three-, four- and five-year-old greed for experience that I should remember, forty years later, the gestures themselves but not the faces and voices of the man and woman making them, enlarged and brilliantly lit gestures, close-ups cut from context by the knife of a selfish, pleasure-seeking eye.

Going where?

Going in steam-trains or cable-trams, sometimes in cabs,

sometimes walking hand-in-hand with Mother or Father across streets where the crossing-sweeper pushes piles of horse-manure from before our feet, going to the places little Melbourne suburban boys of those years go with their mummies and daddies: the Museum, the Botanical Gardens, the Waxworks, Wirth's Circus, Punch and Judy shows, the Aquarium in the Exhibition Buildings, the Royal Park Zoo. The final stage in travelling to the Zoo is done in the last horse-drawn tram left over from an earlier age. Before I have seen a sheep or a cow, and many years before I see a kangaroo, I am familiar with elephants, camels, lions and leopards, with middle-class animals like the giraffe and the hippopotamus, old-fashioned nineteenth-century creatures. Indeed, all these entertainments are, in a sense, left-overs from Victoria's reign. Other animals like Charlie Chaplin are taking their places. The middle- and late-Victorian auras of the London originals on which they are modelled emanate from these pleasure places. Cole's Book Arcade, of which the lofty cast-iron galleries bisect two Melbourne blocks, has the common-sense yet engaging eccentricity that is Edward Lear's and the Englishman's. At the great entrance to the arcade with its architectural air of Waterloo Station, two small mechanical puppets, earnestly and rosily grinning like pot-boys from Dickens, jerk ceaselessly at crank handles which rotate into view successive boards advertising in rainbow colours The Largest Book Arcade In The World and its subsidiary attractions. These attractions have not always to do with books. I remember indoor cages of monkeys, tropical palms and tree-ferns, and an afternoon tea of cream horns eaten to the music of a small whining orchestra and, upstairs, in a first floor gallery supported by brass columns, tiers and seeming miles of gilt-poxed china figurines and curly vases with gilded handles.

Going where else?

Going to visit Grandfather Porter at seaside Williamstown, and being able to remember nothing of him externally except his wheelchair, the afghan that covers his knees, and his white military moustache nicotined tawny at the centre and smelling of wine. I remember my instant perception that, inwardly, he cares nothing for me. I consequently find him valueless even though he gives me a bronze statuette of Kwannon, the Goddess of Mercy. Behind the smudged façades of my parents are stacked almost visible quantities of security, of the emotional fodder and spiritual information I assume to be the truth and everlasting. Behind Grandfather's afghan and stained moustache stretches an emptiness I have not the need, tricks nor impulse to imprint with the patter of childish cloven feet. Anyway, babyish tricks and winning wiles would, I see now, have been of no avail; a blown-off leg, a Boer War medal and a voice like a bittern might have won him back from no man's land to the idiocy of affection, for Grandfather is consciously a Warrior and a Fine Old Gentleman and, deliberately, a Character. English, starting as a drummer-boy in the Crimean War, he has progressed to the wheel chair by such military steps as taking part in the looting of the Summer Palace in Peking, taking for his second wife a crack rifle-shot, and naming one of my uncles Martini-Henry. Militarism seems all to him; his hobby, before the wheel chair, is painting battle scenes. These large canvases illustrate no aspect of his own experience that is unfit to hang on a wall. Rape, gangrene, cholera, blown-out guts and bloody slaughter are absent. The paintings, in every shade of glossy brown, show neat soldiers, their helmets and plumes and cloaks and sabres exquisitely fresh, dreamily involved in some nineteenth-century battle. Caught at a moment of horrorless cessation, the finespun horses curvet like statue horses, their eyes limpid as madonnas'. The warriors pose in attitudes of languor. Here and there a brow is bandaged, the bandage immaculate except for one tiny carnation of rosewood-coloured blood. Usually these picnic-like siestas occupy the well-swept bed of a romantically rocky pass at whose gothic extremity is a golden-brown glaze of sky behind which no one but a superannuated God can be drowsing.

Uncle Martini-Henry, my father's brother, is married to Aunt Rosa Bona, my mother's sister. They too, as Grandfather does, live in Williamstown but in a new house in fashionable Victoria Street. Grandfather Porter and his rifle-shooting second wife, Father's stepmother, occupy an older, shabby, wind-tormented house at the edge of the Rifle Ranges on the bay's edge. The house seems guarded by two small cannon, and filled with cedar sideboards, wine decanters, glass-fronted bookcases and tarnished silver meat-dish covers. Where the walls are not covered with Grandfather's paintings there hang crossed swords and racks of muskets and rifles. Nothing grows in the sandy garden but tamarisks all leaning away from the sea.

Uncle Martini-Henry's and Aunt Rosa Bona's house, Australian Queen Anne in style, is of blood-orange-red tuck-pointed bricks. At the end of Victoria Street, which is lined by immature date-palms in picket enclosures, sand drifts on to the asphalt road from the beach with its tide-lines of shells and its wheeling and marching blue soldier crabs. On this beach Mother and Aunt Bona, squealing and holding up great handfuls of skirts and petticoats, take me paddling. Port Phillip Bay flickers many fringed, age-white eyebrows behind our backs as we return to Aunt Bona's house, the ridge ends of its alp-steep roof and false gables of Marseilles tiles infested by terracotta griffins, its bay windows and fanlights enriched by *art nouveau* leadlights.

At this stage of my recollections Aunt Bona appears continuously to wear a salver-sized black hat occupied by a whirlpool of yellow ostrich feathers. A string-thin golden chain hangs down her front. She and Mother call this front a bust. On the chain is a gold heart, fat as a fuchsia bud, with a ruby in it. Aunt Bona contains love and safety, not merely because of tribal relationship, but on her own account. The watcher perceives this, and that the brew, more diluted than that brimming Mother, and with a dash of wormwood, is nevertheless much the same brew and contains no poison of danger, of withdrawal or denial.

Uncle Tini has a large beetle-shaped opal on his watch-chain, a jinker with dahlia-red spokes, a jinker-rug of simulated ocelot lined by waterproofed black, and a horse called

Dolly. I find this mystifying because Father calls Mother Dolly which is mystifying enough as her real name is Ida. With a mocking intention I am later to recognize as part of her character she calls him Curly. His hair is as unrelentingly straight as mine.

Just as Aunt Bona's fund of certainty is noted by the watcher to be a paler extension of Mother's, the paleness expressed in empty garrulity, so too Uncle Tini's offering of simplicity is seen to be an extension of Father's. Obscurely puzzled and dubious as I am, even then, I am never puzzled or dubious enough to be wary of this simplicity in Father, nor aroused enough from my inborn placidity, when wariness does much later come, to fight it face to face until it is too late, and lives have been mildewed by it. The danger in Father's simplicity is that, years later, step by hidden ruthless step, it has transmuted itself to stubbornness, thence to simon-pure indifference, the final and most killing of self-treacheries. His ultimate destruction of himself and others by unfortified simplicity is something not foreseeable, but instinct, and observation of Father, warn me in time to give attention to my own inherited simplicity and indifference lest they shrivel me too down to an inhuman actor. When I do, much later, guess at the danger Father has passed from his body through Mother's into mine, I watch myself closely. It is hardly necessary. I have been watching myself, by this time, for too long, since the days of the cast-iron balcony. I have watched myself watching the small suburban creature, the uninnocent good boy.

He has a veranda with a view.

The view is unpeopled. It is his, and not a place for people to mar. It cannot be prised apart from his first rainbow, his first skyscape, first clouds and stars and sunshine showers and whirlwinds. It is eternally silent.

Nearer, at his foot, below the veranda, under the plane-trees, the footpath and the roadway do give up, from time to time, the sound of strange bright footsteps, of wheels stopping and starting, of the road-sweeper's shovel as it scrapes under the horse-manure, of the gipsy cries tearing at the throats of the fish-oh, the rabbit-oh, the tinker, the vendor of pegs and clothes-props. He hears whistlers come nearer and fade to nothing to make place for the next whistler and the next. Once he hears a barrel-organ. Once he hears a man singing nearer and nearer and then farther and farther, singing the same words over and over again so that he learns them:

> '*When the moon shines tonight on Charlie Chaplin,*
> *His boots are crackin',*
> *From want of blackin',*
> *And his trousers will need a little mendin'*
> *Before they send him*
> *To the Dardanelles.*'

Behind his back, in the house, Mother sings, at the same time and in the same tune:

'*When the moon shines tonight on pretty Red Wing. . . .*'

In autumn, when the bluestone street-drain is flooded with leaves, he sees, he hears, big pinafored girls, whose schoolbags ride their shoulder-blades, wading the rustles of leaves, and squealing falsely (he recognizes the falsity) or, floppy hats inclined inwards to each other, whispering secretively as tiger-lilies. At twilight, the lamplighter is known to be moving, never near, always far off, at one or other end of the street, unseen with his unseen wand that pins staid large stars into the street-lamps.

He has a house.

It contains many indications of Empire: small silk Union Jacks, a red-blotched map of the world, Pears' Soap, Epps's Cocoa, Lea and Perrin's Sauce, a chromo-lithograph of Edward VII and Queen Alexandra, Beecham's Pills, Mazzawattee Tea canisters and, stamped in purple inside wardrobes and drawers, the assurance *Manufactured by European Labour Only*. The house contains also many indications of a lower middle-class lavishness Australians regard as bare necessities. In the meat-safe are a sirloin, pounds of rump steak and cutlets. In the pantry are a case of apples, a pineapple, peaches, oranges and bananas. The shelves are lined with bottles of jam, with sauces, pickles, chutneys and jars of Rose's Marmalade. On top of the crammed vegetable rack lies a crescent of pumpkin on the cut surface of which is some large back-to-front lettering sucked from the newspaper it was wrapped in. This may be, for all I know, the heading from the news of the Czar of Russia's assassination. It is curious that these mundane and humbly lavish still lifes of food should be so clearly remembered for, never having experienced what hunger is, I have no recollection of ever performing, at that time, the act of eating anything except mandarins, strawberries and asparagus. There is my wooden egg-cup, my own egg-spoon with teeth-dents in its silver bowl, and no memory of egg-eating. There is the Sunday tea-table: white damask glossily starched, and bearing, as the table-napkins stiff as cardboard do, a design of swans and bulrushes; the salad bowl, cake-stands, jam dishes, pickle jars, sugar-castor and celery vase all of cut glass; the tiered electro-plated cruet; the silver trumpets of sweet peas; the butter knives, cake knives, jam spoons and Sunday bread-knife with mother-of-pearl handles, and silver-gilt blades and bowls engraved with florid scrolls and curly acanthus leaves —all the glitter and gleam of the setting for an Australian Sunday tea. I recall seeing the emerald green jellies inside whose fluted trembling are suspended grapes and straw-berries and banana slices; the pink-iced sponge-cakes flavoured with rose-water, the cream puffs, macaroons and lamingtons piled up; the ham coated in breadcrumbs and stuck with cloves at Father's end of the table and, at Mother's end, the highly peppered Sargasso of sliced cucumber, tomato, lettuce, onion and radishes sodden in Champion's Malt Vinegar which Mother imagines is a salad. Although no memory of sitting at the table and eating remains I must, of course, have eaten like a little boy.

He is a little boy.

He has a sheep-dog called Nigger.

Mother has brought Nigger from the country along with her linen sheets, crochet-rimmed pillow-shams, tea-cosies, crested silver forks and teapot and table-spoons, Rockingham dinner service and a collection of aprons graded in size and material to match every domestic duty: black Italian cloth for sordid tasks, white bibbed ones for cleaner tasks, small useless ones heavily embroidered or inset and edged with lace for more ceremonial occasions, symbolic garments of no use and on which no spot is permitted to fall. Nigger, the one living object of the trousseau, is older than the boy, so many years older that his teeth are abraded almost to the gums. Bulky as a wrestler, Nigger prefers a pretence of drowsing and dreaming prone rather than levering a burden of body to its bored legs. Seeming as old as Grandfather, Nigger is not unoccupied as Grandfather is. Wisdom, sympathy, forbearance, and a weary knowledge of which shade of kindness a mood demands, occupy Nigger. The boy kisses him as one kisses life; reluctantly but of polite necessity to kiss Grandfather is to kiss death.

Besides Nigger he has toys. He has a no-eyed Teddy Bear he kisses more than Nigger or anyone, a glass walking-stick, a wooden top, a skewbald rocking-horse with a real horse's tail, a paint-box, a slate with a walnut of sponge attached by a string, Cole's Funny Picture Book, a large india-rubber ball decorated with a shiny picture of a fair-haired boy like him playing with a large india-rubber ball decorated with. . . . The implications of the ball thus decorated tempt him to thoughts of never-ending diminution, to his first thoughts on the nature of infinity. In later life this absurd game engages his attention for a period until he reins back his mind to the fact that he is to deny any donation of other impermanent animals to the pattern his parents, impermanent animals, have donated him to.

He has Mother and Father.

Fortified by these possessions, these seemingly indestructible possessions, his belly full, his body neutralized by excellent health and proper degrees of warmth, he is freed for timeless and solitary behaviour.

He has, above and beyond all and everyone else, himself.

He presses the palms of his hands firmly on his eyeballs to make the phosphenes glide from the luminously veined dark he has brought into being. Glowing oval blots, rimmed with a blurred electric blue, swim out of the ornamented gloom, then, on the point of capture, slip sideways and upwards out of vision, to be replaced by others and others and others, all infinitesimally different—stemless flowers of his own manufacture.

It rains. He sits, neatly as a story-book boy, on the colonial sofa in the living-room. He watches the drops on the pane. For how long? For a little while? To this moment; he sits there watching to this very moment. He sees the drops writing their descents on the glass, wriggling in a pretence that they avoid linking with other drops, next swiftly darting to snatch other drops, to melt together and stream dying out of sight. 'Gentle Annie,' says his mother of the rain, in an informing tone. And then, again, abstractedly, 'Gent-le An-nie,' as though listening, not to the present rain but to a bygone rain and something else. Is Mother, he thinks, listening to her own English mother saying, 'Gentle Annie'? He thinks of the fair boy playing with the ball on the ball he plays with.

It is a sunny day. He has looked at the green fruit on the backyard tomato bushes or at a snail or at the view or under Nigger's tail. Is there nowhere else to look in the world? 'Go and look up the chimney,' says Mother, reminding him of a pleasure he always forgets to remind himself of. He lies on the rag rug, his head on the raddled bricks of the fireplace. In the blue at the chimney-top he finds a daytime star. He watches it, and watches too the black miniature cauliflowers of soot bloomed with indigo that grow in the chimney tunnel. Oh, to grow there! he thinks. Oh, he yearns, to fly there and nestle in the blue-black!

He looks out through the coloured glass panels of the living-room door, first at a ruby-tinged world, then at a yellow one, finally at a world blue as the blue of a castor-oil bottle. Oh, to walk there, to watch himself walk there, wandering off and away, the blue-haired boy holding the blue Teddy Bear, and disappearing among the boles of the blue plane-trees.

Mother has taught him of the coloured streets and the chimney star and Gentle Annie and the skirmishing raindrops.

It is Mother who directs him towards a form of animism shot through with Victorian moral maxims, and leavened by pitiless practicality. Under fly-papers unravelling like sticky curl-papers from the ceiling, and stuck with dead and dying flies (naughty flies?), Mother points out a free fly (a good fly?) wringing its hands clean and scrubbing its eyes. She recommends its attitude to cleanliness, and points out the cruelty of tearing the wings from flies, a thing he has never thought of doing let alone done. With mousetrap, cobweb broom or other destructive device in hand, Mother speaks, nevertheless, graciously of her intended victims, supplying them with such an air of respectability as to suggest they have the power to judge between good and evil, and that they possess souls. The mouse is at least clever, the spider industrious, the bee busy, and so on. Ant, caterpillar, moth, butterfly, the Gentle Annie rain, thunder, the winter plane-trees hung with uncountable ear-rings, Christmas beetles, flowers, have each and all, Mother implies, the natures and souls of human beings. To illustrate this she shows him how to strip petals from the pansy or the violet to reveal the green mannikin with an orange scarf about his neck and his feet in a mustard bath. She tears the lower lip from the antirrhinum to unveil the minute Virgin Mary standing inside with her long-sleeved tiny arms extended in compassion.

Mother teaches what she learned in her country town girlhood: to thread lilac flowers on broom straws, to make a poppy-show of small flowers in a matchbox, to cut from folded newspaper long chains of dancing men, to build houses of cards, to make wheels of interfitted matchbox drawers, to play a thousand simple games. One of these games he . . . I . . . can never forget.

It is night. The living-room fire wanes. I have never been out of bed later. Mother and I sit at the table, I in pyjamas with a cashmere shawl over my shoulders, she in nightgown and grey-blue wrapper. A long bedtime plait of hair hangs over her shoulder. Its end, tied by a piece of tape, lies on the furry table-cloth over which we bend to play Tit-Tat-Toe.

Eyes half-closed in a simulation of being closed, I make spiral movements above the slate on which Mother has drawn a spiral figure divided into numbered sections. I chant dreamily:

> '*Tit-tat-toe, my first go!*
> *Three jolly butcher boys all in a row!*'

The kerosene lamp is glowing and breathing like some warm golden animal. Now and then it blinks. It purrs. It almost utters a dim, kind word.

> '*Stick one up! Stick one down!*
> *Stick one in the dead man's ground!*'

The pencil pecks down softly and bluntly on the slate. My eyes, pretending merely to open, exaggeratedly strain wide open. When Mother adds the figures thus picked out, I win. I always do. I am aware she does not care a rap about winning. Nor, really, do I, but, since I think it will be cruel to her as well as giving myself away to tell her that I know she lets me win, I let her let me win. The fire crumbling apart like incandescent cake, the kettle on the hob droning itself to silence, the lamp exhaling itself and an era towards extinction, I feel, in memory, that Mother's face is never more peaceful. But it is unseen, unrecallable, alas, unrecallable. To be not able to recall that face of peace, at that moment, and yet to recall her face in death and not at peace, is an invitation to regret I dare not accept. Better far to regard the moments of lamp-lit peace as an accidentally charming illustration of mother-and-child indicative of nothing except nothing better to do, and displaying nothing except that mothers cannot help enacting motherhood nor sons sonliness.

Mother is, however, generally too vital and noisy, too young and on the go, to participate often in such scenes of family quietude. She is constantly singing. Years after, heart and head deep in children, her vivacity tampered with, she can still sing. Even on her deathbed she sings.

Her singing is, as often as possible, a comment on the situation of the moment. She chooses a song of which the words, in reference to the situation, have a touch of mockery, of sardonicism, even of sly larrikinism.

For example, the red-and-white ice-cream cart, and its horse wearing a palm-leaf hat from which dangles a fly-veil, and the velvet-trousered Italian with his little brass bell, are still in sight and hearing, two or three doors away, when Mother begins to sing, with a clarity and vigour implying a larky motive:

> '*Oh, oh, Antonio, he's gone away,*
> *Left me alone-io, all on my own-io. . . .*'

With her O-Cedar mop flourishing in a burlesque of housewifery—I can now understand that she is imitating a lick-and-polish slavey—she polishes on each side of the Axminster runner in the passage. The wind-bells tinkle, and she sings:

> '*I dreamt that I dwe-elt in ma-ah-arble walls*
> *With vassals and serfs at my si-i-ide. . . .*'

She is ironing: camisole ribbons, Father's shirts striped like exercise books, my sailor-collared blouses, starched petticoats of *broderie anglaise*, Richelieu table-cloths for occasional tables. As she bashes one flat-iron down on the gas-stove, and takes up the next, and rubs it with beeswax, she sings:

> '*She lives in a mansion of aching hearts,*
> *She's one of a restless throng,*
> *And the diamonds that glitter around her brow. . . .*'

She mocks thus the diamonds on her own brow, the diamonds of sweat; she comments thus on the ancestresses on the side of her mother's family who surely wore diamonds.

Once I hear her and Aunt Rosa Bona wrangle on and on for what seems a long time about an entertainment at Aunt's that Mother has no wish to go to. Her mild, 'No, Bona, really, dear,' becomes by stages a less and less mild negative. It reaches, 'I said, "No!" and I mean, "No!"' From under her tormented wheel of yellow feathers Aunt persists in nag-

27

ging. Suddenly, Mother begins to sing, softly but with a cold impertinence bordering on insult:

> '*I don't want to play in your yard,*
> *I don't like you any more....*'

Aunt Rosa Bona stops in her tracks, puts down the éclair, picks up her gloves, and is gone, shutting the front door with such deliberate noiselessness that, in suggesting a slam of explosive violence, it almost outmatches Mother's own obliquity.

'*The saucy little bird,*' Mother sings, '*The saucy little bird on Bona's hat.*'

Other people's words provide Mother with the means to express feelings at a tangent, to veil in song the fact that she suffers fools reluctantly. She is fearless enough to utter directly and cuttingly but prefers not to. It is often a means also of blunting her mockery of herself. Yet her singing does not always scoff or have a double edge. She burns away her feelings in a song that, however cheap, runs parallel enough to the moment's emotion, however lofty or sorrow-charged or airy-fairy.

Sometimes she takes me to the front room, opens the piano as one opening a coffin, lifts the camphor-scented strips of flannelette from the keys, removes her rings and flexes her fingers in the manner of a concert pianist, and plays with the prissiness of her convent training but with dash 'Rustle of Spring' or 'The Double Eagle March'. I am to discover that she plays very badly. Next, she plays the song she has taught me to sing, while I sing it affectedly, and know I am singing affectedly without understanding why I must.

> '*Oh wheah and oh wheah has mai little dog gone?*
> *Oh wheah, oh wheah is he?*
> *With his ears cut short, and his tail cut long,*
> *Oh wheah, oh wheah can he be?*'

I sing this several times with increasing affectation, mouthing and mincing insufferably in a style entirely my own.

I never hear, and am never to hear, Father sing, although

28

he is probably capable of the National Anthem or 'For he's a jolly good fellow' at Masonic gaudies or Country Week Cricket smoke-nights.

Mother sings as she fills the kerosene lamps; she sings knitting a tam-o'-shanter, polishing the brass front doorstep, mixing my Saturday morning Gregory Powder ('Just before the battle, mother') or slicing lettuce, in the fashion of the time, as fine as mermaid's hair. Sometimes, as when she is darning, the hole stretched taut over the mouth of one of the two wine-glasses mysteriously in the house, and used for nothing but darning, Mother's singing is saccharine and melancholy, 'Poor babes in the wood' or something similar, a lullaby to the fingers weaving the needle over-under-over, under-over-under. Sometimes, the song is wordless. She reclines on the sofa, her head hanging backward under a burden of pain, her hands pressing the hair away from her white temples which I rub with the little pillar of menthol that lives in a delicate acorn of pale wood. As I rub, she drones with a sort of scarcely audible wildness. Sometimes, when the late summer is soaked through and through with the smell of tomato sauce being boiled, and the kitchen seems littered with bloody colanders and wooden spoons, Mother's singing is way-up-yonder, operatic singing. Women, then, seem always to sing about the house: singing and aprons go together, the rolling-pin and 'Bonny Mary of Argyle', the scrubbing-brush and 'Alexander's Ragtime Band'.

On each side of 36 Bellair Street live hearable singers. There is Mrs. Easom on one side (34? 38?) and Mrs. Richmond on the other (38? 34?). At this moment the ear in my mind catches them still at it; Mrs. Easom, loud and rapid as a dictator, committing a tuneful barking into which silences drop arbitrarily to smash like the thick china bowls I conceive her smashing in a series of domestic rages; Mrs. Richmond mewling ceaselessly as though she crouches on her hunkers, not happy, not unhappy, under large, floppy, furry leaves the colour of cigars. There is an impression of unblinking bird's eyes.

Of Mrs. Easom little else remains but the memory of modulated yapping. No face. No shape. No gesture. Tall? Short? Nothing is remembered but her iron-coloured hair screwed around curling-pins of the same colour. The hair *aches*. I possess the untraceable information that she is a widow. This knowledge, another first experience for me, intimates that she disregards some rule of life by being Misterless, and is consequently more powerful than usual women like Mother, and not to be trusted. She has a daughter Elsie who is, I know, fat and warm although absolutely invisible to me now despite the fact that she takes me to my first cinema matinée at Newmarket. I must walk with this cosy space called Elsie, almost certainly holding vacancy's hand, under the plane-trees and lamp-posts, past the Town Hall with its veronica bushes, privet hedge and municipal lawns protected by dead cannon. The crimson plush edging the dress circle has the texture of my Teddy Bear. London, Hobart, Nice, Bombay, the plush on theatre balustrades has the same Teddy Bear texture—how could I not keep on remembering? I remember also two scenes from that first film I see in 1915. Because a house is on fire, red film is used; the actors jerk about in the ruddiness to the cinema pianist's violent music. Another scene is on blue film to point up the fact of night in which a surface of water reflects a moon to the long ripples of music from the front of the cinema. I yearn, as I do when watching through the coloured panes, to be immersed in that red or blue. I yearn for what an inbuilt cynicism forewarns me I shall never have: entrée to any world of imagination.

Of Mrs. Richmond there remains the feeling that she is, until her thorns show, safer than Mrs. Easom. An invisible but indubitable Mr. Richmond surrounds her like a scent. She is, as all adults are in my Kensington recollections, physically nebulous, but so vivid an impression persists of unwinking bird's eyes and sparrow-brown that it is safe to wager her small and intense. In time, very soon in time, she is to present me with the sentence of words that will unveil to me, for the first time, that adults can assume an attitude which seems one of distinction yet contains threats without definition, and perils to be skirted on deceitful tiptoe. This attitude, my parents, in those days, have neither the time, talent nor inclination to display. They may be foolish. They may be wise. They can be accused of stupidity or omniscience. Speaking charitably, their interests may be elsewhere, in, for example, their physical love for each other.

As I write this I mock the superstitious fear that the voices of my parents are pleading just beyond the frontiers of consciousness, 'Oh, forget us, forget us . . .' and, magnanimously or fervently, on my behalf, 'Don't give away your own secrets, my son, my son.' They plead, if they plead, without avail. Forget my father and my mother? I am them. I gush with a million others from the man's body, and become sole victor—while the man and woman still writhe and exult in each other—in a deadly Armageddon at the gateway of the woman's womb. I am ingrained, soaked, veined through and through with their overflow of virtue and sin from which I have bred my own evils and purities. And since, to augment their donations and my own manufactures, I have borrowed lavishly from the inescapable world, I have as many faults and graces as the world, as meagre a supply of graces and faults as the world. Forget? Forget them and thus forget myself and the world? Not yet, not yet.

As for giving away secrets: they are not secrets, and not worth keeping. If secrets, they are not mine. They are what someone else, somewhere else, at all times, knew, knows or will know.

Mrs. Richmond, bird-small or not, owns Pearlie and Victor. Pearlie is some age, perhaps eight or nine, which makes her a foreigner, a *big* girl, an arrangement of not predictable enough actions. She is a female, raw, undulcified by years or maternity. She is bossy, has large green-striped snapping teeth and a hairlike cascade of hair-coloured hair which sometimes conceals and contorts itself in curling-rags made from strips of old sheeting, but mostly undulates down from an enormous puffed-out bow of ribbon, usually workaday navy blue, ceremonially a shade of mauve that has the effect on my senses that biting a lemon has on my teeth. Victor is a horse of a different colour. Victor is my age. Victor is my first playmate and, though scarcely a friend and scarcely loved, is a first reading for the first rehearsal for the first scene of the first act in the long comedy of friends I am still stumbling through.

It is inevitable, it advances autobiography minutely and effortlessly, to come to another and yet another first experience. Even with memory patching what reality must have breached, it is certain that my cocoon is wearing, here and there, thin enough to permit intrusions on a good boy. These intrusions never really more than brush my goodness, though they tear the sheath surrounding it. They do nothing to innocence, for I have never possessed innocence. They give edges to intelligence, they refresh watching eyes. Victor is, for a time, They. Victor is many first experiences.

He is, for example, at eye-level. He is the right size, my size. He is easier to look at than ants and cockchafers. He is much more visible than adults. Whatever Mother and Father, and Aunt Rosa Bona auntishly doting and chirruping under her platter of feathers, may believe, I have never really seen their faces. I have seen no face until Victor's. It is one I can intimately examine for signs of his soul's and emotions' weather. Hitherto, I have caught the climate of people from the rays vibrating out of the space they make animate, from the colours of a voice, from the quality of their silences, even from the manner in which they inhabit the realm of their dark night and their sleep which is, to me, a mere shire in the realm of my dark night and my sleep.

Victor's is the first face to interpose its planes and complexities between me and instinct. This puts instinct on its mettle. We stare face to face at each other. I smell the sap-like scent from his nostrils. What I view, far far back, eternities back, behind the brilliant, curved jellies of his eyes is the future. We know instantly that we have only in common what every human has. Our confrontation is essentially a confrontation of primitive and unashamed warinesses; it could have been the meeting of sophisticated centenarians with nothing to lose and every hope of gaining. Do I gain? I gain indelible information, outside my power, then, to express in words, information on the beauties, surprises, tricks, evasions, lures and lunacies of the mobile mask. I find intimations of his and my and the world's mortality in the pinked edges of his teeth, the wet curling-open or the brutal pressing-together of his lips, the dark grape-like bloom about his eyes, the seeds of yellow wax in his ears, the flushings or wanings of blood under the envelope of skin. Intuitively I know all this will rot like a peach.

Because he is the same marvellously convenient size as I, we understand each other's eases and difficulties of locomotion, and hopes of levitation. We can therefore examine each other's machinery with no more and no less curiosity than we examine our own. We move from the revealed to the concealed.

Peter is the word current then, in our class, for penis. We barter Peters. Since we are similarly pink and white, the only new knowledge I gain is that I am not unique in construction or behaviour, and that Mr. and Mrs. Richmond, as represented by Victor's penis, are not as civilized as my parents as represented by mine. He has smegma. I have been taught to wash. These exchanges are conducted with directness and busy relish. They are also conducted in what goes for deep secrecy, behind the castor-oil plant in Victor's backyard or the latticed fernery overrun with smilax at the side of our house. Nothing has been said ever to me about the possibility of this sort of amusement occurring but I realize that it is one forbidden to adults. Between each incident I, at least, do not suffer from guilt. Once my trousers are on again my mind is with my body and eyes wherever elsewhere is. Guiltlessness and secrecy avail nothing. When, days or hours later, I am what is called 'playing with Nigger', Mrs. Richmond is suddenly there, above me. 'I know,' she says, 'what you and Victor have been doing.' I have met my first dangerous adult. Fathers and mothers rarely seem adult to their children, merely older, distorted by time, and dirty with the soot of years. As children themselves do, they condemn with a blow or praise with an embrace. I realize, quick as a flash, that Mrs. Richmond's attitude has no more end to it than her sentence has. The messing-about believed to be secret and sacrosanct to little boys is knowledge to her. Her sin and danger are that she adds nothing, neither dismay nor sympathy, horror nor explanation. Has Victor broken a child law and talked? Has God uttered? Has Mrs. Richmond spied and, having spied, waited to get *me*, to get me *alone*, to tell me that she knows what I knew?

Despite this sudden disclosure that there is an adult who is sinful enough not to punish sin, I do not waver or cringe. An atavistic extra eye opens within me. I almost shrug in an adult fashion. I certainly go on doing what I am doing— 'playing with Nigger'—deliberately cruelly trying to lever a saliva-slimy chop bone from between his worn-down teeth. He is pretending to be an amiable old dog about it but is really wearily angry, not because I am after the bone which neither of us cares about, but because he smells my nastiness of manner. He would like to savage me for this although he loves me.

I have been able to read Nigger since I could crawl. I begin to read adults more warily after Mrs. Richmond. I read much about all men as I turn the pages of Victor's nature. But Victor and all men are a mere fraction.

Mother teaches me to whistle 'My home in Tennessee' and 'Cockitee kissed the Quaker's wife', and to play 'Chopsticks' badly on the piano. I learn to stand on my head, carry vessels of liquid without spilling, and to compel obedience from objects once intractable: bootlaces, button-hooks, braces, door-handles, my bath-sponge and toothbrush, my water-colour brush, knots, drawers and Venetian blinds. Time is giving me, one by one, the skills by which I shall be able to work myself efficiently to death.

My older visible loves, the hand-washing fly, the modest violet, the busy bee, the Blessed Virgin in the antirrhinum, are joined by others such as the swallow, the cricket, the case-moth and the praying mantis. Mother introduces them and their puritanical but charming morals as though they

34

are persons. To supplement these visibles she sings or recites or tells into existence an unending train of beings: Bo Peep, Moses in the bulrushes, Hansel and Gretel, the Knave of Hearts, God, King Bruce and the spider, Rumplestiltskin, Mother's own Swiss pioneer father waving a cutlass at aborigines and crying out, 'Cut 'em! Slash 'em!', Puss-in-Boots, Grace Darling, Jesus Christ and the loaves and fishes. In this transplendent assemblage the more virtuous are less transplendent than the less virtuous; the animals behaving like human beings are more engaging than the human beings behaving like well-trained animals. Fairies are about, and indicate their presence by replacing with threepence one of my milk teeth left in a tumbler of water.

Into the midst of well-to-do fairies, talking cats, multiplying loaves and gingerbread cottages, floats a hat that is to cause the first quarrel I ever hear.

Mother takes the lid from the cylindrical hatbox of satiny white cardboard. Next, she lifts out sheet after sheet of tissue paper; the bedroom is animated by the snowy rustling, a sound that perfectly favours the texture, and the breathing and floating movements of the paper. I watch, and appreciate, the tenderness of the gesture with which she finally lifts out the hat. It is a thing of fragilities: fragility of colour, fragility of skeleton, fragility of material. Huge poppies of half-transparent silk, opalescently grey and pink, poise as though just alighted on one side and under the brim. Mother puts it on my outstretched hands to prove that this ghost of wire and chiffon is as light as air. Its price must be far heavier for, later, I hear Father swearing at Mother about hats and money. She swears back. Father swears again, more violently, and leaves the house, most violently slamming the front door. The wind-bells jangle hysterically.

'Hell and Tommy!' I hear Mother crying out to herself in two sorts of anger, one of showy and unconvincing noise, the other of pure rage, 'Hell and Tommy! The beast! The brute beast! The fiend from hell!'

From the living-room where I am calmly painting a rosella parrot in my painting-book, I hear her footsteps moving

35

about quickly in many directions while the wind-bells restore themselves to stillness. There is a pleasurable sense of more to come. The footsteps peck decisively to where, neatly dipping the point of my brush in crimson lake and listening like a dog, I await the next move.

Mother's hand descends from heaven, jams a hat on my head, and yanks me from the chair. I make a well-mannered squeak about my painting.

'Not a word,' says Mother, dressed for the street. 'Not a word. I shall buy you a new paintbox. I shall buy you a parrot. That man is a brute beast. He is a bastard.'

She rattles down her wedding and engagement rings into the plate holding the jardinière containing the maiden-hair fern in a pot.

'A *bastard*!' she pants. Without knowing what she means I find the new word interesting, and her noisy game exhilarating.

'I am leaving that man,' she says. 'I am no longer Mrs. Porter. I am Ida Ruff, *Miss* Ida Ruff. You and I and baby will live with Aunt Bona. Or on the beach.' This is more exhilarating a game. The tone of her voice tells me that we shall never live on beaches. To prove this so the front door opens, the wind-bells rattle off a glassy amused phrase, down the passage comes Father. He stands there.

'Keep the bloody hat,' he says flatly to hide an elation in winning by magnanimously losing.

Mother snatches up her rings openly as one snatching up cough-drops, and begins to weep while laughing, a weeping that is not for any reason such as pain or sorrow or even happiness but for femaleness.

The hat? Mother is never magnanimous. She keeps it. It goes back into its box, and is never worn, at least not publicly. Is this Mother's wicked way of also winning by losing? Does she sometimes, in after years, when she is alone in the house, and has some moment to herself in the crack-like interval between some task just finished and some other task just about to begin, lift it (that tender, tender gesture) from the tissue paper? Put it on? Examine her older face in the looking-glass, older under the new old-fashioned object that remains, paid for and unused, as a memento of two stubbornnesses? When she dies it is still in the box, and still beautiful. It may have been too beautiful ever to wear. I doubt that. Mother was a woman.

If I have time on my hands I have also time at my heels.

I cut myself, apparently deeply, between the forefinger and middle finger on my left hand. How? I do not know. Father carries me on his shoulders to Dr. Moss's at the corner of our block. The scar of two stitches is still on my hand. Blood? Pain? Stitching? I recall nothing. I do recall the undulating journey, Father acting the part of a nice camel smelling of tobacco, the plane-tree leaves stroking my head, the head of the tallest person in the world. I remember seeing, far below in the drain, the spent and broken carbide sticks from the swinging road lamps. I remember the Three Wise Monkeys in brass, and a brass pen tray with antlers, on Dr. Moss's table. Dr. Moss? No.

Father takes me to the barber to have my hair cut really short. When Mother dies there is found among her collection of keepsakes an envelope containing a cutting of the earliest floss from my head, and a lock from this more ruthless shearing of which adventure nothing remains with me but the memory of an advertisement for Milo Cigarettes which shows a woman smoking, and shelves lined with shaving-mugs of all sorts with the names of their owners pasted below them. The knowledge that Father carries back the clipping of hair to Mother is knowledge arousing curiosity. Does he ask the barber for it in a you-know-what-women-are way? Does he slyly pick it up from the barber's floor, and slip it in his vest pocket? One knows too much about one's parents to know all the truth.

My hair is cut like a schoolboy's. I go to school.

It indicates the placidity of my nature that it is an easy business, at least for me. For Mother?

Almost certainly dressed to the nines, absolutely certainly wearing a new pale blue linen hat, its starched brim upturned, elastic holding it on, I walk to school with Mother.

Eldest sons must have many first experiences at the same time that mothers have theirs: almost always it is the grown woman who is more mangled by the experience. The walk must have wrenched some of the greener leaves from the foliage of Mother's nature. It kindles me almost to skipping. On my left the airy prospect I have watched for years swings away, with its empty streets silent for ever, and for ever alluring to one side of my being. I carry a brown paper parcel. Newspaper parcels are common, and are not publicly carried. My genteel package contains no Woman's Magazine selection of vitamin-impregnated scraps but, wrapped in a table napkin, beef-and-pickle sandwiches, two slices of thickly-iced currant cake, a large black-and-white humbug, and a small bunch of grapes from the backyard vine. I carry also a blue enamel mug.

It is a sunny morning.

When we reach Dr. Moss's house and monkey puzzle tree on the corner, his pittosporum hedge is creamed over with blossom, sizzling with bees, shimmering with butterflies. Three cabbage moths spar with each other making jagged graphs above the seething hedge. Here we turn right, and begin to climb up the slope. We cross over several asphalt roads and basalt-cobbled back lanes. We reach the brick-walled schoolground. It is, metaphorically, a longer journey upwards than I think; for my mother, returning amputated, it must be a bitterly short one downhill—the uterus torn out, the cheeks of the heart flushed with resentment. Men, even little boys (which are what most men scarcely develop beyond), know more about women than women know about men or little boys. Men and little boys are more secretive than women, prostitute or nun, mother or virgin. I know Mother will be crying, or will have been crying, when I reach home.

I reach home. She has been crying. This is patent, yet she bothers to tell me so, and begins to cry again. She has told me of her tears to prove her motherhood and deprivation, as well as to start me into revealing what she does not know: did I behave like a manly little fellow and not cry, or did I behave like her own flesh's flesh and cry? She desires not either but both. Since I do not tender freely and, in an attempt to divert her, begin chattering about the pink chalk tick on my slate, she must ask. Did I cry? Somehow, and dreadfully, blind as Oedipus but wide awake as Odysseus, I stop her in her tracks. I feel her tears hiss dry like blood splashed on a stove. I sense some tender fibre violently strain and snap in the recesses of the woman who is pouring tea for me into a cup decorated with a gilt clover leaf, and on the saucer of which rest two arrowroot biscuits.

It is not until over thirty years later, my mother nearly twenty years dead, that my father accidentally lets me know what has happened to brake her. As she adds milk to the tea for the cropped warrior son returned from battle, for the bright son from the muddy fields, for My Son the King from his tour of assassin-riddled streets, have I, pleads Mother without pleading, have I cried?

'Fuck,' I say, 'fuck, fuck, fuck, fuck, fuck.'

My sixty-odd-year-old father, relating this, chuckles with dirty reminiscence, his face meantime creasing itself older, and looking too humanly ugly like one of Hieronymus Bosch's. Mother, who dies long before she learns the despicable rules of frankness, that subtlest dishonesty and deputy for truth, has said nothing ever of this incident.

No, I have not cried.

I have had a wonderful time.

I have been injected—deliberately, I now suppose, by some coarse rascal of an older boy—with the word meaning absolutely nothing to me except—oh, truth!—except that I guess it to be a word of the world, a masculine insult that is portable and powerful, an initiation ceremony word, an umbilicus cutter.

A wonderful, wonderful time! Mother can hardly have half-descended her slope of tears before I am in a jubilant and unusual fit of rage. I kick a schoolmistress many times on the shins. My subconscious now tells me she is grey-haired, and skinny to fragility, and that there are cloth-covered buttons on her skirt. In directing me to do something she must have

39

touched me with professional kind firmness. Rage is instant. The shock of malevolent toecaps against innocent older bone immediately calms me to regret and pity which I cannot express to her. I have never kicked a shin since.

There is an odour of children, underhand, tepid, and vegetable. There is the dry sliding and clicking of wooden beads along the wires of counting-frames. There is the squeal of pencils on slates as we draw parallel upright lines, an introductory exercise in handwriting. Mother, armouring me against the world, and hoping for my glory to be displayed, has long before taught me to write far beyond this infantile stage. I act the amateur. If I tell Mother, which I shall not, she will not understand my instinctive duplicity. She will be appeased, and will over-act on my behalf her real pleasure in teacher's pink chalk tick which I bear home to her on my slate with as much wily care as I bear home the filthy word. Tick may, in her final totalling, balance 'Fuck!' for, after all, the damage has been done before I parrot out the gross word; a crack must have run across the pattern of her reality as she retraces her high-heeled steps along the streets she has led her son through on the way to rites she would like to save him from but would fight like a lioness rather than have him denied.

At midday, the blue enamel mug loses itself or has itself stolen. It is the first thing I ever lose. Sometimes, in dreams, on beds in strange countries, I almost . . . almost . . . find it again. To replace the mug I find a silver bar brooch with an owl made of forget-me-not blue stones sitting on it. The day is altogether iridescent and heady and unforgettable.

What drives fever to its crisis is the abundance, an abundance as of Jesus's loaves and fishes, of other children. There seem millions, all of my height, and with my flexibility and speed and wildness. It is like discovering a frantic, sly, new tribe of me-sized and Victor-sized creatures. For some seconds after we are let out at afternoon playtime there is an atmosphere of cringing, of sidelong glances, deadly and assessing. Each instantly perceives on others the bridle-marks of that larger, less knowledgeable tribe that owns them, and

40

that they own. But the hands of the tribe of couples, of mother and father, mummy and daddy, mumma and dadda, mum and dad, ma and pa, are nowhere on the reins. Movement in any and every direction, flight to the corners of the earth, is possible. We do not fly, but we move. We stroll. We hop. We dart. We run. Brilliant-eyed, cold-eyed and hot-breathed, we begin to race, to course in faster and faster circles, not touching each other but *just* not touching each other. The invisible tendrils streaming from us brush electrically against those streaming from others. As I race I smoulder, flame, burst into love with the other animals flashing by me . . . no, not love . . . I flare fervently into an accord with them. Eyes dilate. Faces redden. Mouths open. There is the reek, dangerous and ruthless and cool under the delirium, of innocence. This, my lack, I recognize in those who possess it. Galloping the horses of our natures we wheel faster. We permit ourselves to touch. We begin to laugh, soundlessly and senselessly, each to itself. We begin to screech and scream. Now and again, as I speed about the brick-walled asphalt, Victor Richmond's face blazes towards me and past me. Although I know he and his face are as unfaithful as birds, familiarity gives him and his face greater beauty than the others. Victor and I tear open our mouths to shrill at each other. I see his crimson tongue, pointed and glistening at the tip, farther back swollen and vibrating with noise. It is noise itself in the form of flesh. I am enraptured.

This rapture with the tribe and Victor abates, of course, the next day and the day after and the day after that.

The days pass.

As part of a pack, I watch the pack and its monstrous rules. I perceive what I am not to see objectively until I am a man, that the pack practises pure evils men have civilized themselves from, cruelties not watered down by pity, truths not damped down by discretion. I watch. I commit nothing too much, and decidedly not myself, and watch.

I do not stay at Kensington State School for many months. Above my head, behind my back and outside my watching, my parents are up to something that is to leave me with

Kensington and 36 Bellair Street set out in a corner of my mind for the rest of my life, a sketch never to be coloured in, everything arranged for a game never to be played.

Of these months at school not much except happiness appears to have been considered a place in the luggage of the six-year-old. The Great War still in progress, Union Jacks proliferate. Two larger silk ones appear, crossed, behind the eight-day American clock on the living-room chimney-piece. Others protrude from vases. Lord Kitchener is on calenders. Mother has a Joffre blue blouse. There is a school bazaar. Pearlie Richmond and even bigger girls, disguised as Red Cross nurses, with trays hanging on halters from their necks, sell coconut ice, toffee apples, penwipers made from old flannel shirts, and heart-shaped pincushions of tomato-coloured velveteen. I get a little rolled-up Union Jack from the sawdust of the Penny Dip.

Along with 'Piggy-wig and Piggy-wee' and 'Now the day is over', we in the Infant Class are taught to sing 'Men of Harlech' and:

> *Anzac! Anzac! Long live that glorious name!*
> *Anzac! Anzac! That's where they play the game!*
> *And when the war is over,*
> *And peace again there'll be,*
> *You'll find one name on the scroll of fame,*
> *That's A, N, Z, A, C.*

As well, we learn a set of verses beginning:

> *On the twenty-fifth of April,*
> *Far across the sea,*
> *Our brave Australian soldiers*
> *Stormed Gallipoli.*

Do I understand any of this? I think not. Even inklings are doubtful. The war, with its Kaiser Bill, with its Huns brandishing aloft babies spitted on bayonets, or boiling down Allied soldiers to make soap, is no more than an en-grossing fairy-tale like Jack the Giant-killer. Two lines of doggerel somehow remembered from a broadsheet somehow in the house:

> *Der old Dutch king sits on der pump*
> *to vatch vhich vay der cat vill yump,*

have the same sort of meaning to me as 'Humpty Dumpty'.

But, of course, words such as Anzac and Gallipoli and digger, dropping into my mind and vocabulary as into the minds and vocabularies of all Australians, are the seed-words of a new growth. As overtones and implications and prides swell and burst, my generation and the generation it breeds are inevitably showered with the pollen from these explosions of Australian nationalism.

While huge banners are flapping and cracking ruddily over the horizon, and peppering down their dust of blood and glory and lies not to be disbelieved, while Mother and Father are planning to transplant me, I fall in love. The expression is absurd yet there seems no other. I am already involved in forms of love with Mother and Father, school, Angel and the Little Clowns in my weekly comic paper, with lightning and stars and the colour yellow, with the view from the front veranda, with my Teddy Bear, with an infinity of things. Any difference in the degree of love or its quality is imperceptible; there is merely difference in direction. How am I to tell, as much now as then, which of these emotions all called love, is of most value?

Now I am in love with a little girl.

Name?

Nameless.

Perhaps I never knew her name for its seems illogical to remember the names of people whose physical appearance is unrecallable—Mrs. Easom, Elsie Easom, Dr. Moss, Mrs. Rule the pastry-cook who makes me a cake with crystallized violets on it for my fifth birthday, Mrs. Richmond—and yet have no name for one whose appearance is far more vivid to me than that of someone I saw last week.

About my height she can be presumed to be also about my age. She wears a grey velvet dress with a lace collar spreading over her shoulders. The collar contains an extra hole on the right shoulder that is larger than, and not, a lace-hole. This distresses me, on her behalf, as though it were a wound that can give her pain. From under a straw hat, four long cylindrical curls pour richly and blackly down over the schoolbag on her back. Daisies with woolly yellow centres ring the crown of the hat. Her button boots and ribbed stockings are black. Together we walk down the sloping street from school. We walk with a slowness that is exquisite and treacherous for the more slowly we move the more my ecstasy increases, and increase will make my loss greater when Dr. Moss's corner is reached, and we must part. What do we say? Or are we talking to ourselves in the crystal cages of our hearts as we walk downwards on the strip of unasphalted ground between the asphalted roadway and the drain. This strip is sprinkled with thousands of minute fragments of broken glass and china which catch the light and mysteriously sparkle. I shall never again see such a carven and tender face, never such a white skin, never such ink-blue polished eyes and sooty lashes, never such a circular mole as sits above her lips. It is like a spot from a moth's wing. We walk, and I watch us walk, with trance-like gravity, mildly on out of each other's lives, giving up, as we part, two facsimile wraiths that remain together and continue walking together.

Is she the bear-like bunioned woman in the electric train to a cheap suburb, eyes closed, hairs coiling from the mole above her lips? Is she the drunken nagging voice and the spike heels in the midnight corridor of the sleepless nasty hotel? Is she the corseted harpy haggling over the P. and O. railing with the bum-boat boys at Port Said? Is she death and nowhere, the petal pressed in the monumental black book? Is she . . . oh, let us walk on, let the two wraiths walk on together, she in her grey velvet with the torn lace, she with the most beautiful face in the world, down the slope of jewelled dirt, over Bellair Street, taking to the air above the roofs and towers and spires and trees, while, below in 36 Bellair Street, the Renardi is packed into the zinc-lined piano-case.

The Renardi is packed first. The house then comes apart. The wind-bells are taken down and packed in the bread-crock with other fragilities. Patty pans, gravy-strainers, paste-cutters and egg-whisks are packed in the coal-scuttle. Carpets are rolled up. Linoleum is peeled from the floor: there are newspapers underneath. I find a pin with a black china head. Footsteps, footsteps, footsteps, and tea-chests everywhere, tell me that the house is nothing but a box filled with boxes. Oh, wheah and oh wheah has my little past gone? Mother sings:

> '*My old man said, "Follow the van!*
> *Don't dilly-dally on the way!"* '

She smacks me often in an *en passant* manner but none the less hard, and swears and cries when Father says she may not pack all her pot-plants. She packs them. Father says not to scrub the bloody house. Mother scrubs, saying, 'I'm not going to give that women the chance of saying. . . .'

Nigger takes to his kennel as to a sick-bed. The kennel is packed: pot-plants replace Nigger. I console him with con-sciously sympathetic huggings. He is dubious, even inclines to fear, but affects world-weariness. With subdued red lights in his eyes he permits consolation and is grateful, although aware that my consoling him is, in fact, my consoling me. He licks more consolation on me.

The luggage pantechnicon comes. Moustached men in baize aprons add their footsteps to the house filled with foot-steps. The beds are taken apart.

The wasp-coloured door of 36 Bellair Street is closed.

We are out in nowhere, adrift, without a spoon, a fire-place, a lavatory, a jug to put milk in or a wall to hang texts on.

Mrs. Richmond thrusts out a pink-knuckled hand from her brown shade and takes the key. I turn, horrified, to look at my view. Victor's eyes appear slap-bang in front of mine. The emptiness of a kind of shock in his eyes reflects the emptiness of the shock in mine. As the cab-horse clatters to a halt, Victor and I are made to kiss: I retain to this second the conviction that he has just finished eating boiled mutton shanks.

Dressed to kill, we are in the cab. Like an insignia of eldest sonship are Father's umbrella and three parasols of Mother's, rolled and strapped into a rug, which I am embracing.

DO NOT SPIT says the blue lettering on one of the tiles in the wall of the white-tiled tunnel at Flinders Street Station. We are through the tunnel, have walked along the country platform, and are in our compartment, sorted out and seated, before my distress begins.

I have not yet learned the value of telling lies and have therefore told none, although I am infinitely artful in committing lies by keeping my small mouth precisely shut. Now I am in difficulties. Because I am in my best clothes, in public and an unknown place, I wish to commit the lie of manliness and impassivity while, at the same time, committing the lie of being a happy-go-lucky child not really aware of what is going on, and therefore not subject to emotional disarrangement. I wrestle with myself and the shock of the shock in Victor's eyes, the painful rage which I can no longer guard or watch as closely as I should. It strives against restraint like a living body in mine.

On the platform, Aunt Rosa Bona beneath her hat of turbulent feathers is gaily arguing with Mother who is gaily arguing back, important facts disguised as nothings. Uncle Martini-Henry and Father return along the platform from not convincing Nigger who is, I know without being told and without ever having seen inside a luggage-van, standing in the luggage-van defiantly terrified and wishing for younger teeth and less training in good behaviour. The two men are briefly saying nothings to each other that sound like abrupt practicalities. The train yelps. A bell begins to ring. Uncle and Father shake hands. Aunt and Mother cry out sentences they have forgotten to chatter earlier. Father comes along the corridor, and enters taking out his tobacco pouch. The air is filled with many cries, and a god-like voice soaring above all noise, 'Gippsland train! All aboard!' We are ready. The train is ready. I fight desperately with the body within

46

me. The train begins to move. Like a page from a book the scene on the platform is ripped from view.

'Good-bye, Melbourne Town! Melbourne Town, good-bye! I am leaving you today,' sings Mother, oh, happily, happily.

I can lie no more. I erupt in tears. That they are the first tears I shed cannot be true. That they are the first tears I remember shedding is true. Equally true is that they are the first tears I shed for the impermanence of physical things and material things, for the world and its people, for shapes and their shadows, for sounds and their shadows, for life and its shadows, running and pouring away like water from a tap not to be turned off. Useless, useless, angry tears.

'But,' says Mother, not guiding me to lie a bellyache for my tearful torment of rage, not offering a suggestion of being over-tired, or needing to do number one, for me to snatch at, 'but, Laddie, you'll love the country.'

She leans across and gropes in my pockets for a handkerchief not there. She hands me her own, a composition of lace and eau-de-Cologne. While I soak up distress with this frivolous scrap, Mother smooths my hair with her gloved hand, a firm gesture expressing, 'Stop your nonsense! Stop this minute!' but also, 'Mother understands.' Whether she understands is doubtful: she is returning to the country she loves deeply; I am being plucked by the scruff from the asphalt streets, from the asphalt schoolyard, from beside the ever nameless, ever beautiful girl in the grey velvet dress and the lace collar in which there is an incurable wound, from out of Victor's eyes, from beneath Dr. Moss's hedge pulsating with wings, from the balcony edged in cast-iron.

If the tap cannot be turned off, tears can. Lace has my tears. My freckles are scented with eau-de-Cologne, and there are no tears left.

'Blow your nose,' says Mother. I blow it, observing as I do from my window-seat that we are decorously but busily hastening through a cutting draped in mesembrianthemum and decorated here and there with agave. I hand back the handkerchief and look about with my washed, my scalded

47

and scoured eyes and, for the first time, enclosed in that small, cushioned, luxurious cell, see my flesh and blood as outsiders might see them.

Little brother and smaller sister occupy the two seats next to me. My sister's short, fat, gaitered legs stick out horizontally as her doll's legs beside me. Sister and brother are as clear-cut and unimportant to me as ever. I obediently love them. I do not much like them. There is nothing new in them. Their heartlessness at the destruction of 36 Bellair Street is what I know of them. They live without watching. They do not remember. They do not care. If I am not careful, if I make one false sniff, my brother is going to stop carefully trying to unpick his tin railway engine, and say, high and clear, intending offence, his tone pointing up insult, 'Laddie was crying.'

Father is smoking his best pipe, a cricketing prize rimmed by silver, which he only smokes with slippers on at 36 Bellair Street. There is no 36 Bellair Street. He wears his tan boots and his pepper-and-salt suit, his second best. I am shocked that he has taken off his hat in a public place. He wears a ring with a golden shield on it. His eyes are blue, not watchful, and affect a secret twinkle intimating that he has a disdainful thought he will not share. His mouth moves about the stem of the pipe in a manner pretending wryness, in a self-browbeaten manner. He is glad that everything is over, he and his pipe. He closes his eyes as mine reach his. So *that* man is Father. I cannot guess that, at one stage of my life, I am going to look very like *that* man.

In the seat on his right sits Mother's lever-hasped bonnet box of ginger-coloured tin, formerly her mother's, and stands leaning the rug-rolled umbrellas.

In the window-seat on his left, opposite me, sits a woman. This is she, this is Mother.

At what age does one actually see, rememberably, one's mother, the full-length portrait? Whatever may be said by others, I write now that, with the small suburban backyards of Richmond and Hawksburn and Armadale slipping backwards, each with its lemon tree, and clump of chrysanthemum or Michaelmas daisy, I receive my first complete visual picture of her, and can find no reason not to believe myself.

During the years before I enter that compartment of that train and, with the unquestioned right of a selfish eldest son, sit in that window-seat, I have collected many jigsaw bits of Mother: the corn on each little toe, the 'filbert' finger-nails, the ear-ring piercings in her lobes, the four deep vaccination impressions, like bestial thumb-prints, on her left upper arm, the hair that lets down to her waist, the milk-white breasts with fragile sprays of blue veins on them at which I have seen two babies suckled.

Now my salt-peeled eyes see a woman wearing a dark grey travelling costume frogged with black braid, and a black toque on one side of which two crow-black wings stand up in a vee shape. Watching me watching her she unbuttons her black kid gloves, gentles them off, and smiles. Her teeth are white and strong. A minute semi-circular piece is chipped from one tooth. She loosens her veil, an almost invisible net spotted with flossy pill-sized pompons. She lifts it up over the front of the toque. I see the smile, which is occupying itself with slight variations of itself, more clearly, and that the Swansdown Adhesive Powder and the dry rouge have been used. I see her eyes, greenish-brown with lighter streaks and pinprick speckles of black raying from pupil into iris. These eyes are offering me something they have always offered and will continue to offer.

As though accepting for the first time what I have already accepted and shall continue to accept, I smile. It is a first performance of that sort of smile, and means nothing except awareness that I have given away myself and my tears for nothing new, that I am years older, though still six, and less wise. If a subject has been changed no words have been used to change it. I therefore cannot know if Father and Mother know more about me than I do, or nothing at all.

Mother opens the tin of Swallow and Ariell's Cream Wafers Aunt Rosa Bona gave her at Flinders Street, when I was years younger half-an-hour ago.

My brother and sister stir like serpents, and raise sugary voices, and stretch out their still-clean hands, plump and quivering delicately with greed.

In Mother's eyes the illimitable and never-to-be-withdrawn offer, which is about to be shuttered by more widely social and practical expressions, retains its intensity for a personal second more as she holds the Cream Wafers towards me.

Were I not bereaved she would give me the tin, saying, 'Pass the tin to the others, Laddie. One each. *One*. And mind you take the nearest.'

Since I am bereaved she extends the tin towards me as to a visitor capable of refusing.

Since I am bereaved I eschew good manners and, to my own horror, take three. Will Mother say, 'Greedy guts! There are others. Your eyes are bigger than your belly.'? She says nothing but says it so clearly that I blush. The train screams.

Eight hours later I am a country boy.

Eight hours later, and 170-odd miles from Melbourne, eastward over the horizon of my Kensington view, I am in a shire town, a Gippsland town, Bairnsdale, which is to be the scene of my petty comedy for the next ten years. It is one of those districts of which is said, 'The Scots have the land, the Irish have the pubs, and the English have the accent'. Here, I am to continue to foster placidity almost to the degree of smugness, to hasten neatly and evasively but happily, untouched and ever watchful, seeing everything and nothing, through the shadows I do not see of other people's lives.

To reach Bairnsdale we travel in a first-class smoking compartment which seems to me a miracle of ingenuity, and luxurious to a degree. Once my tears are dried, and my heart merely sore, everything entrances me: the bevelled looking-glasses, three a side, above the green leather seats with buttons deeply set in; the varnished jalousies sticky as honey; the hinged arm-rests the shape of éclairs; the nickelled *art nouveau* hat-pegs that reproduce the two too too sinuous curves terminating in hearts like leaves or leaves like hearts on the stamped metal ceiling; the foot-warmers; the corridor-door that slides sideways into a slot edged with green plush; the morocco-inset table-top that lives under the seat, and can be attached to the wall to make a legless table; the overhead racks of metallic net supporting our portmanteaux and dress-baskets; the two spittoons, shallow copper funnels set into the *fleur-de-lis* of the carpet, through the holes in the bottom of which my father unmissingly flicks the spent wax Vestas that nurture his pipe. None of us spits: in an era of spitters we are not a spitting family.

We pass through a colonial landscape composed, alternately, of almost untouched landscapes older than history, of hills older than the wind and trees older than the British Empire, and of landscapes no older than seventy years—

miles of paddocks grid-ironed by hawthorn or boxthorn hedges, and Anglicized by them and haystacks, hedge-elms, windbreaks of pine, clumps of oaks, willow-edged rivers with my first-witnessed cows wading the shallows, spillings of butter-cup and dandelion, Bo Peep sheep, turnip-fields, maize-paddocks, houses and fences shawled with Banksia roses and honeysuckle. Symbols of nostalgia, names of the Old World are cried out by blue serge porters ringing bells above the geranium-beds, or outside the refreshment rooms and bars, of gravelled or macadamized platforms: Oakleigh, Berwick, Beaconsfield, Trafalgar, Herne's Oak, Rosedale, Sale, Stratford (on Avon), Bairnsdale. We see no kangaroos or emus, those creatures from sixpences or insurance company letterheads, which most Australians, of that year as this, see as frequently as most Englishmen see lions or unicorns. The milestones are blue-enamelled rectangles advertising GRIF-FITHS' TEA in white enamel. Mile after mile of post-and-rail fences are lettered with injunctions to use DR. MORSE'S INDIAN ROOT PILLS, FLUXITE, SHINOLEUM, SILVER STAR STARCH, VELVET SOAP, WITCH SOAP (NO TOIL, ONLY BOIL) and KEEN'S MUSTARD.

To leave behind a minutely engraved and intricately tinted plan, to be compelled by adult practicality to leave it behind unfingered, seems one of the disadvantages of child-hood. How many shadows of broken desires must haunt and flicker among the shadows haunting and flickering in streets and lanes and cul-de-sacs children glimpsed, and yearned to walk to the end of, and never did. To be offhandedly pre-sented with another, a newer, differently embellished plan is one of the advantages.

My first sight of Bairnsdale strikes me breathless and still and smaller.

Space! Infinity! Light!

In Kensington, stuck on an asphalted suburban ridge at the rim of a panorama, I had seemed taller to myself, a spy suspended above luminosity. In Bairnsdale, I feel myself let loose at the centre of an immeasurable sphere. Pure light gushes and surges and soars away from my minuteness in every direction, upwards and ever upwards, inhabited by slicing swallows and creaking swans and stock-still hawks and pinprick larks; outwards to arch over the northern mountains in the thick blue of which are half-forgotten, tumble-down gold-mining towns occupied by mere handfuls of hill-billies incestuous as cats; outwards and east to curve for a century of miles over the farthest eucalypts and their sumless tons of glistening morocco leaves; outwards and southwards over the river-mouths, the swan-haunted lakes, the very South itself, and the world's felloe.

I seem no longer to look through a window or a microscope; I am in the window and under the microscope. That this new universe is no wider than the one I have seen in Victor Richmond's eye is too true to be good, and something, even now, yet to be learned again and again and again. That this immensity is seeming only, and a cage to escape from, and return to, and escape from to return to, will, in course, appear. I am hardly old enough to be unsophisticated: I am still six. I am still sophisticated seven or eight or nine or ten.

Set in that immensity exploding and geysering out in all directions we have a street and a house. In one respect only does Mitchell Street, Bairnsdale, resemble Bellair Street, Kensington: it is a shortish street on the way to nowhere. Rump-steak-scented smoke adorns its chimneys; to the sound of pianos making *Dardanella* or *Traumerei* huge candle-lit silhouettes on the holland blinds peel off their daytime layers to reveal the sad formlessnesses beneath.

Two blocks away, at one end of the street, are the river-cliffs overrun by buffalo grass, ivy and wild honeysuckle. Below, wide and olive-green, the heron-and-kingfisher-and-cormorant-peopled river moves slowly as blood south to the lakes. On the town side it is lined with weeping willows, horse chestnuts, red gums, plane-trees and apple orchards. On the farther side stretch the river-flats chess-boarded by hawthorn hedges, and stuck here and there with cowled hop-kilns of veal-pink brick or thin boards weathered brittle and the tint of platinum. Around these kilns stand conventions of

Blessed Thistle and Heraldic Thistle tall as men, or platoons of maize taller than Aztec priests, among which the Hindu farmers with beaked noses and long ivory teeth stroll in earth-coloured Western hand-me-downs and exquisitely folded turbans of exquisite pinks.

In that direction lies every opportunity for a boy to meet death; by drowning in the bream- and mullet-choked currents sleepy as death yet concealing snags and plumbless depths, by hurtling through the rotten upper floors of the kilns, by eating raw toadstools instead of raw mushrooms, by a surfeit of blackberries or stolen apples, by snakes or scorpions.

At the other end of the street, two doors and a roads-width away from our house, are the Tannies. The Tannies are several acres of land set apart by civic pioneers, who had foreseen all but Progress, to be Botanical Gardens. Under the retrogressions of Progress the scheme has faltered but the small forest of pines, oaks, elms, birches and poplars has grown of its own simple account to a magnificent miniature of Windsor Great Park, an open aviary for thornbills, silvereyes and magpies.

In its direction death for a boy is equally available: to plummet forty feet from the top of a nest-riddled European tree to the summer-hard Australian ground pierced by cicada holes, to be felled by a falling oak limb gnarled and mighty as Gog's leg, to sink mouth-over in the Tannies' swamp which is rumoured to be quicksand, and smells of stale mud and smart-grass, to be venereally poisoned by trying to blow up into balloons the French-letters which the provincial lovers and adulterers of spring and summer abandon on the grass they have flattened like hare forms by their nocturnal activities.

Until my fervour for climbing, fishing, bird-nesting, mushrooming, fruit-stealing and bodily recklessness runs dry, I embrace every one, and others beside, of these opportunities for doom, and come through with little but bee-stings, miniscule Great Britains of scars on my knees, and bare-foot soles impervious as pigskin.

Mitchell Street connecting these two perilous and enchanting areas is a tunnel of elms. Its gravelled roadway, weedy edges, grassy footpaths, open drains of mossy brickwork crossed by red-gum foot-bridges, all seem to me to compose a perfectly situated street in which our house is perfectly situated four doors away from a Chinese joss-house no longer in use, and diagonally opposite The Common.

Mother, no sooner have we left the train, and the station chockablock with milk-cans and crates of ducks, and the sleepier, springier, country cab, makes her nest again. This occurs with the speed of miracle: the cab draws up—hey presto!—the house is furnished, and the kettle boiling. I have what is surely an illusion that the first thing packed in Kensington, in that house with its number, is the first thing unpacked in the country house that has and needs no number: the most useless machine in the building, the Renardi. The piano-case is put in the stable. The shabby stable for which we can never afford the rich kernel of a horse remains the piano-case's, and is one of the fascinating unsuburban things I endlessly, noiselessly discuss with myself as though tracking down the mystery of creation: the differences between Kensington and Bairnsdale. How these differences stimulate me who suffers nothing from them!

There is no porcelain kitchen-sink. Mother now uses a tin washing-up dish, stacking the wet dishes on a large japanned tray. Hot water comes from an enormous iron boiler with a brass tap which sits perpetually murmuring on the perpetually lit wood-fire stove, and contains a marble which has a practical reason but which I believe is there to make the boiler sing.

There is the rustic refinement of two sorts of water, tap-water from the river, tank-water from the rain. Outside the back door, on a wooden platform beneath which naked jade-and-jet little frogs with pulsing throats and golden eyes live in a jungle of three sorts of mint, stands the corrugated-iron tank which receives the overflow from heaven and the rain-gutters along the eaves. The satin-soft liquid is used, after the wriggling mosquito larvae have been caught in a muslin

55

filter, for little else except washing my sister's and Mother's hair.

There is no door with coloured glass panels, a deprivation to be borne regretfully, but there are other doors whose differences from doors known have their consolations: the half-door of the stable, the squealing fly-wire doors, the trap-door to the little cellar in the pantry, the lavatory door with a crescent moon and two stars cut out in its planks.

There is no path of encaustic tiles, merely tracks footworn through shaggy lawns populated, in their season, by dande-lions, pimpernel and cape-weed or mushrooms and puff-balls; no veranda enclosed in cast-iron, but wider, longer verandas on three sides of the house; no indoor copper set in brick, and wearing a chimney, but an outdoor copper in an iron tripod, no pine wash-troughs but a graduated set of huge oval washtubs of galvanized iron. The inside of one of these is stained by the bluing water.

What Kensington lacked Bairnsdale has, what Bairnsdale lacks Kensington had. Bairnsdale lacks a sewerage system.

Beyond the greengage, the cherry plum, the peach and apple trees and the piano-case's stable, at the extreme end of the backyard, coated a foot deep in dolichos which Gipps-landers call lavatory-creeper, and overhung by a loquat tree, is the lavatory, the weather-board dunny for which the modish names of the period include such as Aunt Mary, Houses of Parliament, The Little House, Down-the-back, Lavvy and Shouse. Its floor is covered with chrysanthemum linoleum from the Kensington front bedroom. A bottle of Phenyle, a blue enamel candlestick and a box of matches, a small fringed green mat, and the two texts hung on the whitewashed walls, complete the furnishings. The texts once hung in the Kensington kitchen; looking back, I find their presence in the lavatory an indication of Mother's oblique ridicule. *The beloved of the Lord*, states one text encircled in mock orange, *shall dwell in safety*. The other, interlaced with jasmine, states, *Without me ye can do nothing*. The necessity to make this kind of tangential comment on life never changes in Mother when much else does. It is a form of mental reservation, even of cynical silence, at the core of which must lie an unfulfilled dream of lashing out verbally and with brilliant indecorum.

In the country Mother changes. Or rather, so far as I am concerned, she appears as another kind of Mother.

Since the time I wholly saw her first, lifting the spotted veil back from her powdered face under the winged hat, the cloud earlier concealing her has thinned, shredded away, vanished. She is now a woman almost always in an apron of black Italian cloth, her blouse sleeves rolled back above her beautiful forearms which turn day by day from white to country brown, a woman labelled with the names of days.

She is Monday as she helps the washerwoman whose hands are as pleated and bleached and sodden as some tripe-like fungus, a hook-nosed, hook-chinned, toothless woman as witch-like in appearance as behaviour as she prods with the pot-stick through the smoke and steam at the outdoor copper of boiling garments.

She is Tuesday as she sprinkles pillow-slips, Father's shirts, my sister's starched sun-bonnets, and the boys' cotton sou'westers, for her flat-irons. These have already been clashed down on the top of the kitchen range so hot that a mirage almost forms above its blackleaded surface. While the irons are heating, a peaceful overture to the rites begins. Mother and the washerwoman take each bedsheet separately and, one gripping the bottom edge, one the top, retreat backwards from each other, straining the sheet horizontally taut in a version of domestic tug-o'-war, inclining their heads to scan it for signs of wear, then, this done, mincing towards each other with uplifted arms to begin the folding. On the day of this grave pavane we invariably have for dinner a succulent hash made from Sunday's cold joint. This Mother calls a German Fry—a dish her Switzer father badgered her English mother into learning how to make.

She is Wednesday, her hair concealed beneath a worn, old-fashioned head-dress, once her mother's, and called a fascinator, as she shakes the little fringed furry mats that lie

57

before each inside door, as she mops fluff from under beds, sprinkles damp tea-leaves on the Brussels carpet before brushing it, sweeps the verandas, hunts cobwebs, polishes the brass taps and door-handles, rearranges dust with a feather duster.

She is green-fingered Thursday, and happiest, dividing her violet and primrose plants; manuring her five precious azaleas with the horse-droppings I have shovelled from the road, or cow-droppings from The Common; making a scarecrow that, wearing Father's old clothes, subtly resembles him, and to which, hopping about like a Pearlie Queen, she sings in imitation cockney, 'I wouldn't leave my little wooden hut for you-oo-oo . . .'; crushing a handful of lemon verbena leaves or eau-de-Cologne mint between her palms, and inhaling the scent of her hands which must smell also of earth and thyme and toil and happiness. Thursday reveals most of all that she is country-bred, and that her passion for the country imbues her too deeply for denial: she knows a thousand delicately brutal tricks to circumvent birds and caterpillars, wasps and slugs, frost and midsummer, from despoiling her rows of peas, her lettuce and Frau Karl Druschki roses, her Lazy Wife beans and maiden-hair fern, her hydrangeas and carrots and Sweet William and chives and almost sacred camellia tree. Her bible is Mrs. Rolf Boldrewood's *The Flower Garden in Australia* (A Book for Ladies and Amateurs dedicated by permission to the Countess of Jersey). Her favourite seeds come from *Vilmorin-Andrieux et Cie, Marchands-Grainiers, Quai de la Mégisserie 4, Paris*. So absurd is nostalgia and my persisting desire to complete the circles of experience that when, years later, I visit Paris, I eschew the *Tour Eiffel* and other *turismo* lures first to find the *Quai de la Mégisserie* where I compel myself not to cry.

She is Friday, curling-pinned, slap-dashing vivaciously and deftly through domesticity so that she can dress herself up, flee from her family into the after-dinner twilight, and go shopping. Friday is late shopping night. What she shops for on these evenings is nothing essential, nothing mundane.

The baker, the bloody butcher in a nimbus of flies, the milk-man, canter into Mitchell Street daily; the grocer, the fish-monger, the rabbit-oh, the John Chinaman greengrocer and fruiterer, the iceman and the egg-woman appear once or twice weekly; the knife-grinder, the tinker, the chimney-sweep, the clothes-prop man, the old clo' man, the clothes-peg gipsy and the Afghan pedlar drift through as regularly on time as the seasons, and the dust-laying water-waggon, and the ice-cream carts, and the swallows or their children which build their demi-cups of mud under the wooden shade over my bedroom window. Powdered and scented (eau-de-Cologne or Lily of the Valley), in her best earrings and gloves and dazzling polished shoes, her enamelled watch pinned to her bust, chewing a Sen-sen or a clove, Mother goes shopping for . . . for what? The tumpti-tiddily-tumpti of the Shire Band aloft in the hexagonal bandstand at the end of Main Street? The displays of xylonite hairpin boxes of imitation tortoise-shell? The Gaby Deslys figurines with thistle-down hair? The celluloid kewpies dressed in Bairns-dale football colours? The elegantly cruel spurs and plaited whips in the saddler's? The dusty witch-balls and fuchsia-coloured paper bells suspended over the soda-fountain and marble table-tops of Russo's? The glamour of gaslight, and electric light, and the passing and repassing between the wax dummies in the shop-windows and the spurred and slouch-hatted blokes rolling cigarettes and spitting with neat good manners between their feet as they lean against every Main Street veranda-post?

She returns home at nine-thirty sharp, her eyes glittering, refreshed by artificial light or moonlight or starlight, exhi-larated to girlishness, crying out gaily, 'Tea! Tea! Tea!' and, taking off her shoes now filmed with the dust of roads and adventure, 'My corn is giving me Larry Dooley!' 'I heard a mopoke,' she says, prodding the fire, removing the stove-lid, and pushing the kettle over the hole. 'I saw a falling star. Someone is dead,' she says, or, 'I sneaked a piece of that variegated honeysuckle over Coster's fence: I think it'll strike,' or, 'The band was playing "The Blue Danube" tonight,' and, 'One, two, three. One, two, three,' she sings whirling in her beautifully darned stockinged feet. She reveals what she has bought, other than excitement, from among the moustache cups and hurricane lamps and enamel bowls and winceyette night-gowns and glass-rubied gilt studs of Main Street. Maybe there are liquorice straps or blood oranges or little china canaries we children are to fill with water and, then, blowing down their hollow tails, make bubbling music. Whatever she buys is for us children: transfers, packets of compressed bits which expand to Japanese flowers on the surface of saucers of water, marbles of which I once knew the names, a bag of sugar-coated Paris Almonds, white and pink—simple gifts, payment that haunts now, for her several hours of freedom for the weekly promenade.

Once only does she lose her head, and buy herself a hideous white china rose, beautiful, for some reason, to her. 'When you dance tonight,' I hear her sometimes sing—oh, mockingly—as she lifts the atrocity—oh, gently, gently—to dust about it, 'wear a rose of white. 'Twill show you forgive me again. . . .' What is she really saying in song, for she is saying something?

She is Saturday and, breakfast over, a sergeant-major. Before breakfast, each child has had its weekly dose of Gregory Powder, a nauseous gunpowder-coloured purgative. Now, purged and fed, each child has its Saturday task. Her voice heightened, her movements brisk, she hurries about chivvying us, less because we are really of much help than that our being made to do something has its moral and disciplinary value, and is, moreover, a custom of that class in that era. Mother's humble hoard of real silver, and the electroplated silver, is cleaned with Goddard's Plate Powder and methylated spirits: the tea service, the salt-cellars and mustard-pot, the two cruets, the spoons and forks, the four biscuit-barrel rims and lids and handles, the salt spoons, soup ladles, fish-slice, cake pedestals, the rose-bowl and the trumpet vases. The fire-irons and fender are polished, and the steel knives are burnished with a sort of gritty cocoa rubbed on with a large cork set in a wooden handle like a drawer-handle. Butcher's paper is scissored into squares for the lavatory, and into cut-out filigree resembling Richelieu embroidery for the pantry shelves. Howsoever good I am, howsoever rapidly and competently I perform my part in these duties, I burn to escape and race reinless into the elm-lined streets, the Tannies, the river-flats, the miles-wide paddocks surrounding Bairnsdale.

Saturday afternoon is for baking. This is a labour of double nature: to provide a week's supply of those more solid delicacies Australian mothers of those days regard as being as nutritiously necessary as meat twice daily, four vegetables at dinner, porridge and eggs and toast for breakfast, and constant cups of tea. Empty biscuit-barrels and cake-tins being as unthinkable as beds not made before eleven a.m., Mother, therefore, constructs a great fruit cake, and a score or more each of rock cakes, Banburies, queen cakes, date rolls and ginger nuts. These conventional solidities done, she exercises her talent for ritual fantasy, for the more costly and ephemeral dainties that are to adorn as fleetingly as day-lilies the altar of the Sunday tea-table. Now appear three-storeyed sponge cakes mortared together with scented cream and in whose seductive icing are embedded walnuts, silver *cachous*, *glacé* cherries, strawberries, segments of orange and strips of angelica. Now appear cream puffs and éclairs, creations of the most momentary existence, deliberately designed neither for hoarding against a rainy day nor for social showing-off. Sunday tea is the frivolous and glittering crown of the week; there is the impression given of throwing away money like delicious dirt; there is the atmosphere rather than the fact of luxury; Sunday tea is, above all, my parents' statement to each other and their children that life is being lived on a plane of hard-earned and justifiable abundance. I watch abundance which means that I watch Mother, its actual as well as its symbolic impulse.

At this stage, astute within a vague placidity, so head-over-heels am I in harum-scarum content that my inner eye drifts away from observation of myself so that I become as blurred in outline to myself as my parents once were to me. In this mood, lasting years which all seem the same year, I appear, now, looking back, to have catalogued Mother more than any human being even though that catalogue must have been made in a by-the-way fashion. This may be a natural habit of eldest sons, or mere sons. It may only be the habit of sons who are driven by their natures to write. I suspect so, but am unsure. I do not even know if an eldest son, writer or shearer's cook or accountant, be the best or worst judge of his mother. I never shall know. I am discovering as I write these words that my autobiography, at this period, is my mother's biography. Outside her formal pattern of Monday as washing-day, Tuesday as ironing-day, et cetera, Mother is constantly making time almost in the same way as she makes Cornish Pasties. She makes it, between the crevices of her daily plan, in many patterns, and lays it aside, lays aside tangible and visible samples of the hours: a mound of darned socks, a dozen jars of quince jelly, a dead-straight line of weeded onïons, a varnished meat pie decorated with a pastry rose and its serrated pastry leaves. Sometimes, as men and boys do, as Father and I do, she fills in time. She too fishes in the river, comes mushrooming and blackberrying, shrieks and splashes and dog-paddles at beach-picnics. This filling-in is, however, apparent only: the picnic-hamper holds the too much she has made to eat, there is always time's essence in blackberry tarts and blackberry jam, a dish of stewed mushrooms and jars of dried ones, or a platter of fried bream. In making time thus three-dimensional in many forms she creates the illusion of abundance for us.

She sings still, as constantly, as cheekily, the same songs but whereas, before, the song seems foremost and she a vaporous shape gesturing through some task behind the melody, now it is she and the task that fill the foreground, piling up riches, weaving, like a spider, from the threads of her own strength of will, and love, and ability to serve, a web of plenty. She knows that we can scarcely afford to keep up with the Joneses, let alone impress them. She sees to it that we afford to impress ourselves.

Abundance! Plenty!

To me, now, the years between six and ten are cards of the same suit. The total impression remaining is this one of copiousness. Never for one second do I realize that what I count as such is not so to many. Not only does it seem so in my dreamily watchful, belly-filled, soft-bedded, unruffled home life, it seems more so in that country town outside the family walls, and in the country outside the country town. It is a magnification of Dr. Moss's pittosporum with its bees and butterflies and blossoms and gusts of scent. From waking to sleeping, from January to December, from year to year, it is impossible for me not to be aware of fecundity: the grass thicker than wool and gorged with globules of dew or matted with frost; the late twilight air flowing in currents of moths and Christmas beetles and cockchafers as we play on The Common under a sky closely gravelled with planets and stars; the footpaths and paddocks glaring yellow with cape-weed through which we paddle until boots or bare feet are mustard-coloured with pollen; the birds gibbering and squealing and squeaking a million-fold in every elm in every street at sunrise and sunset, and, late, late at night, when one is in bed, and the candle blown out, the crowing of roosters from every direction, from near, from nearly near, from over the hills and far far away, cry answering cry repeatedly in sounds so threadlike, so distant, so weary, as to be almost the cry of silence itself. I see fecundity everywhere—the seed-boxes of poppies shaking out their pepper, the winter-defrocked trees blotted with nests, the summer trees bearing billions of leaves, the vast mushroom-rings, the grapelike bunches of blackberries overhanging the paths and ditches along the river, Mother's fingers and mine stained emerald with the green blood of uncountable aphides we have squashed from the buds of the rose-bushes.

Fecundity! Plenty! Abundance!

Abundance has its shades.

At the end of the block, opposite The Common, and next to the abandoned Chinese joss-house, lives the Adams family whose design of private existence is so public and so different

63

from my family's that I find it startling, outrageous and sometimes disgusting but, all in all, fascinating. There are never as many Adams children as there appear to be, and I recall only eight by name when I could, without torture, confidently have sworn to twice as many. Perhaps this multiplication is caused by their noise, their weasel-like dartings from place to place, and mostly by the fact that many of them seem about the same age, and strongly resemble each other. They are all knobbly at the joints and bony in between them, they are all knock-kneed, with gipsy-ish cheekbones, flat noses, long flexible mouths set in tide-lines of grime, unwinking beer-coloured eyes completely encircled by pink whites, and netted in wrinkles as though they are middle-aged. Boys and girls alike have spiky dust-brown hair in which burrs, chaff and streaks of jam or tomato sauce stick, and remain sticking, for days. One or other is always shaven-headed because of lice. Granules like dried honey infest the corners of their eyes and the roots of their lashes. As all we country children do in summer, they go barefooted, revealing long tarsier-like toes. In the colder months, when we others wear boots, they wear sandshoes that smell of feet. Their names strike me as glamorous and romantic, particularly the double names of the girls which are always used in full: Christobel Veronica, Rosalie Marigold, Geraldine Emily and Melba Florabelle. The boys' names are Winton, Aubrey, Selwyn and Maximilian.

I am fully although astoundedly aware, from over-hearing Mother and Father, that Mr. Adams earns more money than Father, and therefore understand their possession of many things my parents very clearly express themselves as being too poor to afford. I observe, cold-eyed, that the Adams tribe places no value on domestic customs and rites of behaviour I regard it as almost criminal to scant. In short: there is no fish-and-chip shop in the Bairnsdale of the nineteen-twenties, otherwise the Adamses would undoubtedly be fish-and-chip people. They have fish-and-chip manners.

On two occasions I somehow witness them at table. They do not wash before eating. There is no table-cloth, not even a newspaper one, and no table-napkins. On each occasion there is the same centre-piece, indubitably permanent, of bottles of tomato sauce, jars of sulphur-yellow pickles, tins of treacle, and condensed milk, tins of jam with the lids jagged open and prised up by a tin-opener. All these vessels bleed and dribble on the greasy table. I know, from the conversations of the Adams children, that frankfurters, saveloys, sardines, bananas, garishly iced pastry-cook cakes, fresh bread and crumpets, are their favourite and most usual foods.

I see them feasting on black puddings, kola tonic and vanilla slices, champing loudly and quickly with their decayed teeth, giving no attention at all to any one of the many technicalities of eating Mother considers paramount. Knives are licked, mouths and noses wiped on sleeves, crusts are not eaten but thrown to the floor for the several dogs.

Mrs. Adams, whom the older children call Ma and the younger Mumma, is put out by none of this. She is a taller but no plumper prophecy of what Christobel Veronica and the other girls will grow to, flatter of nose, spikier of hair, with the same unwinking eyes. As aitchless as her children she behaves as they do, dropping crusts lovingly to the dogs, slurping nigger-brown tea from a saucer, straining across the table to stab a knife into a tin of jam, and coating a slice of bread held flat on the palm of her left hand with the glutinous dollops of purple goo thus dug out. Her behaviour, more valid and impressing than her children's because she is a Mrs. and a mother, shows me that there is an acceptable though different sort of family order, a different set of rules, a different conception of what is abundance.

The Adams idea of abundance is expressed in the five bicycles they own, in the several tricycles rusting with the rusting pilchard tins and Hornby railway lines and disintegrating go-carts among the shoulder-high weeds of the backyard, in the pianola and the stacks of unravelling pianola rolls, in the harmonium with *its* decayed teeth, the three banjos, the gramophone with its toffee-coloured convolvulus-shaped horn which seems repeatedly to wheeze out only

Harry Lauder singing 'Roamin' in the gloamin' ' though there are deposits of records tossed like quoits in corners, on to pantry shelves, on to and under sofas.

I am not so much appalled as roused to wonder by seeing nothing in what I think is its right place: bicycles in the passage, fancy dress costumes and crutchless bloomers hanging on the backs of kitchen chairs, a sodden pillow and a doll's perambulator in the gully-trap, an iron saucepan containing the ashes of some long-ago-charred Irish Stew holding open the front door, playing-cards in the lavatory, penny dreadfuls, kitten-decorated chocolate-boxes and stone ginger-beer bottles everywhere.

The bedrooms really disconcert me. When I leave mine in the morning I do not enter it again until I am going to bed. It is a place I should not want to be in during the day. By training I regard a bedroom, then as now, as a spotless, uncluttered place to sleep in. The bedrooms of the Adams boys are junk-shop places to fight in, play in, store things in. Their unmade beds are littered with stamp albums, caramel papers, cigarette-cards and popguns. I am as astounded by a canary in a cage in one bedroom as I am by the presence of rabbit-traps, Meccano derricks, bicycle-chains, boxing-gloves, an enamel plate half-filled with a failure of toffee, and an unemptied chamber-pot in which float apple-cores.

I am more startled, though I affect a form of polite deafness and blindness to it, by the almost formal litany of insult, tongue-poking-out (sharp white tongues) and ugly-face-making that goes on between Mrs. Adams and her children. I am used to the much less waspish form of bickering exchange, hearty and over-masculine, of my country uncles, and know that affection inspires it, and their matching adulthoods ratify it. It is clear too that Mrs. Adams and her children, bitterly screeching at each other 'Greediguts!' and 'Shut up, bum-face!' and 'Stinkpot!' and 'Youse is all barmy as bandicoots!' love each other, and regard their performances as conventional enough. Nevertheless, I am uneasy at this treatment of and by a parent, and am more uneasy because it is not something I am accidentally overhearing and seeing but something they do not consider caring if I see.

I am startled, too, that the Adams children and their dogs and dirt, and any neighbour children and their dogs and dirt, have the run of the whole house, including the parental bedroom, and the use, at any odd time, without asking permission, of anything in the house—slices of bread-and-dripping, tins of condensed milk, the pianola, anything at all.

I am most startled by their friendly habit of offering to let me have a bite or a suck from something they have already bitten or sucked—a pear, a piece of peppermint rock, a cheese sandwich, an aniseed ball. My nausea at the thought of accepting the offer is difficult to obscure even by a polite evasion of lies. Neither my stomach nor I has the moral strength to repay their insulting gesture of *bonhomie* with an insulting gesture of sacrifice. The nausea is caused partly by an inborn fastidiousness, partly by family training, but there is a cause so revolting that, whenever I am subject of one of these offers to share, I need to escape quickly from the Adams circle until I carelessly forget the cause. The Adams boys blow their noses not with handkerchiefs but their fingers. They use the same fingers, not paper, to wipe themselves.

Although horrified when I first see them do this, and then rub the brown from their fingers on to the public lavatory wall, I instantly accept it as one more difference between me (and people like me) and others not like me (and people like me). Twenty years later, as a schoolmaster at a wealthy private school in Adelaide, I see dozens of these unmistakable brown streaks on the white-tiled walls of the lavatory cubicles. Since lavatory-paper, hot-and-cold wash-basins, soap and towels are laid on in the lavatory-block, the excremental score-sheet indicates addiction to an unusual delight. Facing the assembled school at morning prayers I wonder which expensive schoolboy fingers holding the hymn-books are the same pens as the fingers of Maximilian and Aubrey and Selwyn and Winton.

Winton is also the first and only person I ever see write a

67

dirty jingle behind a lavatory door. *One would think*, writes Winton, as thousands have written before him, *with all this wit, that Shakespeare had come here to shit.*

As one rubs shoulders with the world, one rubs shoulders with how many Wintons, how many executants of *graffiti*? The walls of the world are marked by their secretly done writings, their naïve bawdinesses and self-taught pornographies, their agonizing sexual lonelinesses, their exaggerated advertisements of unmentionable delights, their wistful or boastful invitations to fleshly ecstasy, their heartbreakingly bestial, or pathetic, or inaccurate illustrations of the very sources of life itself, of life and unfulfilment and agony. Do men, I wonder, as they scratch with a pencil on the walls of the lavatory outside the Guildhall in Royal Windsor, under the Accademia Bridge in Venice, in the Melbourne Botanical Gardens and the Hibeya Gardens of Tokyo, draw their own organs, circumcised or uncircumcised, big-balled or little-balled, when they illustrate thus their need and dream and dirty human-ness?

In watching the Adams family I learn earlier what I might otherwise not have learned until much later. They are first samples to me, unhygienic habits apart, of the sort of Australian I am to meet many of. Their accent is that of the lowest English working-class of the early nineteenth century. Whatever amendments time and place and the acquisition of material things make, the accent is defiantly preserved. Wealth cannot taint it nor education undo it. It is preserved as much by university professors, schoolteachers, politicians, non-conformist clergyman, business magnates and the owners of thousands of acres as by the wealthy Australian working-class itself.

It is an ineradicable and perverse accent, signal at once of the possible strengths and certified weaknesses of the Australian character, an accent indicating, on the one hand, laziness, vicious sentimentality, self-pity, genteelism, self-satisfaction and lack of self-discipline, on the other, intentions to nobility, unstinted Good Samaritanism, powerful and Puritanical stubbornness, courageous foolhardiness and

68

a brazenly sardonic independence of outlook. These attitudes, this accent, belong to millions living in barbarian's luxury at the heart of many-faceted abundance.

The passion I still have for the prolific aspects of nature develops to its height during these years, and is unlikely to diminish. It is a passion not to be defended.

I am never so passionately aware of the power of the earth and the lavishness of it as on Gippsland midsummer days. Before eleven in the morning the bees are staggering drunk in the madonna lilies. The endless safaris of ants pass each other scarcely speaking. Out and out beyond the town's rim of orchards and asparagus fields and maize crops and pumpkin paddocks, thousands of acres of peroxided grasses shimmer and surge at the bases of an infinity of ring-barked trees pale and lustrous as aluminium. The rotating shadows of the rotating tin louvres of windmills do not cut one swathe in the grassy pelt of fragile tassels, bobbles, plumes and maces. Out and farther out, beyond the Golgotha of the slaughter-yards, lies the cemetery like a spilling of shapes in marzipan, the cemetery and its abundant dead boxed down under the freesias and sparaxis and periwinkle and briers and gorse more abundant than they.

The song and the poem I learn in Kensington kindergarten days truly prophesy the development of the legend of Gallipoli and the Anzacs. The one connection I have with this mystifying and exclusive procedure of war and Gallipoli lies in my Teddy Bear, and the destruction by Turks or Huns or Kaiser Bill of Uncle Arthur Abernethy. An orphan adopted to be a farm-boy by Mother's father, Grandfather Ruff, Uncle Arthur Abernethy is far more famous to me for giving the Teddy Bear than for giving his life for his country. There is no one alive, I think, except myself, who remembers that Arthur Abernethy was knock-kneed and skinny, had unruly double-crowned hair, and is a dead Anzac. Because it is talked of and taught about so much in Bairnsdale I become aware that the Anzac legend, while duller in the telling and over in a flash, is more lasting, more stickable, than showier other Great War legends: Mata Hari, the Angels of Mons, Kitchener and Jellicoe, the Rose of No-man's Land, Allied soldier corpses being boiled down to make soap (or is it soup?) for Hun soldiers. These other tales excite me more, but the growth of the Anzac legend bears them down, thickening as it does to a sarsaparilla-like creeper twining its way through the undergrowth of earlier less nationally glorious legends about convicts, coach-robberies, bush-rangers, Captain Moonlight, gold and aborigines.

In her fireside, sitting-down, story-telling moods, which she can only spare to have with a baby at breast or a crochet-needle in hand, Mother is voluble, sometimes accurately, sometimes inaccurately, about aborigines; tales heard years before in *her* mother's fireside, sitting-down, story-telling moods flow easily, well-remembered and word-perfect, from her unpainted lips. Aborgines steal with their toes; abori-gines eat living grubs and grilled tiger-snake; aborgines are faithful Men Fridays to explorers and, at the same time, treacherous explorer-killers, cruel to shipwrecked white women, and given to abducting and murdering little pioneer boys of my age, not as edible dainties, but for the fat sur-rounding their kidneys, this fat being reputedly best to anoint black bodies to a superior glossiness on corroboree nights. It is such debased aborigines who are pursued by Grandfather Ruff slicing about with his cutlass, and shouting out in a German accent, 'Cut 'em! Slash 'em!' Or they are hunted down like rabbits, and left to the blowflies. Or they are given lavish supplies of flour and sugar impregnated with poison when they come on their begging visits. Or they are invited *en masse* to picnics where they are blown up. I get the impression, even today almost ineradicable, of stove-black mothers and fathers, and neatly ranged Little Black Sambos and Topsies, one minute nibbling corned beef sand-wiches and sausage rolls, and drinking raspberry vinegar, as they sit on hollow logs packed with gunpowder, the next minute sky-high, with the clouds of crimson smoke raining down legs and arms, and hands holding tumblers, and sandwiches with semi-circular bites in them.

'Come, Josephine, in my flying machine,' sings Mother softly and naughtily, 'going up she goes, up she goes. . . .'

They are tales abroad too, during my country town boyhood, of the Old World and an un-Australian past, tales from which emerges a curious hierarchy of actual and fictional characters which I do not then have the perception to distinguish one from the other, or realize are not local but imported. As we children of Mitchell Street play chasey or tiggy or hidey on moonlight nights on The Common or in the Tannies, there is the delicious terror of being uncertain whether, behind a clump of boxthorns or in the diabolic shadows of the oaks, crouches Jack-the-Ripper, Bill Sikes, Fagin, Springheel Jack, Sweeney Todd or Mr. Hyde. This villainous pantheon is supplemented by bride-murderers, ghosts, baby-farmers, Captain Webb, Casabianca, General Gordon, Lord Roberts, the guard at Pompeii, and animals such as the Boer's horse, Llewellyn's dog and Androcles' lion.

Tales we distort for each other, hidden in the long grasses of summer twilight, lead us hopefully to expect, almost to pray for, what we see in the woodcuts and steel engravings of our parents' or grandparents' gilt-edged and calf-bound books preserved from the Victorian era: cloudbursts, fireballs, miraculous lightning, auroras, showers of stars and, most popular and titillating of all, the End of the World. The End of the World is often discussed, and calmly enough, even though it be God's well-advertised and alarming theatrical production with earthquakes and hailstorms and rainbows and tidal waves all happening at once, while graves eject the gesticulating resurrected, and angels cascade down the stairs of air.

Although these tales and legends are compositions largely of depravity, witless heroism and startling tactics of personality, they possess also a seductive mystery. To us country children some of this mystery infects the outcasts of the town, the eccentrics, naturals, cripples and foreigners. It infects the blackies, swaggies and drunkies. All these are creatures from whom we keep our distance. Their solitariness shows: instinct, of which we take far more heed than of parents' prohibitions, warns us that these solitaries are kinds of time-soiled children not to be played with and not to be touched. They are certainly not the sort of manageable adults we cynically allow ourselves to trust without trusting. We can trust these queer ones wholly, for an atmosphere of defence-less amorality emanates from them. We instantly sniff this out for it is our own less visible, less defenceless amorality, and it goads us to eschew pity. Cruelty is safer for us than tolerance, brutal mockery than sympathetic silence. We therefore cruelly mock, either whispering together in hisses to be heard or, if the distance we keep be great enough, cry-ing out at them like mad and sexless hounds. In this we are skilled to the point of professionalism. With faultless malice we have already nicknamed our class-mates and friends— Dopey, Skinny, Fattie, Monkey, Shitty, Stinko, Ferret, Pisser and Twitchy. We have already sharpened our steel voices on each other, packs of boys on packs of girls, packs of one school on packs of another school, packs of screaming State School Protestants on packs of screaming St. Mary's School Roman Catholics:

> *Cath'lic* (Proddy) *dogs jump like frogs*
> *in a pool of water.*
> *When the Proddies* (Cath'lics) *ring the bell,*
> *all the Cath'lics* (Proddies) *go to hell!*

We are, moreover, prepared for whatever may come. The town, for example, so far as we know, is Jewless, but we have long been ready with:

> *Ikey Moses, King of the Jews,*
> *Sold his wife for a pair of shoes.*
> *When the shoes began to wear,*
> *Ikey Moses began to swear.*
> *When the swear began to stop,*
> *Ikey Moses bought a shop.*
> *When the shop began to sell. . . .*

And so on, endless verses.

It is suggested that adults teach children. I suggest that children teach children, and that the 'playing' they do for adults is not the real masks-off playing they do for themselves. Not until I am myself an adult do adults attempt to teach me sin. Too late. Children do not have to teach each other sin: they merely swap sins as they swap postage-stamps or dolls.

At this distance of years it interests me to recall that two, especially, of the odd-people-out at whose backs—always backs and always far-off—we shrill out what are virtually exorcisms, are hard-working citizens. To vilify them we use the formula we use for all our victims: 'Silly old swaggie!', 'Silly old drunkie!', 'Silly old blackie!', 'Silly old dago!', 'Silly old Ching Chong Chinaman!' and the more lacerating, 'Silly old hoppy-go-quick!', 'Silly old four-eyes!', 'Silly old duck's bum!'

To us, one of these two honest-to-God workers is a near-witch, the other as untouchable as a Japanese *Eta*.

The witch is Nurse Mawdsley, the midwife. Except for a long rabbit-skin coat she wears hail and shine, blazing January or soaking October, she seems normal enough, a two-legged woman of authentic rubbery curves, shapely large white hands, a pink and white face on which glistens a young golden moustache, and a loudly melodious voice which, for some reason, sounds purple to me.

When Mother's fourth and, several years later, fifth babies are born, there Nurse Mawdsley is, the doctor in his brass-bound motor-car on her heels, there she is in the house, her rabbit-skin coat with its lining of frayed nut-brown brocaded silk possessing the hallstand beside her navy blue silk hat in the stiff crown of which are innumerable holes punched by her two black glass hatpins. There she is, bossing Mother into keeping to her bed, into eating stewed apricots and junket, and reading Charles Garvice novels. This latter Mother does with, I have no doubt, one eye, while the other and her two ears range the kitchen, and the biscuit tins, and our bowels, and the weeds and slugs stealing a march on the garden. There Nurse Mawdsley is, making tea differently from

Mother, making it, as Father says behind her back, pale as ant's piddle, making it on weekdays in the Sunday-sacred crested silver teapot that was Grandmother Ruff's, and slopping the milk in first and too much but, to our amazement, putting nothing in her own except a slice of lemon which she later eats with refinedly outcurled fingers and rabbity nibblings. This oddity of behaviour, and the fact that she reads *The Bairnsdale Advertiser* and smokes scented cigarettes in the lavatory, seem somehow to confirm that she really is the absurd she who grows babies under cabbages, and after whom we screech, 'Silly old Mother Mawdsley!'

I am sixteen before I know, and then neither perfectly clearly nor correctly, the facts about conception and birth. I think this fairly usual for the class, generation, continent and country town I was brought up in. My parents tell me nothing of sex ever. During the numerous, often elaborate and, to me, increasingly boring, unrewarding and time-wasting sexual interchanges I have in barns, behind hedges and in the Renardi's piano-case with little girls and other little boys, it never enters my head that what we are up to has anything to do with fathers, mothers, babies or me. It is merely a furtive game I have been asked to share in, most often *à deux*, sometimes *à trois*, once a retrospectively funny *à quatre*. Although I am, during those years, a born watcher who has not outgrown watching, I never observe Mother large with child; Mother's waistline being, it seems, not the sort of thing I go in for watching. I am, of course, not yet ten, but the blind spot persists until much later. I am prepared to admit that the subject of babies as an aftermath of sex could have come up; my ear, as so often to this day, is doubtless elsewhere listening to time passing, to myself and the world dying, and the voices of the dead prophetic poets soaring above the unnecessary noises men let men make. Without a chart and without an informative whisper therefore, I assume that Nurse Mawdsley, in some sort of unimaginable but dull collusion with the doctor, is responsible for landing Mother with a new and uninteresting brother or sister. I seek no reason for this tiresome largesse; the fact of it suffices. When, cheerfully sinister, and jocularly dangerous with her purple voice, her fingers hooked away from her cup of ant's piddle, Nurse Mawdsley is fifteen-sixteenths of the household, I do watch her warily. The designs on the wallpaper seem smaller and dimmer; my brothers and sisters seem flatter, as cut from a material without depth; boiled eggs are runny, and have not been wiped clean before cooking. I watch, and keep my mouth shut. When, however, the rabbit-skin coat no longer hangs like a sad beast on the hallstand, and Nurse Mawdsley's furry and majestic bulk is, some time later, seen several safe blocks away, I, in the encouraging company of a First and Third Murderer, am moved to open my mouth wide: 'Silly old Mother Mawdsley! Silly old Mother Mawdsley!' What am I, with the others of my age, shouting against? What atavistic fear? I do not know then, can only guess now.

The untouchable is the night-man, the lavatory-man, the dunny-man, outcast of outcasts. Most often he does come at night to carry away our excrement, degradation in the dark, but, often enough, shamelessly in full daylight. Heralded by a stench and the clashing of metal doors and galvanized iron, his horses pace slowly into the street. Windows are closed. Eyes are averted, and breaths held. As all tradesmen's horses of that era do, the butcher's, the baker's, the grocer's, the milkman's, his horses move from house to house, from tradesman's entrance to tradesman's entrance, without being directed. They stop; they pause waiting for their drivers; they move on, at exactly the right moment, as though by clockwork, Calvanistically long-faced with resignation, their manes in girlish plaits, their eyelashes covered in dust. In summer they wear straw hats through slots in which their ears protrude like hairy leaves. They draw what we call the night-cart or, less prissily, the dunny-cart, a two-storeyed van of metal cubicles each containing a dunny-can. I see the pariah now, entering our drive-gate with an empty can, and leaving with a full one, his naked, conspicuously muscular arms holding the shame-weighted container on his head in the manner of Rebecca holding the water-pitcher at the well in Mother's *Child's Bible*. The night-man wears a hat, decidedly for practical reasons, but also because, in those days, no man—indeed, nobody—goes out of doors without headgear. To do so lays one open as much to social condemnation as to the imagined dangers of sun, rain, falling dew, changes in weather, moon, night air, twilight air or mere air. Hatlessness is more than unhealthy and vulgar, it is capricious to the point of lunacy. When, in 1927, Dick Currie, a handsome and god-like footballer, takes to wearing nothing but his curls on his head, the town is shocked to gossip. Not even the most headstrong of his fans dares follow his peculiar lead.

The top of the night-man's hat is squashed so dead-flat that it appears his skull must also be. His arms are enmeshed in a knitting of flies, and so is his face, his moveless face. He can make no gesture to swipe off the mask of creatures. He does not wince under their abominable little feet as his horses do. He patiently wears the insects as though he has been dipped in them, a baptism setting him permanently apart.

Once, one December, I am in the lavatory; I have lifted the lid from the hole, and am dreamily undoing my braces, when I hear the trapdoor open and, my modesty disturbed, myself struck to unmoving breathlessness, see through the hole the full can slide scrapingly away, and the empty one pushed into its place. Then, taking me utterly aback, and shocking me as something macabre, a hand appears through the hole, five-fingered, human, flexible, with clean square finger-nails, and finically drops a little card on the seat. It then withdraws in its moveless mitten of flies. The trapdoor closes. I can breathe and move. I take up and read the card on which is printed:

> *Enjoy Christmas as best you can,*
> *And don't forget the Dunny Man.*

I rush this mystery to Mother. She is unimpressed. Silly boy, it happens every year. A Christmas-box of half a crown will be left. Crikey! Half a crown! On the seat? Yes, on the seat. In a matchbox? No, in an envelope. Wouldn't a matchbox be better?

76

Mother, who is boiling Christmas Pudding threepences and sixpences to sterilize them, suddenly places her hands in an attitude of prayer, rolls her eyes piously ceiling-wards and, at the same time crossing them, sings in a burlesque choir voice, very *tremolo*:

> *'Hark, the herald angels sing,*
> *Beecham's Pills are just the thing,*
> *Peace on earth and mercy mild,*
> *Two for a man, and one for a child.'*

Since the other children and I cry out against the midwife and the night-man, it is not surprising that we cry out at those who have less reason for our respect and silence. When we are alone, each of us is niminy-piminy silent, angelic as a story-book character, imitating humanity, incapable of egging self to viciousness. However, in pairs, in threes, in groups, we are without fear of deriding the spastic scraping and jerking along like an out-of-gear mechanical toy; of white-faced Miss Read lifting and thumping, lifting and thumping and dragging her giant boot with its foot-thick sole across The Common; of the monstrously fat jelly of a woman who works in Mason and Carter's, Newsagent and Fancy Goods; of Mrs. Rich the pawnbroker who has a little grey goatee; of the pea-picking Dagoes and maize-growing Hindus; of Paddy Power the dwarf who lives by himself in a dwarf hut, and resembles all the dwarfs since seen, in waddle and desperately alert expression; of the old, old, old, black-be-capped and black-slippered Chinkies, the dying Chows, the skin-and-bone last of the Amoy Chinese from the worn-out gold-fields, who sit with swollen eyes on the disintegrating verandas behind the plumed and dusty weeds of the Pearson Street hovels, and are believed to be wealthy, to eat cats, smoke opium, put their big yellow things in little white girls' things, and keep threepences in their ears. 'Don't,' cry mothers and cries Mother, 'don't put that dirty, filthy, revolting threepenny bit in your mouth. It's been in a Chinaman's ear.' What Yellow Peril *canard*, filtering through to frontier town Bairnsdale, could make stick to be widespread this frivolous accusation against senile escapees from Tzu-Hsi, the Dowager Empress, I cannot guess unless ear is a euphemism for another orifice in which the badgered secrete their wealth in times of peril. Anyway, we do not attempt to disbelieve the furphy. We are only too happy to see the fingerprints of the devil on all who are too large or too small or the wrong colour or crippled.

We are suspicious of a devil's simplicity and directness in the hunchback, in the man with the birth-mark that colours his face half-mulberry, half-white, like a mediaeval tabard, in the many women who, because of a mineral deficiency in Bairnsdale's bland, sweet water, have eyes like Pekingese, and goitrous throats ranging from Burne-Jones to pelican. So we scream our counter-charms at them to warn whatsoever possesses them that we are suspicious and superstitious.

Superstitions and fallacies are stock-in-trade, and keep us constantly wary. Though willing enough occasionally to test blasphemy, and find that, as guessed, no thunderbolt strikes the blasphemer, and no voice from heaven booms through a display of lightning, 'I heard what you said about Me,' we prefer to keep on the safe side of sacrilege.

Yet, other minor perils season our dish of days. Warts are caused by licks from dogs, or from handling toads which we inflate to great size by blowing down hollow grass-stalks stuck up their holes. Lockjaw, which we translate as meaning eternal dumbness, occurs instantly—absolutely instantly— that the skin between thumb and forefinger is cut. Lizard and goanna bites may appear cured, but break out, year after year, at the same minute of the same hour of the same day they are inflicted. Each sigh made means a drop of blood lost from the heart, and a day cut from life. One's grandmother dies if one deliberately steps on a crack in asphalt. A guinea-pig's eyes drop out if the animal is held up by its tail. A snake, if permitted to cross one's glance with its evil, lidless own, hypnotizes one to nightmare immobility. A snake, if its back be broken, even before noon, and it be apparently dead, is unable to die until sunset. A snake, if caught unawares, hastily gulps down its young, circles itself into a hoop, tail in mouth, and bowls itself away from danger. To see a white horse sets one snapping out, 'First luck, white horse!' and gabbling the numbers from one to ten, which done, one spits on a forefinger, and marks a wet cross on one's dusty boot or dirty foot. Just as a four-leafed clover is good magic, so is a wishbone, a nautilus shell, a potato with a face, a philippina, a stone with a hole in it, and a white horse. A cast horseshoe is not good magic. It is necessary to pick up the sinister thing, to spit on it and, then, hurl it as far behind as possible over the left shoulder, the eyes meantime being squeezed shut, and the ears covered by the hands, to prevent oneself knowing where and when it comes to earth.

Mortality scents many of our superstitions. Death is an engaging topic, particularly when we have played ourselves to a standstill physically and emotionally in one of the more chilling games such as, *Who's going around my house, tonight?* or, *Sheep, sheep, come home!* and twilight has become night, and fate is visible in our own dying voices and unseen faces.

Death is a riddle to which, in these moods, we question the answers we have been given, and make up many more of our own answers to question. None is convincing. None is satisfactory, not even the possibility of arriving in heaven (which we do not question), as by a later train at a celestial railway station, to be greeted by those who have taken an earlier train. For me the flaw in this alluring notion of which I hear from Mother, and at Sunday School, and Religious Instruction at Bairnsdale State School No. 754, and generally, is the irritating difficulty the older dead and the newer dead will have to face in recognizing each other as they gather by the beautiful, the beautiful, the river, over the ranges, on the golden shore, beyond the sunset or just across the bridge of gold. What, I chatter voicelessly to myself, picking at a scab, what of the young mother who dies and leaves a little baby which lives on, and grows into an old man before it dies? How will the young mother recognize the old man? And he, who was a memory-less baby when she died, how will he recognize her whom he has never seen? What will my Grandmother Ruff, who died when I was a baby she used to

79

nurse, expect of me when I die? What if Mother dies, today, right now, and I live on and on to be a long-bearded hundred before joining her? This, of course, is ridiculous country to be running in: my dying is something I simply do not believe in. Nor do I believe for one moment in Mother's dying.

She is clearly not marked down for death. She is too entangled in life, too busy, too lively, too noisily chatterbox, and has, altogether, too many imperfections disqualifying her from death. I have long since gathered that, apart from the historically wicked Rasputin who is recent, and King John, and Attila, the Scourge of God, who are old, the dead require to be noble, truthful, religious, patient, sweet-natured, and altogether morally larger than life. They possess, in short, all the graces the living do not, and Mother patently does not. Mother is oh-you-tee.

She smacks me and my siblings about the legs with a little soft leather strap which nevertheless stings, and which she calls her cat-o'-nine-tails although it is cut at the end into only four small tails. She never goes to St. John's Church of England except for christenings, other people's weddings and, sometimes, at Easter.

When she drops a gravy boat or scorches a batch of scones she uses her favourite oath, 'Hell and Tommy!' She sometimes swears like a man—as youngest pet daughter of a boisterously happy-go-lucky family well-endowed with shootin' and fishin', if not huntin', brothers she has had every opportunity to acquire a striking vocabulary. Worst of all to me, she is at times coarse—'Lord Muck of Turd Island!' she says almost contemptuously of some pompous fool. Thank God I have caught some of her coarseness; I should be utterly insufferable without it.

As she splashes in the bath with her long translucent bar of glycerine soap or, on state occasions, with the sphere of pink soap that has the same ravishing scent as her talcum powder, Wild Geranium, she sings with blasphemous loudness, 'For those in peril on the sea. . . .'

She steals cuttings of plants through picket-fences, not only as fearlessly as a hardened criminal but also on Sundays, in full view of the afternoon strollers in their navy-blue suits and ox-blood boots, wheeling cane-and-sennett baby-carriages quivering sensitively aloft on high, fragile wire wheels.

She picks up cutlet bones from her plate to gnaw them bare.

She is charming as a royal princess to my sister's music teacher, Miss Brewer, and presses upon her a pot of Pear Ginger, a bunch of zinnias, and a little bouquet of parsley, but says, 'I can't *bear* that woman. Airs and graces! Dressed up like a sore toe, but hasn't had a bath for weeks. Dirty English! Dirty flashness! I shudder to think of her . . . her underneath.' Then she smiles, not revealing her teeth, with the equivocal, dangerous smile of a Becky Sharp by Greuze. 'That Pear Ginger,' she says, 'was your Aunt Mary's recipe!'

I catch on.

Mother cannot bear Aunt Mary either.

'Zin-ni-ahs, oh, zin-ni-ahs,' says Mother in a lah-di-dah manner. I recall that she calls zinnias Old Age.

I recall also that Mother has told me that to give parsley to another woman means that Nurse Mawdsley and the doctor will bring the woman a baby. Obliquely as ever, Mother is wishing Miss Brewer some female ill, is putting the mozz on her.

When the Canon is perceived to be at the front door, 'Oh, bugger, bugger, bugger bugger, *bugger*,' whispers Mother from the pantry where she is hiding. 'Tell him I'm out. The man's a crashing bore. Tell him I'm out, Laddie. Tell him I'm in Timbuctoo. Tell him I'm dead.' Yet Mother smacks me—hard—if I attempt to get away with a lie myself.

Indeed, indeed, Mother has few of the qualifications for death.

Immortal as I see her, her death as impossible as my own, implicated in full-time living as she is, she is nevertheless a gourmet of those side-dishes death lavishly provides.

She loves to feed all of us children, but especially me who listens more feverishly, what she herself loves: tales of death. She ranges from Cock Robin to Hero and Leander, from Lucy Gray to Greyfriars Bobbie, from Babes in the Wood to walled-up nuns, from Mary, Queen of Scots and Edith

Cavell to the bride who playfully hid in the chest that locked itself upon her and all her wedding finery.

I am easily able to spring the fact that Mother has less appetite for these samples of doom, albeit tasty, because she is not herself involved in their making. She is fearfully hungrier for those portents of death which are all about her, and which come near enough to her for her to imagine them part of her own experience. Dogs howling late at night in a certain manner ('Hark!' says Mother theatrically. 'Listen! Those dogs! When they howl like that. . . .' Her eyes dilate. '. . . *death!*'); a meteor streaking down the slope of heaven; a black moth or a bat entering the house; three ominously spaced and resounding midnight knocks on a door, and emptiness, nothing, no one there, when it is opened; to Mother all these foretell death or have foretold it truly to her friends or to time-out-of-mind great-aunts and second cousins. Just as I believe (almost) that snakes cannot die until the sun goes down, so Mother believes (almost?) that Great-uncle Tom died in Sierra Leone just as the sun went down or—I forget which—just as the tide turned or the moon set or the last leaf fell. In her scrambled repertoire of songs, which includes many about the kind of prettified nineteenth-century wars Grandfather Porter painted, is a song illustrating this belief. The few recallable lines go something like this:

> One held a lock of thin grey hair,
> One held a lock of brown,
> Closing their eyes to the earth and skies,
> Just as the sun went down.
> One thought of mother, at home alone,
> Feeble and old and grey,
> One of his sweetheart he'd left in town,
> Happy and blithe and gay. . . .

Of Great-uncle Tom, who had sent her a sleeping doll large as a two-year-old human, its body of pink kid dressed in the most delicate embroidered muslins edged with lace, from which its china face and limbs white-and-rosily emerged,

82

Mother says, 'I was sitting, quiet as a mouse, on my little stool under the pomegranate tree by the well. I was nursing Charlotte. I called her Charlotte, you see. There I was, quiet as a mouse, and there wasn't a sound anywhere. And I was thinking of Uncle Tom, the way one does. The sun was just setting.' (It may have been the moon setting, or the tide turning. This detail eludes me.) 'And, as I sat there thinking of Uncle Tom, Charlotte suddenly twisted about in my arms. As though she were in pain. Of course, I didn't think anything much about it at the time, *very* strange as it was. But, months later, when we heard of Uncle Tom's death in Sierra Leone, it all came back to me in a flash. I remembered. And it was at the very moment that Charlotte had moved that poor Uncle Tom. . . .'

You can guess the rest of Mother's nonsense.

Were I to be hounded into presenting, before some unimaginable tribunal, illustrations of Mother displaying her love, I should ultimately present what I have here and now chosen to present to the tribunal of myself. Doubtless, in an ultimate analysis, whatever I consider pertinent, and attempt to present dead-pan, and as objectively as possible, turns out to be as sentimental and nostalgic as the rather twee picture of Mother playing Tit-Tat-Toe with me by far-off lamplight or, with the engine of yet another day at last turned off, drowsily suckling a baby—now a broken man older than Mother ever becomes—by the dregs of a fire, three coals like carnations, in a kitchen smelling of peace and a cut lemon.

This Mother is the same Mother who excitingly chills our blood by whispering to us as we sit on the side veranda watching the owls swoop by in the twilight:

'In a dark dark land there's a dark dark town; in the dark dark town there's a dark dark road; in the dark dark road there's a dark dark street; in the dark dark street there's a dark dark lane; in the dark dark lane there's a dark dark house; in the dark dark house there's a dark dark room; in the dark dark room there's a dark dark coffin; in the dark dark coffin there's . . . a dark dark GHOST!'

Her telling us children these tales, this rubbish, is part and parcel of a never-pausing and never-ending expression of her love; she shares with us her own fervour for, and genuine half-fear of, the supernatural and the ghostly and ghastly and completely absurd, just as freely and directly as she shares herself from Archer to Zany, her private derisive vulgarity and exquisite public manners, her blowtorch temper and cool, deep reservoir of patience, her blind honesties and trivial dishonesties, her charm and her stupidity, her fantasy and her practicality, her pretty ideas and her silly whims.

Unlike Father, who has nothing of himself to give, or only the shadows of virtues, and weaknesses not fit for children tough as children, Mother is perpetually generous with herself. This is either because she can freshly remake herself, good and bad, and therefore inexhaustible, or because she is by nature indestructible.

No! Mother's chance of death is so poor as to make death for her unbelievable. She has none of the marble nobilities, none of the bronze-laurelled virtues. She is too human.

Grandfather Porter's death is, however, quite believable and, though with a different intonation, for the same reason. He is *too* human.

His death, long expected, nevertheless catches the family napping *circa* 1920. It is enacted solo, informally, and with a modesty edging on secrecy. These are unlooked-for and outrageously unexpected tactics in a man of stubbornly military character who has lived for a number of years on little more than reading, port wine, cigar smoke and imperial behaviour. Defrauding his ten children and his second wife, an ex-beauty and ex-crack-rifle-shot called Katherine Hayes, of a rip-roaring death-bed scene, Grandfather is one moment alive in his wheel chair, smoking a cigar and nagging away about a paper-knife for which Aunt Kate (Grandfather's second wife Katherine), Aunt Gwendoline (Father's half-sister) and Aunt*ie* Nell (Father's spinster sister Helen) are searching in other parts of the house. The next moment Grandfather is dead, and in no need of the knife for which people are fruitlessly searching—it is under the wheel chair —selfishly dead, without giving proper notice.

Upon hearing the news which arrives by dramatic telegram I am disappointed to witness no tears from Father or
even Mother, and none of the cries ('Alas! Woe is me! Gone,
gone, gone!') books have led me to expect. I am rattled also
to observe that my parents seem too illiterate to know what
they can do in lieu of more articulate expression of emotion.
They do not blanch, bite their lips, press hands to hearts, or
clench their jaws. Father begins to strop his razor, talking of
trains as though there were fifty a day to the city instead of
two, the early morning and the afternoon two-thirty. Mother
begins to pack Father's portmanteau with the South African
labels on it, addressing stern remarks to underpants ('I was
sure I'd darned you, you nasty thing'), and starched collars,
and Father, who addresses replies to his own lathered face in
the looking-glass.

'Oh, Curly! You can't, you *can't* wear this black tie,' cries
Mother at the tie, glaring at the tie. 'It's frayed to billy-oh.
Get a new one at Buckley and Nunn's.'

'Have to do,' says Father to the face he is slicing foam from.

'Buckley and Nunn's. It won't take any more than a
quarter of an hour. A half-hour at most. *Before* you get the
train to Williamstown. Get a good silk poplin.' Her voice
becomes aerated. 'And while you're in town you can get me
a packet of verbena seeds.'

Father says nothing so deliberately that Mother says,
'Verbena seeds!' sharply as a slap.

'Going to a funeral,' says Father. 'No time for traipsing
through. . . .'

'Listen carefully, man. I've put your corn-cure—are you
listening, Curly?—your *corn-cure* under your handkerchiefs.
No, I think *two* packets. Pretty things, verbenas. There's a
new strain out called . . . called. . . . There, I've forgotten the
name. But I'll write a list.'

So this is death and bereavement!

Observing the bereaved I am not convinced, despite the
potency of the telegram, of Grandfather's death.

However, something impressive does happen. A week
later Father returns enriched by a new black tie, silk poplin,

Buckley and Nunn's, and a black armband. This latter really is something. In the absence of tears and wailings, in the absence of a blood-curdling recital from Mother whom I expected to seize the opportunity of an authentic bereavement as inspiration, but who, when nudged in the direction of clarifying doom, says no more than, 'The dear old man has gone to join the angels in heaven. He'll meet Grandmother Porter. Eat up your swede, it's got nutmeg in it. Which you *like*,' the new tie and the armband are the only proofs to convince me that Grandfather really is dead.

More convincing proofs arrive some weeks later, four of Grandfather's paintings of enchanted and blood-free battle, and one of a Moorish interior alive with mild, minute Arabs with eyes the size of pin-heads. The Arabs are wrapped like parcels in robes with papery folds. Some are striped like humbugs. Some Arabs stand, some incline, some half-kneel, some are flat on their faces, among the slender pillars, and under the archways shaped like playing-card Spades. Each head is turbaned differently, as if the painting illustrated *Twenty Ways to wind your New Turban*.

'Hell and Tommy!' says Mother, and puts the paintings in the spare room where they almost cover the walls, and induce a feeling of claustrophobia.

There also arrives a case containing books, and a note in curly backhand:

For Laddie. I hope he gets as much pleasure and benifit from these as his dear grandfather did. How is Owen? K.P.

Owen is Father's second name.

I feel pretty sure, now, that Grandfather's wife, my father's stepmother, Aunt Kate, clearing the Williamstown house with its wind-gnawed chimneys of the dead's lumber, decides fortuitously on me as donee a split second before the rubbish-man arrives. In her world of whist, rifle-shooting, spicy gossip, crayfish suppers and horse-race gambling, books are junk which she transforms into a gesture of uplifting affection for the gilt-headed and cat-smug boy she dislikes because he talks in polysyllables, writes poetry about sunsets, and paints in water-colours the flags of the world, regimental badges and the guild signs of London, all copied from 'Chums'.

'Why did Aunt Kate send Grandfather's books to *me*?' I wastefully ask Father.

'It's about time you went to the barber,' says Father.

'Because she can't read, can she—O-wen?' says Mother unpacking the books, and bursting into, 'I'm called little Buttercup. . . .'

'She can't spell benefit,' I say of the woman who, in handing on Grandfather's books to me, hands on the very material that is ultimately to quicken in me the infusion of footloose blood Grandfather has himself handed on to me. The books are calf-bound. Cigar-ash is spilt here and there between the lithographs and woodcuts and steel engravings. The pages have been cut with the paper-knife lost under the dead man's chair. Among the books are works later to have much effect on my life: Mitford's *Tales of Old Japan*, Bird's *Unbeaten tracks in Japan*, Mac Farlane's *Japan* and Reed's *Japan*. It is natural to assume that the old man with the tobacco-stained moustache whom I did not like, who gave me the bronze Goddess of Mercy, loved Japan as I love it.

Father's black insignia of tear-less mourning, the oil-paintings in the spare room, and the books indicating my idea of earthly Paradise, are certain enough proofs of Grandfather's death but the clincher is the fact that, overnight, Grandfather becomes gloriously ennobled. He has hitherto been, I have been thrilled to overhear, a selfish old scoundrel wasting his time with books and paint-brushes, improvident, a bore, a know-all, a blatherskite, shrewd as a bagful of monkeys, a malingerer, ungrateful, always half-seas-over and, in some undefined fashion beyond the reach of law, responsible for that dear, sweet woman's, his first wife's, death, Aunt Frances's stammer, Auntie Nell's weak ankles and nervous twitch, and Father's meagre finances. Now, though not worthy of tears and cries of sorrow, he is no longer worthy of abuse. The prickly bushes of his petty failings and capital sins explode into blossoms of virtues I try to avoid overhearing accounts of. He is a witty old boy, a brave soldier brave to the last, and a thorough—a *fine*—old English gentleman, an exemplary husband to his first wife—that virago and flibbertigibbet who could not keep a servant longer than a day, a kindly father without whose inspiration and patience Aunt Frances would never have spoken a word or Auntie Nell—*Aunt Helen*—ever have walked a step.

He becomes, in fact, more boring dead than I ever found him alive, when I dutifully repaid his reasonable boredom with me by my unreasonable boredom with him.

How ruthless and hard and vile and right the young are.

I am as happy, during the four years, between the ages of six and ten, that I spend at State School 754 in the country, as I briefly was in the suburban state school. I love facts, and the excitement and processes of getting facts. In short, I love school, and am, fortunately, hurried from grade to grade—once passing through two grades in one year —at a speed fast enough not to have my ardour for supplies of brand-new information, and more intricate problems, and more decorative knowledge, whittled down to boredom. I perceive, absolutely without surprise and almost without interest, that I am younger and much more clever than the other boys and girls in the class, that is much more clever, and for a space of several years only, at school work. Much of this variety of cleverness sticks about me like a nimbus of fuzz, until the storms of puberty unpick it, and I become intellectual rather than intelligent.

It never enters my head to consider that this short period of being convinced by what I am told, of being swift in perception, and retentive of memory, is my fault or my crown. I am loudly informed from the platform, by accredited adults I have no reason to doubt, that seven eights are fifty-six, that Berlin is on the Spree, that Henry the Eighth had six wives, and that William Wordsworth was an English poet, and decorously and unquestioningly adopt this information. Teacher says so: that is that. All I have to do is to sit with my hands clasped behind my back, and listen, and remember. I do. It is dead easy. This a-rose-is-a-rose-is-a-rose attitude to primary education serves me well.

Once, but never again, my passion for abundance and mental industry tempts me to greed, and I learn all the verses of 'Harry Dale the Drover' instead of the one verse asked for as a night's homework. I discover, next day, less by directer means than a kind of pricking of the thumbs, that this showiness is a dirty indiscretion, a traitor's ploy, and socially offensive.

I immediately cotton on to the fact that intelligence thus lightly used, and one-upmanshipishly displayed, is a birthmark giving me a two-coloured face, is goitre, a hump on the back, webbed toes, and makes me stink like the night-man. Once again, I learn what I knew on my very first day at Kensington School, and have carelessly forgotten, that it is more intelligent to appear less intelligent. I henceforth rein myself in, and publicly give back only what I have been given—fifty-six for seven-eights. It is incomprehensible to me that others have time enough to proffer fifty-four or sixty-three or silence, responses striking me as perverse, undisciplined, and as elaborate tricks. I do not realize, then, that my suspicions are largely correct, and that the pleasures of thus exercising the mind are not, for ever, to be for most of my schoolfellows: bodily pleasures will do, a cave and a curtain will do.

I am, fortunately, as indifferent to my success indoors at school as I am indifferent, fortunately, to my lack of success in the organized games of the schoolground. I do recognize some protective value in, and receive some physical pleasure from, swimming, running, climbing and fighting, and therefore am able to swim like a frog or Byron, can run and climb as well as less brainy boys, and fight with uninhibited ferocity when circumstances nick a hole in my thick fleece of serenity, and let out a gush of hate. I cannot consider fighting in competitive Manly Fun any more than I can consider pitting my running, swimming or climbing body against other bodies. Nothing, then, or now, arouses me or will ever arouse me from a perfect disinterest in ball games. I see other boys showing every possible sign of coarse pleasure in football and cricket and shinty, in boxing and wrestling; I see their burning eyes and hurtling bodies and interlocked limbs, and know they are freeing themselves from something, but cannot understand precisely how the relief occurs, because my relief from much the same sort of something occurs in different activities. The boys' anticipatory conversations, endlessly repetitive, bore me; the games bore me; the post-mortems composed of excusings, recriminations, vainglory and downright lies horrify me.

My disinterest, openly expressed and lived up to, angers my father. It is a spurning of his unexpressed hopes that I should equal, perhaps even surpass, his own skill for competently kicking, bowling, catching, throwing or striking at balls of various sizes.

Throughout a middle-class boyhood, private school education, and young manhood, Father has every opportunity to burnish his skill, and empty-headedly seizes these opportunities. He wins several electro-plated cups on stands of fake ebony, half-a-dozen medals in jewellers' boxes lined with royal-blue satin, and a meerschaum pipe in a meerschaum-pipe-shaped container lined with vermilion plush. His particular passion is cricket, a game he plays so successfully as a young bachelor on a two-years' visit to South Africa that a farewell dinner attended by sixty cricketers and cricket-addicts and hangers-on is held in Cape Town on the evening before he sails back to Australia. To the seat of honour at that dinner is as far and high in life—or, rather, in what Father considers worth-while life—as he goes. It would have been a fitting chair for him to have died in, at least for the games-playing part of him to have died in. He would not then have nonchalantly bowled down other human beings as though they were wickets and he fate.

I first become aware that he is famous to himself when he becomes aware (or has he been patiently waiting?) that I am old enough—no, *big* enough—to be taught some tricks with bat and ball. He is too late. I am not to be corrupted; and my precise and glass-clear and abominably priggish analysis of why I will not play with him, my own Father who buys my porridge and boots, begins a period of years of wry antagonism. He is too late because, first of all, I have already watched, and found out that games of this formal sort are, from my point of view, only for those people whose supplies of energy and vanity can be burned away inside the framework of a game, only for those who have nothing to do, and who have the time to waste to become proficient in wasting time. I have no time to waste. Father's idea of daily practice with bat and ball shocks me because it means less time for swimming, tree-climbing, reading, drawing, less time to loll and think long wonderfully useless thoughts, less time to watch myself and the world. He is too late because I am born with some lack in or addition to my faculties which makes it impossible for me to pit myself against another in games at the finish of which there are only two prizes, Winner or Loser, both meaning nothing, games that smell of wars conducted on gentlemen's agreements, their sincerity hollow, their intentions cut-throat. Finally, and most tellingly, he is too late because, by the age of ten, I am dubious of the weight of his honesty, and the safety of his simplicity. Time is to prove this wariness all too prophetic. It is not until I am thirty-five years old that I meet, face to face, an actively evil person, a highly intelligent, complex, dishonest and destructive woman but, from having observed my father, a man of mediocre intelligence, simple, honest and, ultimately, as destructive as cancer, I have learned to make out the signs of the blind wrecker.

I am able to sniff out many of my father's imperfections because he has passed them on to me from his own father. It is a heritage I have to keep my eye on for many years, a heritage including a blindness to the points of view of others that amounts to insulting indifference, a lack of imagination, a stubbornness, self-satisfaction, and bland selfishness. I attempt, still, sometimes successfully, sometimes not, to amend this heritage in myself. Father, at thirty-six, merely conceals these flaws by a convincing pretence at hearty participation in the rites of public living—he is, for example, a Mason; he plays golf; he plays cricket; he plays masculinity and respectability and being a good husband, a good father and a nice man.

A form of wordless heroism?

I am trapped by blood, convention, daily proximity, the law, and the fact that I am utterly incapable of earning my own roof, porridge and boots. I love Father but know him to

be an unfurnished man. What contretemps of inner existence
has made him continue unfurnished, year after year, I do not
know. I do not know because, having no imagination, I do
not understand people. I understand no one, and never have,
and never will. What they will *do* is too easily foreseeable; for
me it is nearly always impossible to know *why*. Rape, murder,
suicide, gambling, budgerigar-keeping, any-bloody-thing—
they can tell me why and, 'Yes, oh yes, I do so understand,'
is what I can say. But—really—I do not. About Father, I
suspect (but am nevertheless doubtful) that his sensual desires perpetually gnaw at and consume any will to discipline,
any thought of sacrifice. These itchy desires must long ago
have consumed ambitions and hopes.

He may possess secrets too sweet for the rest of the world.
For all I can judge he may well be—it is difficult for an
eldest son like me to put the correct price on a father like
him—the most cynical man I am ever to meet.

He is undoubtedly a man not earthed although he appears
to be, for it is a prefabricated and carefully inspected personality that fronts the world. Brought up middle class he
chooses to become lower middle class, and to assume the
identity of the lower middle class, that class whose contribu-
tion to ethics is self-respect. The Australian form of self-
respect, however rough-and-ready, heart-of-gold, come-and-
take-pot-luck-with-us, and matily extrovert is, essentially,
genteel, ingrowing, self-pitying, vanilla-ice-cream hearted,
its central fear a fear of the intellect. Father simulates all this
in such a *trompe l'oeil* manner that he convinces himself too.

What he does do: work, eat, sleep, make babies, go to
Lodge, brush his eyebrows, bowl balls, dress, bathe, and so
on—these make a harmless pattern. What he does not do
makes another pattern for which I find no adjective. He does
not whistle or sing or directly express an opinion or collect
things or write letters or—until decades later, and then only
the 'relaxing' rubbish of Westerns and thrillers—read books.
He sits by the fire, his eyes burnt down to glass, and set in a
quizzicality of wrinkles. If I ask how Old Mother Mawdsley
plants the seeds for babies he tells me to tuck my shirt in. He

93

has a number of such replies. After any question, his blue eyes twinkling at some inner judgement he seems to have had to make of the questioner, he says, 'Aren't you supposed to be doing your homework?' or, 'You've got indelible pencil all over your lips,' or, most often, 'Ask your mother.'

I stop asking him, and with him, stop asking serious questions ever, even of myself.

I repeat, by the age of ten, I am dubious of the weight of his honesty, and the safety of his simplicity. Does he realize that I have inherited this obliquity of indifference, this stubbornness, and am also fortified by these qualities against *his* indifference and stubbornness, and am too clever by far to ask one of the questions that would alter the indirect glint in his eye to some other sort of glint, even gleam. If I were to flatter the skill on which his tiny fame is built by asking, 'Would you show me how to bowl a left-hand googly?' is he cynical enough to reply, 'Your neck is as black as the ace of spades,' or, 'Ask your mother'?

I wish, now, that I had been dishonest enough, and unselfish enough, and sweet-natured enough, to ask that question, just as I wish I had been honest enough, and selfish enough, and vicious enough, to ask, 'You spent your boyhood practically living right on Williamstown Beach. Why can't you swim?' or, 'You were thirty, and healthy as a trout, in 1914. What did you do in the Great War, daddy?'

His responses to a genially dishonest question about one aspect of his masculinity (the cricket, golf, pipe-smoking, Masonic side), and a maliciously honest one about another aspect of it (the non-swimming, not-going-to-the-War side), would have been as enlightening to me as a writer as to me as a son and a different kind of male.

Years later, I spend some weeks fighting, with my own middle-aged obstinacy, his seventy-three-year-old stubbornness which is taking the final form of starving himself to death in a posh hospital. From somewhere he dredges up his last mortal words, and gives them to me, using the long-unused nickname of my boyhood, 'Thank you, Laddie, thank you for everything.' As a finale to a ludicrous death-bed scene, and a father-son relationship, and a life, it is, with its Yankee-Jewish-Metro-Goldwyn-Mayer sentimentality, a farewell both startling and mysterious. Irony? Cynicism? Pity for me, uselessly pitting my strength of will against his in the battle to make him keep on living? Good sportsmanship? Charming manners, and being a nice man? His dead face, of course, was then there to be seen. Dead faces, despite the novelists, despite even the poets, are nothing more than the faces of the dead which say nothing, nothing new, nothing worth recording or shedding tears for.

'Ask your mother!' says the unfurnished man with his eyes, exactly the colour of mine, twinkling. Sometimes, rarely, he is harried by Mother into attempting to make something—he has an enormous sea-chest of elegant tools. He begins a dog-kennel, a piece of trellis, and, once an extension to the cow-shed. Hurriedly and badly (deliberately badly?) he makes part of what he has been begged to make. Leaving the tools scattered about, he abandons the job, puts on his silk shirt, and white flannels, his cricket boots, and his I-am-a-man cricket cap, his cap of invisibility, and is invisible. I finish the dog-kennel; the trellis remains unfinished, and wistaria hides its imperfections; Mother finishes the cow-shed, all us vertical children simulating helpfulness, the latest baby, now weaned to a titty-bottle, horizontal on an afghan, Mother crying out, 'Hell and Tommy!' and, 'Hell and *bloody* Tommy!' or singing as she hammers away:

> '*Oh, don't de-ce-eive me, don't ever le-eave me,*
> *How-ow could you you-oo-ooze a poo-er maiden so!*'

She has named the cow Dolly—which is the name of Uncle Martini-Henry's horse, as well as the name Father calls Mother. The implications in naming the Jersey after herself are too fine for me to pin down. Something is doubtless implied—I know Mother. Her quirk of calling straight-haired Father Curly is a sauciness one can expect from her, but it is also the expression of an attitude many Australians have, an attitude tending towards aspersion. It also seems to me to be Early Edwardian for Ida and Harold to become

Dolly and Curly, to suggest the gaiety and liveliness of their courtship and young marriage, the cosy safety that the watcher on the cast-iron balcony in Kensington feels behind his back as he gazes, not only into his future, but into the actual direction of the scene of much of his future.

Mother completes Father's unfinished cow-shed, and it is 1921, and she has only eight more years to work and sing, and suffer without ostentation, and grow older, and die without completing unfinished Father.

In 1921 Father is a cricket-playing Mason who does not sing; Mother is a mother with one more child to be born; the long horizontal banners of calico with WELCOME HOME on them no longer need to be hung along the eaves of front verandas with their trimming of cast-iron crochet to greet soldier sons or husbands returning from the Great War healthy as trivets, or shell-shocked or gassed or one-legged or all three, for they have all returned older who have not died younger, and are beginning to limp or creep from door to door along the elm-shaded streets, with trays of wide boot-laces, golliwogs, packets of pins and hairpins and darning needles, jew's harps, milk-jug-cover beads, imitation amber cigarette-holders, and Japanese fountain pens made of bamboo, with toffee-coloured glass nibs ribbed like lemon-squeezers; I am ten, and in my last year at State School 754.

State School 754 is as architecturally solid, purposeful and comfortable as many schools built in Australia in the 1880's and 1890's. It is of red brick circumspectly enlivened by a geometric fancy-work of primrose-coloured bricks, clinker bricks and lines of black mortar. Its alp-steep, alp-high roof and false gables are regularly inset with smaller ventilator-gables, attics for starlings whose untidy nests protrude from the louvres, and whose baby-ribbon-blue egg-shells are found in the school-ground caught on the shores of the archipelagos of plantain and shepherd's purse that litter the sea of gravel. Since each class-room has its fire-place, on the shelf of which sit wheat growing in saucers of damp cotton-wool, and pickle-jars decorated with shards of broken china embedded in putty, there are many chimneys. Above these shafts, of terra-cotta, and ornate, in the terra-cotta manner, as Oscar Wilde's Tite Street house is, the bell-tower soars up, pricks up its weather-vane, and trident lightning-conductor, to overtop the elms and oaks and plane-trees and peppercorns we are forbidden to climb. Higher than all is the red gum, hundreds of years old, which stands, muscular, masculine and primitive, at the edge of the several acres of playing-fields, a pelt of couch grass and onion grass through which generations of small soles have abraded deep, narrow, winding paths.

Inside the school, there is the smell of chloride of lime, chalk-dust and cedar pencil-shavings. The white tongue-and-groove ceilings seem miles up; the rows of hat-pegs and wash-hand-basins in the tiled-floor cloakrooms seem endless (here there is the smell of carbolic soap entwined with the P. and O. ship smell of Brasso); the wide central corridor, lined with the indoor casement windows and glass-panelled doors of the classrooms, symbolically objectifies primary school life, for at the distant eastern end are the classrooms of the Babies at their sand-trays, paper-folding and uncertain singing; at the western end, peak of achievement, is the Sixth Grade singing 'Wind of the Western Sea' in three parts, diction momentarily refined and poetic—*wined* for *wind*—and voices still unbroken, and sexlessly melancholy.

Perhaps it is because I love Saturday and Sunday somewhat more than I love school, that Friday, the door opening on to them, seems the day of the week I recall most, the last hour of Friday afternoon, 3 p.m. to 4 p.m., summer.

Friday afternoon. Summer. Beneath the half-drawn blinds flows the faintly peppery scent from the miles of desiccated grass encircling the town. Outside, in the European trees, the cicadas, which have been unremittingly at their vast chorus since eleven in the morning, are running down like dentists' drills. Inside, the end-of-the-weekly tasks are done. The inkwells have been emptied and washed. The blackboard has been blacked. Teacher's strap is well-earned-resting until Monday when, once again, for the thousandth threatened time, no boy will have the foresight or the resin to rub resin on the palms of his hands. We all believe that, not only will this simple treatment protect us from pain but that it will shatter the strap into fragments as it strikes our palms. The class, twenty of us, drones contentedly with the droning blowflies—twenty of *them*. I drone, I listen to the droning, and watch myself and those others.

Heads weighed forward by foot-long curls or gushes of nitty hair, the pinafored girls inject stitches, with infinite ladylike languor, into soiled poly-angles of huckaback— huckaback bibs and comb-cases and nightdress bags and scissors-covers and sauce-bottle jackets. The girls' glass bangles tinkle as their soft, soft lips purse and part, purse and part over teeth smudged with mignonette-green. They had a bath last Saturday night; they will have a bath to-morrow night. Their hankies live about the elastic of their bloomer-legs, dirty mauve handkerchiefs into which they weep gently as overflowing cups when they lose their polka-dotted hair-ribbons, skipping-ropes with wooden handles ringed like Alice in Wonderland's stockings, little copper cable-bracelets with locks to which the keys are already long lost, and their hexagonal pencils, one end of which writes blue, the other red. Boys lose shanghais, bazookas, pen-knives, tops, water-pistols, tin soldiers, and the greenish glass marbles formerly stoppers in lemonade bottles. While the girls prick on at their huckaback, the boys—flannel-singleted, galatea-bloused, bare-footed, all of them uncir-cumcised, un-vocational-guidanced, un-medical-inspected, un-intelligence-tested—publicly 'model' on their modelling-boards plasticine ivy-geranium leaves and, under the desk, long skinny snakes, or small male sexual organs which they show each other in the curve of their grimy hands without looking at each other.

Teacher, sacrosanct on the platform, sits seemingly harm-less, nearly human in posture and silence, but only to be trusted out of the corner of one's eye, at the table covered by its ink-blotted maroon serge cloth. What does he, in alpaca coat, winged collar, and boots with toes turned up like a

98

London bobby's, or she, in pearl-buttoned voile blouse, and patent leather belt, write or dream or privately agonize about?

Matters not.

Huckaback, plakka, love letter, poem never to be published, lying letter to creditor, formless daydream, fretful vision of expected lustful satisfaction or foreseen loneliness, all in that schoolroom are earmarked. All occupy a set place in a scheme of rigid relationships. Nothing is equivocal. Boys dress as boys, girls dress as girls, teachers as teachers, and no one, least of all the teacher, suggests that any of one group should pretend to understand or magnanimously sympathize with any of another group, or should betray instinct and the facts, and, with democratic dishonesty or psychological pusillanimity, overlook the palpable differences in age, power, intelligence, position and class. It is still a world Victorian enough for one decisively and safely to know one's exact place.

To middle-aged (reactionary?) me this summer-embalmed sense of safety, individuality and realism sums up State School 754, Bairnsdale, in the twenties of—it seems unbelievable— this century. Was it all, ultimately and really, a system giving a more accurate foretaste of Life than education tries too analytically to offer now?

The Headmaster, with clattering false teeth, dribble-marked waistcoat, and dandruffy clerical grey shoulders as sloping as a hock-bottle, is a rarely vouchsafed God whose weekly sixpence prize for the best essay on *Thrift* or *Honesty* or *Patriotism* has an air of the Victoria Cross. He and his staff, however crabby, crazy, sawny, pernickety, tempestuous, motherly, scatter-brained, hot-blowing and cold-blowing, are God and the archangels, feared and revered, a human God and human archangels, wiser intuitive psychologists and proxy parents, more dedicated and less materially molly-coddled than the subsidized, production-belt experimentalists of today, the political fancy-men, the fad-sellers, the childhood-betrayers, the confidence men on a soft cop. These seem not to know, as children know, and teachers of forty years ago know, that children are both wicked and wonderful, needing to have their bottoms tanned so that they are not seduced into destruction by unjust tolerance. Teachers of my childhood are, of course, vilified for a number of imagined failings; children are the world's most accomplished scandalmongers, liars and gossips. Those teachers are, however, never traduced for a moral misdemeanour, unless lack of ability to control children can be seen as morally improper.

I recall Miss Harvey, distended and pink as a cabbage rose. She lets us sing 'Abie, my boy' and 'I'm forever blowing bubbles' as we march into the classroom, and is often as funny as Louise Fazenda in the silent films. Half-hidden, however, beneath the petals of pink frivolity and funny-bone behaviour, are steel-bright disciplinary thorns that force us to discipline ourselves to rule unsmudged red ink lines (for it is the era of red ink and the red pencil), to recite with elocutionary panache 'The Slave's Dream', and to fill in with greasy coloured crayons those elaborately difficult shapes, the maps of Tasmania, Canada and Ireland. She involves us in no dog-in-the-manger sex instruction, no trumped-up commerce between wise child and sullied adult. We children tell parents and teachers nothing unfit for them to hear. They are prudently equally mum. We do not bore and confuse each other by trumping reality with small half-truths.

In Grade Six, we meet Mr. Daniel Samuel Treagus who possesses the showier disciplinary arts of Satan as whom he is as ferociously handsome, limber and shapely, from his sharply pointed widow's peak and circumflex eyebrows of charred black to his sharply pointed boots. 'You wr-r-r-riggling wor-r-r-rms,' he brays metallically. 'If the gr-r-r-reat angel Gabriel himself . . . nay, if the Lo-r-r-r-rd Himself stood on this platform, you'd defy Him. But you'll not defy me. Not *me*! Oh, never, never, never-r-r-r!' He knows we know he knows that, under his brimstone gaze and demoniac flourishings, we will not defy a caterpillar. How we parse for him! And swim! No mere television image of terror he—he hypnotizes us with ringing human noise, a dashing blackboard manner, his stinging leather strap, and the intensity with which, fully clothed, hatted, booted, he paces the river-bank, bearing a pole from the tip of which, on rope and leather belt, there strains fish-like a flailing one of us boys, a dog-paddling nine-or-ten-year-old. There is no mixed bathing. Among his little men, Mr. Treagus raves like Ezekiel, back and forth, back and forth, on the buffalo grass, terrifying kingfisher and platypus and us, sweating, patient, feared and trusted.

What else do we learn besides swimming and parsing and 'The Slave's Dream'?

By heart—curious, sad expression—we learn a million useful uselessnesses: the countries of the British Empire on which the sun never sets, 'Daffodils', the rivers of North America, the products of India, the dates of kings and battles and executions and broken treaties. We sing 'God bless the Prince of Wales'. We draw sprays of pittosporum, and flower-pots lying on their sides by wooden cubes. We chip-carve teapot-stands and bread-boards. When we read *The Boer and his Horse*, the girls cry, and the boys swallow the tops of their windpipes; when we read *Three Men in a Boat*, the boys laugh themselves flaccid, while the girls pick their noses disdainfully or decorate with red pencil scrolls what they have already written in purple ink in their copies of *Geoffrey Hamlyn*:

> *Black is the raven,*
> *Black is the rook,*
> *Black is the one*
> *Who steals this book.*

Every Friday morning, our copy-books are given out to us. With steel nibs, in ink watered down to duck-egg blue, we prophetically write, thin upstrokes, firm downstrokes, *Procrastination is the thief of time*, *Look before you leap*, *Pride goes before a fall* and *All that glisters is not gold*.

Time, at least, makes *that* ink no paler.

Mother's father dies long before I am born; I am six months old when her mother dies by either, and probably certainly, the bite of a venomous garden-spider, or by being poisoned, as I once overhear some aunts maliciously suggesting, by another aunt.

Grandfather and Grandmother Ruff act out their lives and proceed to their graves in a past that is forced to do without me, and therefore without my opinions. Since my opinions are largely formed by observation, I am unable to have any on my unobservable maternal grandparents. I must take them on trust from Mother's lips. I cannot make them smaller or meaner, nor entertain any mental reservations about them. Consequently, they remain tall for ever, standing distant and dramatic on the horizon of time. Their ancestors take on something of the same monolithic quality, the same legendary air.

On Grandfather Ruff's side, I see the wide-shouldered Protestant shadows of forefather landowners falling through snow-cold air upon the high, brilliantly green fields of valley farms. Their actions are seasonal, and devoted to animals and their needs, rather than personal, and devoted to their own frivolous or moral needs. They are earnestly on the go to an orchestra of cow-bells and rich lowings more than to the clink of wine-glasses or church-bells. They are little interested in learning that they are the victims of God because they are engrossed in not being caught napping, and made the victims of glaciers, spoiled cheese or making hay in a rain-storm. Money is grown as carefully, and is as carefully picked and hung away, as onions are.

On Grandmother Ruff's side, I see shadows less broad of shoulder, taller and lither shadows inhabiting a world in which money is treated with dangerous indifference. It is there, like mercury in a thermometer on which one turns one's back, and goes to Colnaghi's to order treasures not ever to be paid for. One day it is there measuring the footmen, the coachman, the grapes in the glasshouse, and the exact place on the social graph. The next day the bulb cracks; the mercury runs and rolls away in minute beads no effort can recapture.

Grandmother Ruff, fag-end of this faded-out and empty-pocketed aristocracy and, to judge by daguerreotypes, an ardent-eyed beauty, marries Grandfather Ruff, an escapee to Australia from the Sonderlund War of 1847, in Melbourne's then fashionable suburb of Brighton. They take up land in Gippsland, at Sale.

Sale, forty miles west of Bairnsdale, is, in my boyhood, a provincial cathedral city set smack-flat on grassy vast plains, cow-ridden and sheep-blotched, perpetually curry-combed by winds from every quarter, and decorated with park-like areas of bush. It is here, in 1889, youngest after-thought daughter of a spawning of eight children, that Mother is born. Father's parents being as prolific as Mother's, my boyhood is well-provided, not only with ancestral aunts and uncles but also with the husband-uncles and aunt-wives they marry, for all of them are attracted by the fulfilments and hazards of the double bed rather than the exhilarations and omissions of bachelordom or spinsterhood. Since most of these couples are also copiously productive, cousins of all ages congest this stage of my life; braggart striplings with deeply-dented, silver-grey felt hats tilted back on their teak-brown napes, chatterbox young women in fuji silk dresses as striped as the Kodak girl's, skiting boys in sou'-westers of drill, head-tossing girls in ribbed battle-ship-grey stockings, and frilly Indiarubber babies like tempestuous Queen Victorias with bonnets awry.

In this tribal ant-heap, most of the more devil-may-care or forthright members are of Mother's family. It is easy to spot, in these Ruff aunts and uncles and Ruff-descended cousins, a similar rowdy insouciance to Mother's, a similar warmth and febrile intensity, a vivacity bordering on vulgar uproar which does not, however, coarsen them, and leaves their inner delicacy unspoilt and their tenderer hearts private to secrecy. Since many of the Ruffs have stuck to the district, and are a mere forty miles away, there are many chances to visit them and enjoy them and watch them. Watch I must for, though I have maximum *esprit de corps*, the fatal seed to breed the writer—that plant all ears and Argus eyes—has already taken root, and cannot yet be controlled. However much I abandon myself to the lunatic goings-on of children, to the stitch-giving hullabaloo and the blinding and deafening excitement I love, one, at least, of the Argus eyes never blinks, one ear never fails to pick up the sentence that is a ray of light showing up the swindle of appearances and the falsity of logical conclusions. Then, and to this day, however happily I am jostling and being jostled on the jammed highway, nearby watching, the cool one stands, burdened and in the shade: the umbrella, the bundle and I.

Mother's second eldest brother and his family, whom we from Bairnsdale visit most, live in Grandfather Ruff's pioneer house where he and Grandmother die, where nearly all my Ruff uncles and aunts are born, where Mother is born, where Mother is married with waxen orange-blossoms in her hair, and departs for the honeymoon in Ballarat wearing a costume of violet material on March the Twenty-second, 1910. On March the Twenty-second, nineteen years later, she is to leave the earth for her honeymoon in nowhere with all women's final bridegroom.

The house and its surroundings arouse me to the fact of the continuity of family flesh more persuasively than does the presence of my cousins in the flesh. The bricks on the veranda floor are abraded and blurred by the feet of boys, younger than I, who are now bald and grey-moustached uncles, by the soles of little girls—lean Aunt Sophia, pigeon-plump Aunt Bertha, talkative Aunt Rosa Bona, my own mother Ida—who now have little or bigger girls of their own. Here is the wide open fireplace, with its kettle-hook hanging down on a great chain, before which Mother and Father are married. Here still remain a knife-box, a salmon-kettle, a rosewood tea-caddy, a shabby pie-crust table, *millefiori* door-handles and silver muffineers; simple domestic treasures which travelled by sailing-ship from the Old World, and by bullock-waggon along the convict-made road from Port Albert to Sale, frangible and fragile enough inanimates that the death of those who bought them or inherited them animates more than the possessions of the living. These lifeless things, by outliving their owners, speak to me clearly of and for my grandparents; the large oil-paintings of sugar-sweet rustic Switzerland reveal Grandfather's sentimentality, for nothing but a Teutonic sentimentality can have stirred him into lugging these wistful atrocities across oceans, and along rugged roads, into raw Gippsland. Family report says nothing of his looking upon them as a more sordid investment. 'Grandfather loved them,' is said still, in the twenties, of Grandfather who died in the 1890's, a three-bottle man returning sozzled from a Masonic dinner, and thrown from his horse at his own gate. Grandmother's dressing-case with its worn crested-silver and etched-glass contents, its scissors and hooks and bodkins and tweezers and stilettos, its phials and brushes and combs and tiny flasks, reveals to me, more than Mother's accounts of it, Grandmother's fastidiousness. It suggests too that she yearned to keep a portable memento of the showier ancestry time has winnowed away, a fragment remaining for my avid and nauseatingly soulful attention after she herself has been winnowed away by spider or aunt.

In 1921, the acres surrounding the early colonial house of rosiest brick have not been subdivided, and much of the nineteenth century past is there for my entertainment and refreshment, a nostalgic tourist in my own piddling inheritance: the well overhung by the pomegranate tree beneath which Mother sat holding Charlotte the doll while Great-uncle Tom died in Sierra Leone; the long hedge of hawthorn, boxthorn, quince and elm trees; the pump; the Black Hamburgh grape-vine grown from a cutting of the Hampton Court monster; the oaks grown from two Richmond Gardens acorns; the lofty William Bon Chrétien pear tree from which six-year-old tomboy Mother falls, unharmed, unjarred even, and laughing, after a descent that jars almost to cessation the hearts of onlookers; the great-great-great-grandchildren of the bantam rooster that, in the Ruff's humble saga, immortalizes itself and little-girl-Mother by leaping into the hanging-down back-flap of her *broderie-anglaise*-edged drawers as she comes out of the lavatory which is also still there still swaddled in jasmine and mandevillia.

The old-fashioned garden and farmyard, with something of everything, is pure picture-book, and a child's paradise: bantams, turkeys, geese, ducks, Guinea fowl, Rhode Island Reds, beehives, cows, lambs, dogs, cats, a parrot, a cockatoo, a tame one-legged magpie, haystacks, fruit-trees, a sunflower-paddock, a maize-paddock, currants, gooseberries, raspberries, strawberry beds, clumps of bamboo, lavender, guelder rose, a row of elders, primroses, peonies, snailflower creeper, bleeding heart, and ten kinds of violets.

It is easy to see where Mother's delight in growing things has been fostered, a practical delight she has handed down to my two sisters and me.

Indeed, so deep is my pleasure in the work of the garden that, if there be a dimension after death in which grieving for the loss of the world of senses is possible, I shall grieve for no person however once agonizingly desired and passionately beloved, for no emotional adventure however uplifting, for no success however warming, no infamy however exhilarating, for nothing half so much as I shall grieve for the loss of the earth itself, the soil, the seeds, the plants, the very weeds. What this preference implies I do not know, and can only wildly guess. It is a love almost overriding my love of the words that could express that love. It is a less demanding love than the love of words which are more treacherous than plants, more corrupting than picotees, harder to control than a rosemary hedge.

It is difficult enough for me, an unmistakable Australian, albeit of the Awstralian rather than the Osstralian variety, to convey in words to other Australians the exact temper of the clan gatherings at Sale, gatherings of no importance, unrecorded because unrecordable, forgotten before begun, proof of nothing that cannot be unproved, and which, allowing for family verve and offhand solidarity, can be nothing else in the world but Australian. It is much more difficult and almost impossible to entrap this temper in a net of words for non-Australians because it is compounded of the most complex, double-sided and deceiving, and maybe even deceitful, elements. The unwritten rules of behaviour are infinite in number, finely shaded, and subtle to the last fraction of a degree. They are not to be broken. If broken, the rules of forgiveness leading to re-establishment are equally of air and iron. I learn these rules with rather less ease than my contemporaries because, in the back streets of my being, a duel is developing and increasing in fervour between my instinct which knows why something is so, and my henpecking intelligence which wishes to analyse why something is so.

See a crowd of us herded together for morning tea on some occasion—the Sale Show, say—which has brought eight or nine adults, and twice as many children, together at the old house. The men wear their best watch-chains, their opal tiepins, A.I.F. badges and Sunday suits of hand-tailored navy-blue twill or pepper-and-salt Donegal Tweed. They wear these, and stiff collars too, although the temperature is ninety-nine in the shade. The triangles of coloured silk handkerchiefs, largely Paisley, protrude from their breast-pockets. Boots squeak. On the back veranda, the old cedar table seemingly as large as a tennis court is half-covered (the men's half) by their panamas or high-crowned, deep-valleyed felt hats.

'Hurry up with that bloody tea, you bloody women,' the uncles shout. 'Stop your bloody gossiping, and hurry bloody up!' This means many things: that women are merely wives, that the men want their tea, that they recognize that the women are working while the men are idle, that they politely acknowledge this fact, that each husband is saying to all the other women what he would only say to his wife if the other wives were not there.

Next to the men's hats, the women's handbags and new gloves, beige or white, are laid out with the girls' new beige or dove-grey gloves. No female of them would consider appearing ungloved in really public public. They all wear new dresses that smell new. It is still early enough in the day for these garments to be merely on them, rather than that they have settled into the dresses. The women's hats, with imperceptively quivering, semi-transparent brims, bear bunches of gleaming artificial cherries, clinking glassy grapes with a talc-like bloom, or coffee-saucer velvet pansies. The girls' hats are ringed with linen forget-me-nots or pink silk rosebuds. Bangles, aquamarine brooches, and necklaces of amber abound. Everyone is on superlative and high-flying behaviour, which translates into the fact that there is a considered holiday truce in any current feud, and that certain dangerous truths are, this day, to be circumspectly skirted. There is an uproar of chiacking.

'Shut up, you great lazy beasts,' the aunts cry back to the uncles. 'Who's robbing this coach, anyway? Just be patient, you hulking buggers.' Crying out thus, the aunts do not slacken their gossiping with other aunts, and do not halt their busy hands for a second.

In the midst of what appears a typhoon of angry insult and savage cruelty, the boys stand rigidly upright, too clean and too silent, with comb-marks in their hair. They would like to be wrestling or spitting or grabbing each other by the balls, not for fun but to startle the engrossed and selfish adults. The girls titter spuriously at each other, touch each other's mother-of-pearl buttons, and show each other the lace-trimmed handkerchiefs pinned with miniature gilt safety-pins to their velvet bodices, or more fashionably stuck through their rolled-gold bangles.

When tea is poured, 'Christ all bloody mighty!' shouts Uncle X, pointing with a huge segment of walnut-knobbed chocolate sponge, through the gabble, at Uncle Y's shimmering tie. 'Jesus bloody Christ, look at it, will you! Look at the poor bloody bastard's tie! No, no, don't look! She'll blind you.'

Uncle X is thus telling Uncle Y and everyone what Uncle Y and everyone know—that he is more than happy to see his favourite bloke again, and that he likes the tie very much.

'Take no notice of the silly bugger, Y,' says Aunt X. 'It's sheer jealousy. He's only jealous!'

She is making it clear to any aunt who, later, could take it upon herself to think—and say—otherwise, that she has no part at all, albeit harmless her husband's attack, and that she sides as a sympathetic woman with the attacked albeit unharmed.

'It's a *lovely* tie,' squeals Aunt Z, entering the field to compliment Aunt Y tangentially, for Aunt Y, she knows, has bought Y's tie. 'Lovely! It goes with your suit beautifully. Perfect combination. Perfect taste. Don't take a scrap of notice of the silly bugger. Jealousy, that's all. Pure, unadulterated jealousy!'

'*Jealousy!*' Uncle X rolls his eyes ceiling-wards. 'Jealous of that poor bastard's bastard of a bloody tie!' His shouting over, he looks fleetingly, but with meaning and expectancy, out of his raillery, at Uncle Y who is the acknowledged family jester.

The ground having been prepared by Uncle X, principal stooge, with some assistance from Aunts X and Z, Uncle Y is now ready to perform. He puts down his ham-sandwich with elaborate preciseness. He brushes his finger-tips together to remove crumbs or a pretence of crumbs. He clears his throat in the manner of actors acting throat-clearing. His face puts on the pursed-mouth blandness of a superior being.

'X,' he says, curling his fingers like a tea-sipping shop-girl, and assuming an accent of rum truffle richness, 'X, mai deah, *deah* brothah-in-law, whai not be honest with me? Ai know you dote on the tai. Ai'd hev given it to you. If you'd asked naicely. If you'd been frank and open. But you're a cad, suh. You're almost a bally boundah. Your language is *foul*. In short, suh, you're a bastard of the first water, and as cunning as a bloody bagful of you-know-from-where rats. Ai see through you, mai good fell-oh. No tie for you; no bloody tie at all.'

'Yes, yes,' says Aunt X and Z, 'we all see through you, my boy. You can't pull the wool over our eyes.' Then, changing sides, partly because X has now been put in the position of underdog, partly to give Uncle Y, the wit, the funny man, the sad case, the dag, the trimmer, the one-never-lost-for a-smart-come-back, a further opportunity to set them giggling and squealing, the aunts over-act cajolement, 'Now, come on, Y, don't be an old meanie. Set the poor silly bugger an example. Open your heart. Don't be stingy. *You* know he can't afford ties.' This is obverse but graciously astute acknowledgement of Uncle X's keen business sense, and materially successful career. 'Give the poor bugger the tie before he breaks down. Come on, Y, off with that tie.'

And so on.

Exchanges of this coarsely-textured, bravura kind are merely one ingredient of the clamour, and interrupt nothing else. The eating continues as does the passing of teacups, and ham-and-piccalilli sandwiches, and thick triangles of short-bread, and strawberry tart, and the correction of children's manners, and the false praising of other women's sleeves and necklines and jabots. Each one skilfully carries on, at full belt and the top of the pitch and the same time, several conversations: hay harvest, biscuit recipes, bed-wetting, other people's pitied misfortunes and enjoyably scandalous carry-ings-on, pig prices, milk yields, births, deaths and marriages.

Beneath the over-large gesturings, the mock black-guardisms, the trenchant side-comments and satirical laughter, lies a calm reservoir of feeling. This is a reservoir, not too deep, not too large, but strictly family and private, to be tapped only in situations of the gravest kind. It is, in-deed, rarely tapped because individuals, and smaller families within the larger widespread family, prefer to be independent, even secretively proud, in solving their own problems.

Anyway, at the age of ten, I am so in love with the hubbub and braggadocio and seeming confidence of the family that I see them as a skylarking herd to whom nothing is ever a problem, to whom a problem has never presented itself and never will. I see them, of course, only as guests in Bairnsdale or hosts in Sale, when they and we are on show, or in holiday mood, at riverside picnics, renting adjoining beach-shacks at

Seaspray on the Ninety Mile Beach, at carnival times, camping or quail-shooting or salmon-fishing or hare-hunting, and taking steamer-trips down the rivers, through the lakes to the ocean and the endless miles of wide, radiant beaches that rim it. It seems perpetual high noon, dazzling, the air like molten window-panes, and vibrating with family laughter, a laughter never menacing, twopenny-ha'penny, vicious, shallow or hollow, but jetting and splashing out in a happy-go-lucky fountain. I know, now, that what I see and hear, then, conceals behind the jocular uproar, behind the camaraderie and zest, all kinds of selfishness and procrastination, guiles, mendacities, multi-coloured sorrows, anguishes of every variety, even down-right tragedy.

Knowing all this now, I am nevertheless able to see them all, still not found out by Life or me, on that Show Day forty years ago, loud-mouthed and showing-off, over-hearty and carelessly high-spirited, and yet keeping meticulously to the hidden rules. Those rules! Take one rule only; take the rule that governs swearing.

Blue the air may seem to be, but it is only blue of a certain tint. *Bloody*, *bastard* and *bugger* are the only three swear-words they, man or woman, permit themselves and each other to use in mixed company. These words are used in the tone of voice that fillets them of offence, and gives them the quality of endearments. Beyond these three words lies the country of broken rules, of outrage and disgust and Puritan anger. Egged on by my nature to listen and watch, I note too that the swear-words most loudly and often used in the early scenes of clan-gatherings are excited substitutes for expressions of affection taboo to the blushing Australian tongue, for the revelation of deep feelings not to be admitted in a more gracious form. As day wears away to its end, and night falls, and voices soften, the women do not swear at all, the men swear far less, and in a muted way. An aunt who swears like a cockatoo at eleven a.m., at eight p.m. surprises no one by saying, without venom but with firm intention, 'Really, you great hulking men ought to control your language. It's eight o'clock.' My uncles do not comment on this inconsequential remark, but it is understood as consequential, and has its effect. Later in life I am able to observe those of my uncles or cousins who drink, and are usually as foul-mouthed and bawdy as they come when in male company, pruning their conversation of even some of the acceptable swear-words in the front of a barmaid whose attitude they have not yet discovered.

However much I enjoy the hurly-burly and higgledy-pigglediness of these Sale holidays, however many rules I realize, or am forced to kotow to, however much my awareness of being a small fraction only in a multiplication of ancestral flesh, my keenest enjoyment comes from being able to find on every hand three-dimensional evidence of Mother's tales. This is a means of extending myself, of spreading myself backwards in time beyond my own birth; it is the beginning of thought about myself. Hitherto, I have thought far less about the being most concrete and important to me— myself—than about other people, and the world of appearances. Now, in Sale, I appear to myself not only as the me I am discovering but also as Grandfather Ruff chasing aborigines around and away from the very house I am holidaying in—'Cut 'em! Slash 'em!' I cry through my whiskers; I am Mother being born in the room I share with a brother and two cousins; I am Father carving, in his courtship days, on a post in the barn, his own and Mother's initials, H.O.P. and I.V.R., inside a lopsided heart. The past thus surrounding me contains innumerable questions to which I attempt to find answers: here, for example, is the pomegranate tree Grandmother planted above the well; I am part of Grandmother; Grandmother is dead; I live, and the pomegranate tree lives; as I break off a pomegranate, what is the slender but indubitable connection between it and Grandmother and me? Naturally, I find no real answer. I suspect then, I more certainly suspect now, that there is an important answer.

Sale is tied by innumerable threads to many bits and pieces of my later life; I am repeatedly being reminded of Sale by fragments of the world: the waters of Tunbridge Wells have the same gassy taste as the waters of the artesian fountain in Sale Park; the Aimée Vibert roses of Kew Gardens are as white and prolific and untidy as the Aimée Vibert roses by the side-gate where Father used to kiss Mother good night during their courting; the lilies-of-the-valley I pick in a glade in the Forest of Fontainebleau remind me instantly of the lilies-of-the-valley I smell for the first time in the garden-bed by the old pump. Again and again, my boyhood in Sale comes back to me: blood oranges in the railway buffet at Alessandria, chocolate cake at Groppi's in Cairo, a particular sort of cherries in Athens, white violets under the gingko trees of a Kyoto temple, an outsize salmon in a niffy, open-fronted Soho fishmonger's.

It is just such a salmon, in size, that Uncle Fred Ruff has caught on the Ninety Mile Beach, at the Honeysuckles, when we are surprised, Uncle Fred and seven or eight of us boys, by several women in long white dresses and floppy hats appearing over the sand-dunes. Baying blasphemously, his Rodinesque, hairy hands suddenly clamped in the classic gesture of modesty, for he is as naked as a statue, Uncle Fred caracoles with lolloping buttocks into the ocean, we frog-naked boys with our hands similarly but almost unnecessarily arranged, cantering behind him. There, once decently obscured in the soap-suds of surf, but nevertheless keeping our hands in position, we all glare, Triton and his minions, until the ocean- and sand- and sun- and shock-dazzled women start into life again, and, scuttling back over the noon-flowers, disappear like routed Touaregs among the dunes. On the wet sand between the startled and the shocked lies the salmon from the Soho fish-slab.

One day, autumn I suppose, while staying in Sale, Mother and I walk three miles to the cemetery. We have a two-fold purpose: to leave flowers on Grandmother's and Grandfather's grave, and to pick mushrooms. On the way we pick so many along the edges of the ditches that we reach the cemetery with a full basket. At the grave, Mother arranges the chrysanthemums she has brought. Although I am fully aware that she is just not crying, she does not give me the pleasure of the convential tears I conventionally expect so I wander off to watch a nun who is apparently performing what I guess to be a Roman Catholic ceremony at a plot of many nuns' graves surrounded by yews and dominated by an image of the Virgin Mary in white marble. Investigation proves that the nun's moppings and mowings and swift dartings in a half-crouch are no more than the movements of a nun making measurements with a tailor's tape-measure. Is another nun about to die?

As Mother and I are leaving the cemetery, the nun is climbing into a cab at the entrance-gates.

'Gracious God!' says Mother to herself, but loudly enough for the world to hear, as she recognizes the nun. She brushes nothings from the knees of her skirt, takes a little run of excitement, and calls out, 'Sister Philomena!' Sister Philomena is the nun who teaches Mother singing at the Convent of Notre Dame de Sion when Mother is the one Protestant pupil there. We travel back together in the cab.

I cannot recall the conversation which is rapid-fire reminiscence laced with the names of Sisters and Mothers and the girls who were pupils when Mother was Ida Ruff. It is conversation not to listen to, for the sentences have no full-stops and reach no conclusions. My attention goes inward, playing with a name they mention several times, and which haunts me to this day—Bridget O'Loughlin. Who was Bridget O'Loughlin? What were Mother and Sister Philomena saying of her? Where is she now? Occupied with this fascinating name, I do not know by which steps the women in the cab arrive at giving a performance I cannot forget. Suddenly, to my complete amazement, from Sister Philomena's soft and ageless face encaged in brutal white, emerges a clear-cut scale of beautifully formed notes. My own mouth falls open, partly in amazement, but mainly because hers is ovally open.

'Ah! Ah! Ah! Ah! Ah! Ah! Ah! Ah!' she sings. I see her tongue quivering like a human being's. Next, she smiles. Her teeth are so white, so very even, that they must be the first false teeth I ever see if they be not the only flawless teeth I am ever to see. The smile persisting, she says, firmly, not intending to hear refusal attempted, 'Now, Ida, you too. Come, girl.'

Mother immediately folds her hands in a dutifully school-girlish right over left on her lap.

'Ah! Ah! Ah! Ah! Ah! Ah! Ah! Ah!' they both sing, Sister Philomena gently agitating one black-gloved hand in time. The gloves bear little scabs of super-human darning.

'A-a-a-ah!' sings Sister Philomena, schoolmistress, going higher and sweeter.

'A-a-a-ah!' sings Mother, going pink and faintly cross-eyed, and, I know by her twitching fingers, really trying hard.

'Good girl! You were always a good girl, Ida. Now, "Through forest boles." One. Two.'

And, as the cab, the fringes above the doorway quivering, the wheels turning through the freshly gravelled road as through sugar, idly makes its way between the red-hawed hedges and the Kelly-green paddocks and the ditches overhung with fennel and chicory, ' Through forest boles the storm-wind rolls,' they sing with soaring melancholy, rocking and bounding circumspectly opposite each other on the leatherette seats, 'Vext with the sea-driven rain. . . .'

It is the first incident in my life that I consider unconventional or, rather, it is my first recallable experience of un-self-consciousness. This correctly presupposes developing self-consciousness in me. That the happening occurs at the time I am being nudged towards self-consciousness by self-investigation, is to prove of great value. 1921 is the last year, for many years, of my early poise, and is, therefore, part of the design of me, the last year of unflawed non-innocence. I am soon to begin that long, tempting and often shocking journey through the experiences of others which is, year by year, to wear the soles of non-innocence thinner and thinner.

I should, ultimately, die innocent, if I live long enough to wear down, to have wrenched from me, to lose in a half-dream, to give wantonly away, the supply of non-innocence I brought on to earth with me. To assure myself of this desirable end, since half-way house is nowhere, I am constantly uprooting myself, climbing out of the cosy pockets, avoiding the insured cave, the bed-sitter in Babylon, the air-conditioned foxhole with T.V. In short, I do not and must not rehearse for death under the popular anaesthetics.

However, I am still ten and, though I have caught fleeting first glimpses of myself as something rather more than an animal, I am still largely a creature of the five senses.

It is my sense of smell that presents to me, so early, one of the insoluble problems of communication, of communication by word of mouth or writing. I find myself trying to put into words, not only for others but for myself, the nature of various scents, of the difference between the scent of Mother's cabbage roses and her Frau Karl Druschkis, of the odour of a jam roly-poly baked in the oven and a jam roly-poly thumping about in its pudding-cloth in the iron boiler.

It is impossible.

Sometimes one scent appears to duplicate itself, as one situation of living appears to duplicate another, and gives one a chance and a false sense of saying something—the rotting flowers of the iris smell like cat's urine, Early Nancy smells like plum-blossom, peonies like tobacco, marigolds like coffee. This seeming simplicity is unsatisfactorily complex.

It is simple enough, at this age, to recognize but not describe to others the smell of other people's houses, to be—like an animal without words—pleased at, wary of, or affronted by, that smell. One aunt's house smells of home-made bread, mignonette and the sun-hot slats of wooden Venetian blinds. This is pleasing. The house emitting an unrelieved odour of Brasso, carbolic soap, floor polish and phenyle pleases less. The house smelling of old indoor-dog, stale cigar-smoke and the death of moth-balls is one I am not happy to visit. The smells of Bairnsdale come and go, alter with the wind and the weather, and come and go. The south wind, a thing of half-past three in the afternoon, is striped; it carries a diluted odour of the ocean, of mangel-wurzel fields, and a current that waves, like a dirty chiffon scarf, now in front of, now away from one's nostrils, the stench of the slaughter-yards. I am becoming conscious of the fleeting, the impermanent, the here-today-and-gone-tomorrow.

I see an Honour Board, *For God, King and Country*, go up in the school-corridor, and on it the names of my school-fellows which are also the names of their killed fathers—here-today-and-gone-tomorrow.

I see bush-fires, far-off on the foothills and mountain-sides, jewel-like at night, glowering under a mustard-coloured awning of smoke by day. Then the slopes and crests are deceitful and lovable blue again.

I see the river in flood, the water like milk coffee, apparently thick as treacle, and bearing along, not with violent speed but with power too patent and too arrogant, the ballooning bodies of cows, and a rooster, a muck of drenched feathers, masculinity shocked at cataclysm, crouched on a barn door that glides, and revolves like a gramophone record, and glides, and revolves, and glides inexorably out of sight.

I see that October is a month in which flowers of one colour take the gardens and fences and old sheds: lilac, wistaria, thistle, dolichos, cherry pie, cineraria, rhododendron, primula and columbine. Next minute, the tide of mauves and purples has gone; it is multi-coloured November.

I taste the dust of the dried horse-manure that the slender willy-willies leave on my lips and teeth as they circular-waltz from nowhere giddily up to me, and through me, and on to nowhere else. I feel the white dust spirt silkily up between my toes which are soon to paddle no longer in dust for, still barefoot, I know that barefoot days are dropping behind me with the abated flood, the extinguished bush-fire, the willy-willy in a hurry, the flowers of October, the scents of cabbage roses and slaughter-houses.

It is my sense of hearing that collects most telling indications of what is happening to me. I have been living, detached from myself, in a dream composed of fascinating elements, of other people's noises, of the oceanic sound of wind in the pines of the Tannies, of tradesmen's wheels turning into Mitchell Street. Now I am tossing and turning on the outskirts of the dream. I am either beginning to wake to my own fascinations, my own inner noise, or am twisting down more deeply into a dream in which I am of increasing interest to myself as a figment of my own making.

I begin to hear time running away in sumless various fashions; it dawns on me, a startling revelation, that each one sound I hear is one sound fewer to hear in my destined total of sounds to hear. At night, the town's electric light plant, pumping on and on like a heart, is my own bedtime heart, each beat more one fewer of the total beats left. At midnight the town's heart stops dead. Silence falls so violently, with an increase of blackness in my bedroom and the edgeless world, that for a while nothing can be heard but silence. Then, far away, I hear a last rider galloping across the wooden planks of the Wy Yung Bridge, over the river, out of the town. Beyond that scatter of hoof-beats suggesting flight and fear, far far beyond it, on the outskirts of darkness and silence, rises the sound of farm-dogs howling to each other across the miles, and answering each other, and the echoes of their howlings and answerings more remotely howling and answering in the foothills and creek-valleys and waterless gullies.

Time is being pumped away, galloped away, howled away, echoed away, ticked away by the drawing-room clock and the kitchen clock and the clock of *bisque* china in Mother's bedroom and the frost clicking its needles as it knits itself to itself on the sheets of corrugated iron of the roof. Since I am fundamentally more realistic than imaginative, and inclined, at this stage, to find words more convincing than anything else, it is the words of a school song that most clearly express my feeling.

While, from his platform, Mr. Daniel Samuel Treagus, beaked and saturnine, beats time with a dark long hand enriched by its home-grown glove of glossy black hairs, the class clasps its dirty hairless hands before it, and dolefully sings:

> '*Row, brothers, row, the stream runs fast,*
> *The rapids are near, and the daylight's past. . . .*'

'The stream runs fast,' I say to myself. 'The stream, the

stream, the stream runs fast.' I am, in short, for the first time, aware of getting older. I no longer hear my voice squealing and shouting on The Common at twilight, although the voices of the others now and then swing like vocal shadows across the pages of the books I am reading: *Robinson Crusoe*, *Chums*, *The Last of the Mohicans*, *A Tale of Two Cities*, *The Sorrows of Satan*, the *Bible*, *Fox's Book of Martyrs*, Grandfather Porter's books on Japan, *Quo Vadis*, *The Boy's Own Paper*, *The Girl's Own Paper*, *Chatterbox*, *The Stones of Venice* . . . anything. I am indiscriminate because I have no power of discrimination. I am lost and drugged.

'Bookworm,' says Mother—there is her pride in me somewhere, her tone suggests. Father looks, 'Bookworm!' at me—there is his contempt of me somewhere, his look suggests.

I go foundering on.

I no longer hear myself singing, 'Oh where and oh where has my little dog gone?'

Would I sing if Mother were to ask, or has that singer gone with the little boy and the Teddy Bear into the blue world behind the glass pane? I do not know. Since she does not know that I do not know whether I would sing, she does not test acceptance or refusal by asking me to sing. When does she last ask, and I last sing? I cannot remember. Why does she ask no more?

There are now five children. The shawls that were mine when I was the solitary and adored king are showing their age, yellowing like ivory, and growing thinner, on the latest baby. Still, Mother has not played that silly song for my brothers and sisters to sing. Some délicatesse in the mother-eldest son relationship? I doubt if I should have cared had she played *my* song for the others; but I merely doubt; I am far from sure. It is, anyway, one of Mother's fine touches that she does not give the same sort of love to each of us any more than she gives the varying plants in her garden the same kinds of care. When I am three and four and five and six Mother points out the constellations to me: Orion, The Whale, The Hare, The Scorpion, The Cup, The Southern Cross. I look up and up, so earnestly and for so long, at her finger stirring the broth of gems, that I become dazzled and giddy enough to conceive myself staring downwards into bottomless beauty. I know by name the stars and planets she knows by name, and have since learned no more than what she teaches when I am a child.

Not once do I catch her at the same exquisite exercise with the others: perhaps an eldest son exhausts a mother's fire, burns out the last of her virginal flames with the more outrageous flames of the newer, untried masculinity that supplements and at the same time destroys the father's older, tried-out and chewed-over masculinity. Nor, I say, do I catch her playing the stupid song at the Renardi which, older now, its keys no longer sacred under a strip of camphor-scented flannelette, sounds younger as my sister works with mechanical determination on Czerny's Exercises, 'The Merry Peasant', 'The Blue Bells of Scotland', 'The Minstrel Boy' and 'Partant pour la Syrie'. In this last particularly, but in them all, I hear too the trickling away of time, and State School 754, and, month by month, week by week, hour by hour, my tenth year.

As my tenth year slides backwards under my happily and slowly opening mind and my happy and wary heart, it bears away much that is ordinarily seasonal and will slide in again for a few more years on the flood-tide of other years: the wire-netting fences furry with thistle-down, the spiders' webs trapping beads of water into their own pattern from out of the Scotch mists, the fire-bell clashing theatrically through the blast-furnace air of bush-fire days, the springtime paddocks smelling of vanilla from the purple drifts of Chocolate Lily, the steel-lined bleatings of crows as they gorge on the crickets infesting the crevices of the midsummer ground crackled like Ming, the hush-hush-hush sweeping sound as rusted water-carts spray the dusty roads.

The same tide, too, tugs away, as the flood did the humiliated and dying rooster on the barn-door, things and beings and situations I am never to see or hear or touch or experience ever again, except in recollection. Regret somewhat tenderizes recollection of much that is not, really, worthy of regret or recollection or record.

Nigger's death seems worthy of record. He dies, fully conscious of his dying, content to die, and behaving with the flawless farewell manners Mother and Father could well have taken a death-bed lesson from. Tears are shed, largely by me and Mother who have used Nigger most, and for a longer period, as a warm means of entertainment and solace. Mother pleases me by shedding tears at the same time as I do, and in quantity proportionate to the fifteen years she has known Nigger; I understand her sorrow enough to be not impressed by this display. I am astounded, in much the same way as I am when she does not bewail Grandfather Porter's death, by her next move. She buries Nigger's clumsy, doom-heavy body which is movingly worn bare in patches, like an old carpet, against a trellis and, immediately—the distressing thing—plants sweet pea seeds above it so as not to waste the richness of its decay. Although the succeeding years of enormous and almost vibrant blooms are called Nigger's Sweet Peas, and become the smelly animal's fragrant memorial, this is by no means Mother's intention. Her tears shed, her sorrow expressed, she thinks and acts on *Waste not, want not*. The world, I perceive, has two faces. I am putting my lips near the rim of the beaker brimmed with disillusion. Without ever drinking too deeply I am nevertheless to find my lips near this draught again and again.

A travelling troupe playing *Uncle Tom's Cabin* comes to town. It sets up its marquee, weather-dirtier, smaller, more torn and more patched than any circus tent I have so far seen, in Main Street, on the weedy space in front of the Rechabite Hall. The Fire Brigade building is next door. It is therefore on this area, every Thursday evening, that the firemen are to be seen vehemently racing about in their flannel under-shirts and withered braces, or writhing in Laocoön-like and muddy entanglements with the writhing and spirting boa-constrictor of a hose while their well-Brassoed, golden helmets hang neatly and peacefully as saucepans on the inside walls of the Fire Brigade Hall.

When I pay my threepence for a Saturday matinée place on the cheapest benches, my feet in the firemen's weeds, it is impossible to realize that I am paying threepence for a first experience from which the ripples ringing outwards are to affect so considerably some years of my later life that I am, for a while, to make the theatre my profession. Since these ripples are to have some effect almost immediately, it is interesting to note that I am, while engrossed in and enticed by *Uncle Tom's Cabin*, also very disillusioned. As a whole it strikes me as a deceitful business. Although rich in serenity, I am poor in money. Or, rather, my parents blandly admit themselves poor—an uncomplaining attitude I cherish. I do not like Mother and Father being taken down. It is on their behalf less than my tougher own that I mentally disparage Topsy's husky and offhand singing of something like:

> *Ching-a-ring a-ring a-rick-ed,*
> *I is so berry wick-ed;*
> *I's de gal dat nebber was born,*
> *Larkin' all de day from early morn. . . .*

As she gyrates and capers stiffly, I know that she does not care if we payers-of-threepences really believe her to be Topsy. I know she is bored, and not in earnest. She sounds old. Her burnt-corking is patchy, and much more non-deceiving than that I have often seen on the Adams boys and girls who are dabs at blackened faces, tow wigs and horse-hair moustaches. It is this non-deceiving that I find deceitful, the lack of illusion disillusioning. I have paid my parents' money to have illusion and be deceived. Eliza, a plump woman, squeezing a bundled-up doll to her melon breasts, and hopping with wooden noises among ice-floes of kerosene-tins painted white, proves to me nothing but doll, bare planks, and kerosene-tins; the pack of hounds baying in the wings, which are painted with black-grained, cocoa-brown panel-ling, convince me of two men; Eva has a nose much resem-bling my arrogant own and, instead of a rose-bud mouth, a long thin curling one. Disillusion, however, has its cause as much in the shabby antics of these run-down and already out-moded barn-stormers as in my own suddenly awakened vanity. Although I say nothing to anyone, least of all to Mother and Father who must be spared my disillusion, and scarcely even to myself lest I unwittingly give away the secret I tell myself, it is clear to me that I can outbay the man-hounds, devise more floe-like kerosene-tin floes, write more dramatic dialogue, blacken myself blacker than Topsy and Uncle Tom, and act her and him and Little Eva and Simon Legree himself off the stage. In fact, delicious poison has been sipped from a cracked and dirty cup.

Some weeks later, I have an opportunity to sip again. It must be in August or September because there is reason to remember that the Silver Wattles are in full furry bloom. Another touring company, rather less seedy, comes to Bairnsdale. This company's production is called a Chatauqua. To the exact nature of this entertainment memory provides few clues. It is held in the Lux Theatre, which is also called by older locals Payne's Hall, a vast, railway-station-like structure of brick. Here, on Wednesday and Saturday nights, moving pictures are shown. Miss Vogt, whose taken-off bangles are revealed lying in a glinting pile on the piano-top at interval, when she invariably plays her *entr'acte* repertoire of 'La, la, Paris!', 'Little Grey Home in the West' and 'Joseph, oh, Joseph', is the cinema pianist. Nearest her and the screen, still in the tradition of legitimate theatre, are the dearest seats, the front stalls. The less eye-cutting back stalls, which are not separate seats as the front stalls are but long squeaky benches, are occupied by the less prosperous citizens. The pictures flutter and wince as snowy-faced actors and actresses with heavily kohl-rimmed eyes mime and mouth in jerky haste behind a sort of pale rain. On other nights than Saturday and Wednesday the Lux Theatre houses, from time to time, bazaars, flower shows, baby shows, roller-skating, evangelist meetings, conjurers, mind-readers, ventriloquists, acrobats, school operettas, church cantatas, and the Bairnsdale Dramatic Society's productions of *The Patsy, Nothing but the truth* and *Are you a Mason?*

Of the Chatauqua performers I most vividly recall a woman who sings songs I cannot recall. She remains in my mind as one of the three females who, in half a century, impress me as having incandescent, overpowering and final beauty. The other two are Greta Garbo, and the nameless little Kensington girl who haunts me like Lucy Gray, like all the lost children of ballads and life. The singing woman is called Sylvia and, it is now certain, owes her radiance to a china-doll make-up, to her blindingly bare shoulders and spine and bosom, to the seeming millions of stage-lights, and an evening gown of black sequins fitting her unstinted undulations as tightly as fish-scales of luminous jet. Her white white arms and white velvet neck ravish me to disbelief as she gracefully stirs the air with an immense fan of yellow ostrich feathers (how much more loin-warming than Aunt Rosa Bona's hat), and sings higher and higher and unbelievably higher with a piercing spun-glass voice in front of a rippling back-cloth of bulbous white marble balustrades and Corinthian pillars cuddled by pillar-box-red roses. I ecstatically watch from the wings through the slits in my wombat mask. I am a wombat. I am an actor with two lines to speak.

The Chatauqua producer, obviously a shrewd racketeer well aware of the audience they will draw, has cajoled sixty children, costumes provided, from the Headmaster of State School 754, to take part in an Australian fantasia called, I think, *Dot and the Kangaroo* or *Someone and the Bunyip*. There are certainly a kangaroo and a bunyip, and groups of wombats, platypuses, goannas and koalas. These are boys in shoddy disguise. Bigger girls are Gum-nut Fairies in grimy pink *tutus* of cheese-cloth. Little girls, among whom is my sister, are Wattle Fairies in yellow *tutus*, and wearing wreaths of real wattle blossom picked along the river bank. Dick Verco, the school caretaker widow's son, fourteen, and the oldest and most hulking boy in Grade Six, is King Bunyip. He wears a rather doggy mask, fanged and ferocious in a half-wit way. He sits, up-stage, centre, on a rustic throne, while the unrememberable plot proceeds in front of him. To his left huddle the ten wombats, I, as First Wombat in the foreground, the smallest and youngest in the class, awaiting the moment of glory, the moment of legitimized skiting. It comes.

King Bunyip, in whom, by now, I almost believe, turns his crazy-dog mask with its papier-mâché fangs towards the wombats. Under my stuffy and sour-smelling headpiece I exquisitely suffer an excitement, a corrupting *frisson*.

'Ow, Wom-bats, heark-en!' says King Wombat in a sing-song broken voice. 'Say, moi subjects, is ower roil decision roight?'

I start into life. I move. I advance with calculatedly dramatic slowness from among the sweating, stinking, half-blinded wombats—one, two, three paces. I drop to one knee, the down-stage knee. A shrill and affected voice I have never heard in my life before comes from me as of its own unsanctified volition:

'Ai pray that your august maj-es-tee will permit mai brothah wombats to confer on this mattah.'

After an unrehearsed and mind-jolting pause, during which I observe with irritation and shame that my Wattle Fairy sister is scratching her elbow in an unfairylike manner, the caretaker's fatherless bunyip-son says:

'Yes, ow, wombat, we give ower permission.'

Upon this I rise over-gracefully, poise itself, and—the difficult bit—back towards and, alas, into the wombats. I turn, as though on conference bent. We all nudge and bump our cardboard heads together, acting like a group of Garricks. We chatter, 'Rhubarb, rhubarb, rhubarb, rhubarb!' and stop as abruptly as though decapitated.

In the silence I turn, retrace my three paces, and kneel. Once again the high-pitched voice produces itself:

'Your maj-est-ee, mai brothah wombats and Ai have conferred. We one and all applaud your august decision.'

My moment is over, a moment too petty for anyone but me to remember; it is of the past; it is gone; the petty moment is now for others: 'Hurray! Hurray! Hurray!' raggedly shout my brother wombats in voices unlike wombats, boys or anything. To our dismay King Bunyip's mask slides from his face to reveal the sweating, the glistening, the suddenly wrinkled face of Dick Verco with its faint moustache.

The next time I recall seeing that face thirty years have passed. I am now a man—at least, a man of sorts—too much a man, too little a man. I have travelled, been married, been divorced, have talked too much here and too little there, have taken my part in experiments with many lives and many bodies, have had dispassionate or stormy adventures in lying, in drunkenness, in adultery, in pederasty, in being charming and kindly, in being vile-tempered and arrogant, in being cruel, in being self-sacrificing, in being human and too human, in being inhuman and too inhuman. After many years, many of them showily enough public, I have returned to Bairnsdale to scout and spy on the setting of my childhood, and to walk, in hand-made shoes costing eighteen guineas, with a sense of walking through an old dream, the streets I once ran through barefoot. I turn a corner. It amazes me that, instantly, without hesitation or the faintest doubt, I recognize the man loping towards me, down-at-heels but lusty, deeply wrinkled, large-bellied, going bald, grey at the temples—it is King Bunyip. A Catherine Wheel of questions indicative of a peculiar shyness rather than a vanity fizzes into existence in my mind. Will he have read my poems and stories? Of course not, I think, as I stroll, for stroll is what I find myself doing with conscious, almost self-conscious, nonchalance. Will he have read, or heard, of me and the Hutchins School, Hobart, scandal? Will he have read what I say about Australians in Occupation Japan as I step with a Manila hangover on to the tarmac at Mascot Aerodrome out of the aeroplane from Iwakuni? Shall I raise my voice, and fruitily speak my pretty piece, all smiles and heart-warming handshakes, 'My God! Dick Verco! After all these years! How marvellous to see you, dear boy! How absolutely *marvellous!*' I decide nothing. He will not know me. The two middle-aged men draw level, are passing.

' 'Ullo, 'Arold,' says Dick Verco, King Bunyip, whom I have not seen for thirty years.

'Hullo, Dick,' I say, as though I have seen him every day for thirty years. No more than that. We go our ways. I am, as it were, home again. I am with those who knew me when I was to be known. I am with those who knew me as a boy: to them my scandals and hand-made shoes and foreign travel and footloose life and miniature fame and addition of years are no more than a form of fancy-dress, to be admired or not admired, but making little difference to me, and none —none at all—to them.

' 'Ullo, 'Arold!' is perhaps what I ultimately use up my eyes and ears and hours for.

My two forays into the world of grease-paint and illusion now stir me into activity of a kind unusual to me. After a little shrewd day-dreaming, itself unusual enough, I write a play: *Briar Rosebud* or *The Sleeping Beauty*. I write it, in violet ink, across the pencilled cones and pannikins and geometric patterns and sprays of coprosma in an old drawing-book. Knowing much of human vanity from observation of myself, Mother, Father, my brother and sister and everyone, it does not enter my head to be surprised when other boys and girls make no objection to rehearsing, dressing up and, ultimately, performing on a dray lent by the Queen's produce-merchant father in the side-paddock of the King's father's orchard. It does surprise me—now, this very moment—that, at the age of ten, it is possible for me to abandon, abruptly and decisively, my public vagueness for high-handed actor-manager behaviour: a foretaste in myself of what I am, decades later, to denigrate in others. This means, of course, that I play Prince Charming, first, because I consider myself the best actor, second, because I have induced a cattle-breeder's pretty daughter to enact Briar Rose, The Sleeping Beauty, so that I can kiss her awake. This is not the reward I have primarily set the theatrical machinery in motion to get. Something inescapable, and really not-to-be-desired, has set me in motion as engineer of the machinery. Nevertheless, the kiss seems to become the reward because the Sleeping Beauty does not like me, and will not let the kiss be rehearsed. All else about the production falls into a foreseen pattern of success, because I have not the imagination to foresee failure, nor the impatience necessary to attempt something that will lead to failure. The kiss, therefore, remains the one thing to accomplish.

So engrossed am I with *Briar Rosebud* or *The Sleeping Beauty* and its promised kiss that the tide of time whirls the last days, the last day and the four long, long, long and wonderful years of contentment at State School 754 away from me almost unnoticed and in a trice. The last bell rings. The stream runs fast. The rapids are near. The afternoon grows old and golden. The last bell stops ringing. I hurry home with my prizes, one of which is irritatingly another copy of Lamb's *Tales from Shakespeare* and the same prize I get in Grade Five the year before. I hurry home, no longer a State School boy, to hand Mother the prizes which give her much more pleasure than they give me. Does she remember, I wonder, my return on my first day of State School life, in Kensington, centuries ago? Does she remember the first pink tick and the mouthful of dirty words? The big brown china teapot awaits, and the plate of pikelets, and the safety.

Taking advantage of Mother's expressed pleasure and her happiness-weakened condition, I press her ('Don't talk with your mouth full, you wretched child!') into sewing the three curly blue ostrich feathers she has saved from a pre-marriage hat on to my princely cap, a never-worn smoking-cap she made for Father of ruby-coloured velvet heavily embroidered in gold thread. Biting off the final thread she planks the glamorous object deliberately back-to-front on her own head, crosses her eyes, and sings with nasal fruitiness:

> '*I'm Gilbert the filbert,*
> *The knut with the k,*
> *The pride of Piccadilly,*
> *The* blasé roué . . .
> *Oh, hades, the ladies*
> *Who leave their wooden huts*
> *For Gilbert the filbert,*
> *The kernel of the knuts.*'

This, I know, is somehow mockery of me, as though, while happy to be possessed of a son with a different set of tricks to the men who are her brothers and the man who is her husband, she is also wary of the full value of the different set of tricks, and is deviously suggesting that I keep open a wary eye too.

Next Saturday, no one comes to the performance except the five or six or seven, the uncountable younger Adams children.

The cast, and I, have expected no audience at all. We have all sold penny or threepenny tickets, printed by hand on rectangles of butcher's paper, to whom we can beguile—parents, big brothers, silly old ladies and reluctantly soft-hearted shopkeepers. The twenty-eight shillings, a preposterous sum, is audience enough for us, for we are heartlessly realistic, and want the adults' ratification only in cold cash, not their presences which would rouse us to embarrassment, and make us into parents' children when all we want to be, in this more elaborate game, is children's children.

The Adams audience arrives like Brown's cows, but bickering professionally and hoarsely without looking back at whom they are bickering with. Some are in a sort of fancy dress with the straw jackets from lager bottles tied about their legs like the gaiters of Japanese peasants. Their mouths and tongues are, one and all, black with liquorice. They bring their own haloes of flies. Several skinny dogs follow them as following a rubbish cart.

This audience, however scruffy, is perfect, and eggs us to fearless overacting, for we are gratefully enraptured by their black gaping mouths which show they find us almost un-recognizably gorgeous in gold-paper crowns, numberless strings of beads, Christmas tinsel, mothers' opera cloaks, our lips and cheeks reddened with geranium petals.

Zealously, and with perfect justice, the audience applauds most their sister Christobel Veronica who plays the Bad Fairy with such conviction and dash that I forget not to forgive her her impromptu additions to the script. At last the moment for my own appearance approaches. Briar Rosebud, the cattle-dealer's daughter, the exquisite princess, squeals, 'Lo! I have pricked my snowy finger on the evil spindle!' and subsides into sleep, while everyone else on the dray also affects heavy slumber. Holding my hand on a tin sword stuck in my sash, I count ten to myself; I come from behind the clothes-horse screened by tarpaulin where I have waited watching in my cloak of old chenille curtains, and the smoking-cap decorated with blue feathers.

'O-o-o-o-o-oh!' The Adamses, crawling with flies, sigh long and rapturously under the pear trees. I restrain a bow, or even a glance in their direction. I move to the Sleeping Beauty who is slumped, mouth agape and eyes screwed tight, on a deck-chair hung with lace curtains. I say the one line I have created for myself. It is by far the longest line in the play.

'I, Prince Charming, have voyaged through many climes. The hedge of thorns attempted to bar my path. It was bewitched to lovely roses as I turned my trusty sword upon it. Lo, who sleepeth here? Oh, indeed, thou art very very beauteous, oh, lovely princess. I shall press mine lips on thine.'

Ah!

I bend to press. The Sleeping Beauty's eyelids quiver like moth's wings. Her lips push themselves together. Pity instantly infects me. She doesn't like me, I think. Her posture suggests helplessness. I eschew my reward. Instead of kissing her on the mouth, I touch my lips—just, no more—to her jaw. Her eyes open abruptly, too abruptly. I see in them an expression I do not like, and seem to recognize the dislike I fully expected to see. She sits up. She says her line, the last in the play:

'Thou hast broken the dread charm, oh, Prince Charming. We shall live happily ever after. Let all in the palace rejoice.'

Upon this, all who have lain for twenty seconds sleeping their hundred years' sleep, awake, arise, advance to the edge of the dray and, facing the Adamses and the dogs, sing all the verses of:

Briar Rosebud was a fair princess,
      a fair princess, a fair princess,
Briar Rosebud was a fair princess,
Long, long ago. . . .

She dwelt up in a lonely tower,
      a lonely tower, a lonely tower,
She dwelt up in a lonely tower,
Long, long ago. . . .

As we sing, the Adams audience, still on its hunkers in the frizzled grass, joins us. The reiterated, 'Long, long ago . . .' becomes sweeter and sadder, verse by verse.

To look back on that group of twenty children in their out-of-date shabbiness or fake finery, opening and closing their geranium- or liquorice-stained mouths to make ardent noise, is to look back and trick oneself into a sentimental curiosity. Are they, as they sing themselves into a dimension a little above the earth and a little out of the hour, aware of which future is beginning to sprout or has already sprouted within them? Or do they not know and not watch themselves and their prophetic hearts at all but merely sing and sing and, having sung, descend from the dray, and walk from the orchard, careless of their destinies? The Queen with her gold-paper crown, *diamanté* bracelets on her freckled arms, and alive with idiotic rippling giggles, commits suicide twenty years later. War swipes out of sight the King, the Court Jester ('Dost thou know, thou august majesties, when is a door not a door?') and some of the audience. Years later I listen to the Bad Fairy, Christobel Veronica, already ravaged by the cancer that is to destroy her, talking and talking, and unable to stop talking of bad weather and sickness, a middle-aged cow-cocky's wife in a scarred and dirty Chevrolet jammed with her children who could easily be herself and her brothers and sisters of long ago—of long, long ago.

Briar Rosebud or *The Sleeping Beauty* is almost over. One thing yet remains for me to learn, and one thing yet to do.

A few days later, the day hot and the elm-leaves flaccid,

the Sleeping Beauty, reverted to the cattle-dealer's pretty daughter, appears, apparently accidentally, at the base of an oak tree in the Tannies. I am on a bough collecting the brittle husks from which the cicadas have elbowed their way on their journey from a hole in the ground to flight in the burning air. This will be the last time I collect these fragile carapaces containing nothing, the last time I will be up a tree, humming to myself on a bough.

'Hello,' says the Sleeping Beauty. 'Come on down. I want to talk to you. A bonzer secret.' We are all affecting the new words brought back from the Great War.

I climb down, warning myself of something I cannot pinpoint. There are children playing everywhere about, in and under the trees, as many, as busy as the children in Breughel's *Children's Games*.

'This is a bonzer secret,' she says. 'Come over behind the boxthorns.'

'No,' I say, getting an erection, for I have been behind the boxthorns with other children, but certainly not in the full blaze of December mid-morning with eyes everywhere. 'No, I don't want to.'

'I don't want to see your thing,' she says. The erection gets harder. 'It's only a secret. Cross my heart, hope to die, it's only a bonzer secret.'

I walk with her behind the boxthorns.

Arrived there, she says, sharply as an old woman, 'The secret is: why didn't you kiss me?'

So! I consider pretending that I have no idea of what is going on but realize that, since this appearance of hers is not accidental, it is not worth my while to begin an involuted game she will not play. She has a purpose not to be thwarted. There is nothing to say but a truth I know is not a truth.

'I did kiss you.' I cannot look at her and her terribly clean flounced dress, and her patent leather shoes. I wish I had no erection, and that I did not have Bathurst Burrs hooked into a design on my oldest, patched flannel shirt. I wish I had my boots and socks on, and trousers I was not growing out of. 'I did kiss you.'

'Not properly. You didn't kiss me *there*.'

'I did,' I lie.

'Not *there*, you didn't.'

'Where?' I say.

'You know where?' she says, and touches her lips. 'You didn't kiss me there, after you asked so much.'

'I did.' The lie is becoming monotonous, even to me.

'You didn't. Oh, no you didn't. Don't you want to kiss me?'

I have my opportunity to tell the truth. I select another lie. 'Of course, yes, of course.' I wish she would go away. I wanted the kiss that was withheld, not this confrontation of words about kisses no longer wanted.

'Well, you can kiss me ten times. You can kiss me *there*. But only ten times, as a secret.'

I want no kisses, but I kiss. We do not touch each other with anything but our everted mouths. My erection subsides. Her lips are wet. I want to wipe my mouth but dare not. Each time our lips part, she counts. Nine!

'This is the last one,' she says. 'Only ten, I said, see.'

Only ten!

Anxious to be done with this cold-blooded, fully lit and socially dangerous nonsense, I incline towards her for the tenth time, my lips, wet from hers, pursed well forward. As her face approaches mine, something lights up in her eyes, and then clouds over. It is as though someone is walking there behind the glaze. I sense danger but not danger's nature. With a swift, sharp snapping, she bites my lips, hard. Tears spring to my eyes, and my hands go out to hit. She whirls away, untouched and wicked and mad, runs, runs screeching in her starched flounces and patent leather shoes, screeching, 'That'll teach you! That'll teach you!'

She is right. I learn what I think is only something about a little girl of eleven or twelve. I do not know, then, that I am learning something about women, and that little girls are women.

I am appalled when Mother says, 'What's wrong with your lip? It looks as though someone has been biting you.'

I go red or white, I cannot see which or tell which, and put on my shadowed expression, my ever-ready mask of the absent-minded dreamer which serves when I have not a suitable lie at hand.

'I bit myself,' suddenly seems a brilliant and simple lie because it *is*, in a sense, true.

'Oh?' says Mother, not 'Oh!' but 'Oh?' My expression grows more shadowed.

'Your little friend with the tip-tilted nose came to see you,' says Mother, and I know she is looking at me.

'Oh!' I say, realizing immediately that 'Oh?' would have been safer.

'I told her I thought she'd find you in the Tannies. Did she find you?'

I do not answer. I have picked up a book and taken up the attitude of one lost to the world, a bookworm, a vague one, a dreamer.

'Harold!' This is dangerous, very. 'Did the little girl find you?'

'No,' I say. Bugger Mother and Briar Rosebuds and women!

'Indeed,' says Mother. 'In-deed, oh, indeed.' She starts to whistle 'Cockitee kissed the Quaker's wife'. I sit tight and go on staring at the book. Engrossed as one turning a tablet of the Ten Commandments, I turn a page.

As aftermath of my first theatrical production there remains one thing to do.

In one of Father's tobacco-tins I carry the twenty-eight shillings to Miss Rodda, the Deaconess. It is to be a donation to some mission. Miss Rodda lives at, maybe even runs, the Church of England Girls' Hostel, an institution which, at this moment of recollection, I am unable to guess a reason for in the Bairnsdale of those days. It cannot, surely, have been filled with spinster Deaconesses and Sub-deaconesses.

The Hostel, nevertheless, is there. It overlooks the river and the river-flats, and is a spread-out stone house among vast ex-lawns with curving swathes scythed in them, and tangled herbaceous borders, and beds of degenerating self-sown flowers. A latticed octagonal summer-house is being unpicked by and, at the same time, sustained in a swaddling of bougainvillea near a waterless fountain overflowing with periwinkle. Half-drunk with charity, carrying my offering as horizontally as the Host, scrubbed and polished and starchily crackling as a good boy, I walk up the wide terracotta-tiled path. I skirt the oval bed overrun with cannas and docks and bindweed in front of the ascent of slate steps. At the door, I pull the white china knob. Far-off, behind baize-covered doors, a bell tinkles. It is still vibrating when Miss Rodda appears from out of the slippery, Turkey-carpet-patterned linoleum, and recognizes with a flattering flutter, as though greeting St. John himself, the dear, good, clean, clever, well-mannered, bread-and-butter-faced child who can say Corinthians 13, without taking a breath, at St. John's Church of England Sunday School. The delicate crane's-bill scissors, the keys, the silver propelling pencil and the cork-screw hanging on a chained ring from her belt rattle in a religious way as she invites me in. Dear-*kind*-thoughtful-*good*-little-boying me, she takes me into the front room. Before settling down to counting the money packed in the tobacco-tin, and writing a receipt at a roll-top desk in one corner, she makes me sit in a heavily breathing and gently wheezing leather arm-chair which contains a suède cushion, its wide hem cut into fringes, and on which is stencilled a squat peacock with a perfectly circular tail and that slight squint, sinister and lunatic, that the toys made by Girl Guides and Country Women's Association members seem always to have.

From out of a shallow bowl of Benares brass she selects a stale apple a little less bruised and speckled than the other apples.

Holding it—Portrait of Country Boy with Apple—and my Panama hat which is attached to the front of me by a cord clipped on to my blouse, I stare at the marble chimney-piece which I am to wet with tears of agony eight years later.

When the mother of Briar Rosebud, the giggling Queen with the freckled arms, the produce-merchant's daughter, descends from the dray to walk out of the orchard to suicide, I descend in sword, sash and feathers to begin my walk towards the room in which my mother is to die. The room in which I sit, trying not to move so that the leather will not wheeze, and holding the imperfect apple I am never to eat, and not listening to the Deaconess's bright platitudes, is the room in which I am to stand listening and listening to Mother's ill-chosen dying words.

I return home with the receipt, and a cutting of woodbine the Deaconess gives me for Mother who is, once again and for the eighth last time, sterilizing sixpences and threepences, a thimble, a silver ring, and the tiny china babies with black polls that are all to go in the Christmas Pudding. Neither she nor I knows that I have just come from the last room she is to enter in the physical world. I do not know that by next Christmas I shall believe in Santa Claus no longer, in people far less, and shall have in myself as much more faith as I have lost in others.

Mother does not know that I have much innocence to acquire for she, as a victim of her motherhood, has forgotten what she knew as a child, and considers me innocent.

Intelligence is never innocent.

I know that, soon, oh, soon, in five weeks, four weeks, three, two, one, in no time at all, I shall be the youngest boy in Bairnsdale High School.

In 1922 Bairnsdale has five schools which are disposed throughout the town so as to form, accidentally, the plan of a cross, one school at each extreme, one at the intersection of the arms of the cross. Three of the five schools are in Main Street.

At the western end of Main Street, opposite the final outrider grocery, is the State School. In the middle block, between St. Mary's Cathedral and Kyle's Bakery, is the Roman Catholic School, St. Joseph's, at the intersection of the arms of the cross and the stranger intersection of the scent of baking bread and meat pies and cheese cakes, and the scent of incense and the sound of the Angelus. At the eastern extreme of Main Street, beyond the last shops, the last hotel, the smithy and the police station, is the School of Mines. A tannery reeking of hides and skins and wattle bark, and a brooding public park of oaks and elms and poplars, once the pioneer cemetery, separate the School of Mines from the town's edge and the river which defines it with water and weeping willows, wattles and cress-beds and reeds, wharves and peach orchards and the butter factory.

On the town's northern rim is the Presentation Convent, unseen behind lofty trees and a twelve-foot corrugated-iron fence in which there is a vast wooden gate, heavy as that of a castle or prison, eternally and irrevocably locked. Through a small door set in this gate, wealthier Roman Catholic girls, black-gloved, black-stockinged, all in black like Sicilian working-class women, and with faces set in a womanly, almost maternal, expression exposing at once both modesty and boldness, disappear to what we Protestants imagine are curious rites.

To the south is the High School on a rise overlooking Macleod's Morass, rood after rood of shallows spiked with reeds and bulrushes, and city-busy with swans and plovers

137

and ducks and water-hens. The morass fades out into acres covered with noon-flowers, dazzling as silver-foil in mid-summer. These acres in turn give way to asparagus fields and orchards through which the olive-green river grows wider and wider as it creeps to the lakes. The High School is of bricks, and is draped in Virginia Creeper, wistaria and bougainvillea. Surrounding it are the playing fields: a cricket pitch, a football ground, tennis courts, basket-ball courts and, in one corner, under some red gums, is the horse-paddock for those pupils who come from outside the town on horseback or in jinkers.

Legally, I must attend school until I am fourteen. Since Father cannot afford to send me to even the modest sort of private school he went to himself, I must fill in my required four more years of education either at the School of Mines which is for boys only, and teaches technical subjects such as carpentry and metal-work, or at the High School which is for both sexes, and is a corridor, rarely used in those days, to the University.

As an obedient son I almost never run against my parents. I am disobedient to Father about cricket, and to Mother about reading to idle visitors or neighbours a poem I have written, or displaying a water-colour I have done. I am not disobedient about much else. It is easier to be obedient to these grown-ups deft in the mechanical tricks of existence, and to hold my fork properly, and put it down properly, and to wash my neck, and polish my boots, and say my prayers, than to be disobedient and wrong. I prefer being right. My parents, anyway, have known me long enough not to waste time in asking me to run against myself. They trust me. Moreover, Mother is too busy and Father too indifferent to think up lures or lies to trap me into being an imitation child young before my time: my-son-who-plays-a-nice-bat or my-son-who-writes-poetry. I am therefore left to my desired and happy condition of an obedient son—that is before their faces. Behind their backs I am scarcely less obedient; I run against them—behind their backs—only in matters not fit for adults to know about. Even in these esoteric, and often erotic, performances disobedience is far from specifically so because I am doing not what has been forbidden but what has been not forbidden. The silence and apparent ignorance of my parents is the silence and apparent ignorance I obediently return them in my disobedience to the unexpressed. Behind their backs or before their faces I rarely run against myself.

In attempting to recall who makes the decision for me to go to High School rather than to the School of Mines I draw a blank. My parents' attitude in this, as in the overall matter of education, remains the secret they make it. I may risk the statement that the decision is mine. Since, in going to High School, I am neither running with nor against myself, I can only have made the decision on no grounds other than a curiosity about High School subjects whose names sound exotic and romantic to me—Civics, Algebra, Physics, Chemistry, Geometry, French. Certainly, neither I nor my parents have any thought of what lies beyond schooling. Admittedly, I have decided, without any consideration whatever of the place education, training, opportunity and backing have in the affair, to be a famous actor, a famous writer or a famous painter, perhaps all three (I can see no reason why not!), but with a bias in the direction of writing. If Mother or Father has dreams for a precocious, cocksure and offhand eldest son, they are unrevealed, and never spoken of in my hearing. If they ever talk, late at night, in the lofty Venetian bed all white and nickel, with regret or distress for what they cannot do to manure 'a career' for that son, no one now knows what is said. I think, and fervently hope, there were no dreams to be marred, and no talks to cause bitterness.

I proceed at a hand-canter, dispassionately and fearlessly on into my own future.

The first day of High School life begins.

The gravest insult I can offer my parents' memory is the magnanimity of forgiveness. Perhaps they may have forgiven themselves; I am too devoted to their memory as samples of human beings to forgive them. Forgiveness, at any rate, is something one throws to those one regards as too contemptible for one's hate or one's love. One of the things I do not yet forgive Father and Mother is their planless existence in which two, at least, of the children they have are trodden underfoot. My parents are physically competent enough to have many more children; they have no right, their finances being what they are, to have so many; no right to let themselves fall into long range selfishness by being taken unawares by their anatomy.

Modernized animals need money; man does not live by love alone.

If I do not forgive their planlessness, which wealth would scarcely have modified, I must, in fairness, be grateful for the plan of warm and secure existence which lay at the centre of planlessness, and so occupied the hours that one did not look out on the surrounding wastes. Here I can speak of my parents with admiration and gratitude though without reverence. Food, warmth, shelter are all always there: sirloins and strong boots and thick blankets. That the central plan is one of well-tested attitudes inherited by my parents from the late nineteenth century, and faithfully adhered to, rather than attitudes originated by them and tried out hopefully on guinea-pig children, is maybe a good thing. It is a plan still working in 1922, still diverting attention from the future, although it is to begin to falter several years later when there are six children, when Mother's vitality languishes and Father's mask thickens, when they cannot but be aware that they have taken nature at its own hoodwinking word, and blandly gone on playing an old game of which they do not know the modern rules. But, in 1922, the plan works.

It means that Mother takes me to the tailor to be measured for my navy-blue twill suit, my red-trimmed blue blazer with the crest-embroidered pocket, my black alpaca coat for the more grilling days. It means that, as I walk the mile and a half to the High School on the first day of term, I am correctly dressed and capped and shod, that I wear the conventional school socks, and have the exactly correct quota of books. As I walk, proud as Punch, and dying for the curtain to go up, no Mother walks with me as she did on that first Kensington day.

Winton Adams, also a first day High School boy, pretending not to see me so that he can pass me and be seen, scorches by me on his bicycle which has, doubtless for the occasion, a glittering new lamp, a new luggage-carrier and a new brutally melodious bell which he rings repeatedly as he circles back to show me all these and his new silver watch and his new fountain-pen, his new mouth-organ. He, too, is in school uniform even, surprisingly, to boots. I perceive that his clothes are what Mother calls hand-me-downs or slop-clothes; his serge has a tinge of purple lurking, the trousers are too baggy, the coat too tight here and too loose there. His knees are dirty and, since he wears no garters, his socks are already coming down.

It is not clearly apparent to me, in those days, that, as in my parents' non-planning there is a core of purpose, so in the Adams non-planning there is also one. Winton is sustained by watch and bicycle and mouth-organ, and must look askance at my lack of these aids to spirit, as I look askance at his clothes. Our differing snobberies are not spoken of but are there, parallel and definite. I am to walk to and from the High School four times a day, six miles a day for five years, and am never to own a bicycle or a watch, but am always to be well-dressed even though darned. Winton is never to have tailored clothes, is to revert to cheap sandshoes while flourishing expensive gadgets: a Kodak, a cricket bat signed by the Australian Eleven, a Mah Jongg set. His parents and my parents have both handed on some of the unused evil, some of the affectations and sillinesses left lying around in death-rooms by *their* parents.

Of these things, at the beginning of 1922, as I climb carefully—my new suit not to be marked—through the lichened post-and-rail fence surrounding the High School playing fields, I scarcely have even inklings. During the five years at High School much is revealed obliquely to me. Although my self-confidence never wavers, it has wildly growing self-consciousness ever ready to assist in making it waver, ever ready to assist the brutalities and snobberies of the other children.

At that time I am Australian lower middle class. My place in the shire town's social scale is fixed by Father's income which is revealed, even to people like Winton, by what one has not got. While I avidly go on gnawing and gulping at my minute world, watching it with ferocious intensity as though it really be as vast and wonderful as I find it, I am being watched by eyes which see nothing vast, nothing wonderful, merely a gradation of price-tickets. Whether I become conscious of this watching because the new *milieu* and its denizens engage my older attention more closely is, at this distance, hard to know. Yet there is, in fact, at the High School, a system of callously simple, provincial snobbery. I could well be its victim because, having, so to speak, my father's income, I qualify for victimization by the tongues and tenets of children who have their fathers' bigger incomes; there are all about me the children of graziers, bank managers, lawyers and doctors, as well as of richer but less acceptable people, the owners of emporiums or tanneries or jewellers' shops, those in trade.

Because it is just as absurd a fact, my own different brand of snobbery—that of intellect and manners and shameless self-confidence—nickel-plates me against other snobberies far less sure-footed and far less insolent than mine. I am, of course, wily and meticulous in disguising this insolence because I like people almost equally as much as I like myself and solitariness. I believe no more in my crystal notions than I do in human clay and its fecklessness and amateurishness, but I do believe in both.

On that first High School day an incident occurs wherein my own nature compels me to behave in a manner which appears as much to have been born with me as to have been fostered and which, more or less, for better or worse, I still possess.

There is an initiation ceremony, a naïve, mild and unimaginative one. We new boys have already heard grisly exaggerations of it. Behind the sports pavilion is a corrugated iron water-tank. Here the initiation rites of holding the new boys' heads under the tap to be baptised take place. Presently, the moment for this ducking approaches. There is no need to round up the new boys. We have rounded ourselves up from the moment of our arrival, about twenty of us in our new clothes. The more frightened ones, whose eyes and the tones of whose voices give them away, express their fear of gossiped-about brutality and legendary almost-drowning by saying they are not frightened. The older boys, in their group, have been turning the tank tap on and off as though testing some dreadful machine. They stop this. With almost self-conscious uproariousness they advance, muscular, pimpled, knickerbockered lions on us rattled, short-trousered Christians. There is, to my pleased amazement, none of the savagery I have braced myself to put up with. I am not expecting my arms to be torn off, but I am expecting strenuous horse-play. Our names are asked of us, and are mocked unwittily. Meantime, with the gentlest simulation of manhandling, we are arranged in a rough and ready alphabetical queue. Winton Adams is the first to go to baptism. He wears this distinction brazenly enough but is ready, is half-cocked—I know him with that slanting, sliding look in his eyes—to fight. There is no need. From near the end of the queue I am able to see what happens. Winton is inexpertly upended by several older boys and, with his feet in the air, has his head thoroughly saturated under the tap. Watching, I find that each successive ducking is done with more clumsiness, with more deliberate clumsiness. Not only heads but necks and shoulders are now being soaked. I experience a flash of combined distress and anger, and then rapidly act on its inspiration. I make no bones with myself. I take off my coat, my hand-tailored coat that is the symbol of Mother's practical love and her snobbery, and Father's money. I hand it to Winton Adams who is less soused than anyone, and has the manner of one about to be asked for his autograph. The thought of taking off tie and shirt rears a head too dangerous to be encouraged for, although aware that, as the youngest and smallest boy, I can play on youngness and smallness, I know boys too well to try too much. I am already on treacherous ground. Anyway, it is too late. The witch-doctors grab me. As I am upended, the voice of the agitator, the bitter voice of the rabble-rouser, squalls:

'W'ere's the coat, eh? W'ere's the coat? It's not fair. All the others had coats. W'ere's the coat?'

It is a question no one really cares about having an answer to, but I am reversed so that my feet tip the ground again, while the bell-wether repeats his question. My atavistic inner eye, the jungle eye, opens round and clear as a moon. I see myself, as though watching from yards away, the smallest, the youngest, the neatest, Daniel in the lions' den. I make my choice for the little one. Selecting my vocabulary with old-maidish precision, intensifying the clarity of my voice, I say, hoping that my voice sounds piping:

'I have very wisely taken the precaution of divesting myself of the garment. My parents are far too poverty-stricken to have it marred by immersion in liquid. They would batter me into insensibility.'

This is an imitation of some schoolboy in *The Boy's Own Paper*, and my first attempt at debunking myself for a useful purpose, at playing the funny boy by parodying my own addiction to long words. Disappointingly, none of the lions laughs. *Poverty-stricken* is too jarring; *immersion in a liquid* and *batter into insensibility* win the day. There is no laughter, but I sense a relaxing, and no fangs. Relatively gently I am ducked, scarcely as myself so much as a new-born 'funny little codger'. It is a double baptism.

By this act, which could not have been foreseen despite my taking over from Mother a quirk for self-mockery, I make myself more of a character than I know. Watched I may be as I return to Winton Adams, and take my coat from him with the air of a highwayman taking his cloak from his jackal, but no one is watching me more narrowly than I. It is obviously obligatory to do more than merely put on a coat, and commit thus an anti-climax. With a gesture of counterfeit fastidiousness I act picking a thread from my sleeve, embellishing the gesture with, 'Tut-tut-tut! Untidy child!'

This is just what is needed. The big boys who have already been tricked into hoisting me into the air like some cuddly thing, a kitten or a Teddy Bear, now lose interest in my successor who is being doused to cries of *my* words—'Immerse him in the liquid! Immerse him!' I have become notable quickly, as much if not more to myself than to the others. Some of the older ones surround me and, in a way that could be vicious, question me in the hope of polysyllabic answers. I give them, trying to make myself appear smaller and younger and more piping as the words get longer, and the replies more purposely stilted. This bookish manner, this confidence-man behaviour, is to be my social stock-in-trade and smoke-screen for all my High School life, and even for some years after, for it becomes so ingrained that it does not easily scrub off.

Hypocrisy has an infinity of subtly graded shades.

My High School hypocrisy is, at first, crude enough but its persistence polishes it, giving it an air of truth, and often makes me, if I relax to a careless and intemperate display of it, a crashing bore. It takes the form of presenting myself as a special sort of word-crazy clown always ready to entertain the mob when, really, I am no more than a contented and earnest child with a bi-focal view of the crowd whom I am contemptuous of and in love with. It is not that being an entertainer irks me. It is worth the pinch of effort it takes to build up a character whose unshakable preferences, concealed behind the words they are couched in, come to be amiably misread as lackadaisical eccentricities. This is not a method of buying popularity, which is as tiresome as its opposite, but a means to privacy.

Sometimes I become so deceived myself by my assumed disposition that I am carried away, and am in the danger zone and being naughty, even cheeky to masters and mistresses, before the brake can be applied. Getting into trouble of this kind with those in authority has advantages: it makes my cleverness in one direction and my incompetence in the other direction less offensive to the majority whose abilities are the obverse of mine.

My old black beast organized sport, and in the particular form of cricket, immediately appears. Father, had he seen my performance of wriggling out, would, I feel, really have battered me into insensibility.

Because sport is compulsory, and I am obedient, I go calmly and uncomplainingly to the wicket for the try-out. I am cold-bloodedly ready for anything, especially deceit. If I pray, it is that I have not caught the disease of cricketing ability from Father.

A busy-body master who plays cricket with Father starts to correct my grip on the bat, and then stops, saying, 'But, of *course*, your dad will have shown you.'

I say nothing, and replace my hands in the position I now assume to be wrong.

On that first occasion, and two or three succeeding ones, I do very clearly remember being intent on not hitting the ball, on not making a run. This is more difficult to accomplish than I think. To my chagrin I am not skilful enough to miss the ball always, and I make some runs. Fortunately, by making runs, I learn how not to make them. It is soon accepted that I am a mug, and that I must get no nearer the playing field than the score-sheet. This is from purgatory to limbo but it is not yet far enough away for me. There is no need to act myself out of keeping scores. Spotlessly neat and precise I may be when dressed up as a schoolboy, but my handwriting is thick, blotty and outsized. Two ruined score-sheets earn me my *congé*. For the remaining years of High School life I am permitted to eschew the playing field; it becomes accepted that I go swimming, am in charge of the library, can spend my time pruning the school roses or executing an historical mural or hammering away at the scenery for a school operetta. I do a number of things of no greater and no less value than playing football or cricket except that a personal contentment comes from doing them, as personal contentment comes to others from playing with spheres. Whether this singular behaviour means that I am losing sight of myself is doubtful. If I am losing sight of myself, I am not of others as I peer out from behind my screen of hypocrisy.

Hypocrisy also colours my relations with the less worldly and the perceivably less intelligent masters and mistresses. For as long as my voice remains treble enough, and the years have not begun to deform me into a big boy with pubic hairs and a dirty mind, I affect little-boyishness. Is this a version of Father's Masonic manliness? This act, however, I am too astute to put on for those gifted teachers who sweep me off my feet, as adults should sweep children off their feet, but it is an act I can perform with a skill years since lost along with that untainted non-innocence that motivates the act.

I go on being stimulated by High School for the same reasons State School stimulated me: day by day, drop by drop, the information I cannot get quickly enough, falls into the edgeless and bottomless cistern of my mind. I want to be older for one reason only, to be filled to the brim with knowledge. Being made by the years taller or fatter or richer or speedier is, at this stage, nothing to my purpose. Most of all I want the . . . the *Something* that will empower me to say all I feel. Being a child I foresee *Something* turning up This Year, at the latest Next Year, in the way competence in the management of egg-spoons and shirt-buttons and bootlaces turned up. I do not foresee that This Year is to become Sometime, that Next Year is to become Sometime, and that Sometime is perhaps as near as I shall ever get. I am prepared, now, to face Never.

Next, suddenly, lightning suddenly, while I am still a child, a branch is lopped from my being, and a portion of my childhood ends for ever.

I see what poets are.

Long shafts of light pour from them through the galleries of the years, and cohere in a single greater shaft. This shaft does not blind; it scarcely even dazzles. It is an illumination in which not only the years and the poets themselves are radiantly visible but also the poet's skylark or daffodil or ocean. I see that the poet's possessions are everyone else's, and that he is saying what everyone else cannot say or read or even think clearly of. His skylark is the skylark I hear singing high above the river-flats; his daffodil is the daffodil

Mother grows; his ocean is the Southern Ocean I can now stand before at Seaspray or Lakes Entrance shouting as emotionally and vulgarly as Byron.

What shocks me, then and now, is that, as a writer, I have been outraced before I begin to run and that, if I wish to outrace, I shall never be able to stop running. Tranquillity and hope and conceit save me from chucking away my dream of communication, and taking up cricket. I can be said to set my mental jaw and set off for the foothills, utterly unconscious of the peaks I am yet to scale to see even remote Sometime on yet another horizon.

I cannot swear now if Shelley's 'Ode to the West Wind' is the catalyst; the circumstances of the time and my own nature make it more than possible. Ballads Mother has taught me: 'Lucy Gray'; 'I remember, I remember, the house where I was born' and, 'We are seven' do not lose their power to haunt nor do the jingles heard or learned at State School—'Harry Dale the Drover', 'The Village Blacksmith', 'The Loss of the *Royal George*' and 'Hiawatha'—lose their attraction. They are nevertheless revealed as unlit lamps and, as such, are put away for ever on the back shelves of my boyhood. The lit lamps thickly line the way I am to take; I cannot keep the fingers of my mind from their flames; the pain of the scorch is fresh and delicious and agonizing; but it leaves no scar; when I cry out, it is only in my heart, like a man.

This silent cry is of ecstasy for what has been done, and of despair at being forestalled, and being thus forewarned, that neither This Year nor Next Year am I to have the ability and the wisdom to light a lamp of my own. Although one branch of my childhood is in this fashion lopped for all time, the rest of it still inhabits the body of a child which occupies itself with childish matters.

I am discovered to have a flair for acting. This offhandedly happens when, as smallest boy in the most junior form, I am elected by a drama-crazy schoolmaster to play Tiny Tim in a set of scenes from *A Christmas Carol*. Limping and piping— an old one for me, this—with fervour, I so believe I am Tiny

Tim that I wistfully pipe and movingly limp for days after the performance is over. Father would like to, but it is Mother who boxes Tiny Tim's ears; others bare their teeth in distressed forbearance, and could scream. Thus earmarked, not merely for a degree of ability but for the caprice of immodestly relishing that ability, quite without skiting but in a shameless transport, I am thence always in the school operettas or dramatic productions, and work my way up from the Emperor Hokipokitippitoptop's parasol-bearer in *Princess Ju Ju*, through the rip-roaring Pirate Gub in *The Pirate's Daughter* to Ko Ko in *The Mikado* and Sir Andrew Aguecheek in *Twelfth Night*.

If ever I am nostalgically moved by High School it is in recollection of those moments when foul-mouthed boys with boils on their necks, and girls with bandy legs and false teeth, disguised in glittering rubbish, painted like beautiful idols, and flirting their spangled fans or brandishing wooden cutlasses, raise their clear coarse voices in song and dialogue, transforming themselves for a space to a grotesque and moving loveliness—for a little little space—before life transforms them to the burdened and confused, the mean and bitter, the stupid and cruel, the sentimental and unpitying, the defeated and destroyed, the dead.

While I am more than willing to caper and squeal as someone else, I am more than reluctant to take part as an orderly imitation of my essentially level-headed self in the speech-making and contrived cold wars of the school's Debating Society. There is a smell of organized lying-to-come in the very choice of subjects, and more than a smell of the scoring-board, of runs to be made and goals to be kicked. This is not for such as I. I prefer to be the silly-ass cissy boy, the funny man chattering and giggling on the side-lines. Anyway, in matters of this public kind, my nature has decided for me that I am the Kipling cat that walks alone, and mum, and dead-centrally, down the avenue lined with fake Yesses and Noes. I have enough Yesses and Noes of my own, authentic ones, and no time to dally with abstract ones.

I continue drawing and painting. At one period sweet peas

149

are an obsession until the problems of reproducing them floor me, and I take to easier subjects such as the Coliseum which, for a while, I am continually, almost constantly, executing. Massive grandeur is less a problem than fragility. Finally, Böcklin's *Island of the Dead* becomes the subject I copy over and over again in every medium affordable, and so many times that I could now forge it in the dark.

Between school-work and play, between drawing and learning to smoke, between Sunday School and fruit-stealing, between poking away with my mind at the encrustations and interknottings of Browning, between staring into the stars or the faces of insects and flowers or the flaming hearts of fires or the cold hearts of children, it is impossible to stop myself from writing. When *The Bairnsdale Advertiser* holds a short story competition for children I win my first First Prize, earning more money than I have ever had to myself, ten shillings, for *The Golden Tortoise* in which it is astonishing and amusing to find today a number of prophetic suggestions: my continuing affection for the Orient, for many-jointed words, and the outrageously fictitious quality of truth. With the ten shillings I buy Mother a xylonite hairpin-container, Father a tin of Light Havelock Flake-cut Tobacco, my brothers and sisters a large bag of the sweets then popular: Milk Kisses, Silver Sticks, Helen's Babies, Coffee Stars, Aniseed Balls and tiny glass tubes of Silver Cachous. I am an unimaginative boy. For myself I buy a kaleidoscope which happens to catch my eye when I am in despair of thinking of something to buy myself, and a reproduction of Maurice Griffenhagen's painting of two Arcadian bucolics fervently kissing in a poppy-field under an autumn moon. Mother sings about the house, at least when I appear, sad songs about Edwardian autumn moons, thus making me suspect that I have amused or disconcerted her by my unpremeditated choice. It seems to me now, that this gift-shedding after my little windfall, is hardly an unselfish move for it gives me great happiness, happiness of a rather buying-oneself-out sort.

At the State School I have had no special friend. There,

neither the idea nor the need arises. Unself-consciousness requires no looking-glass, has no secrets or complaints to share, and wants none of the duties of friendship. At High School, by the age of twelve, I find myself with an assortment of friends, for I am losing the earlier purity of independence and one-ness that protects one from the charms and fatigues of friendship. These friends resemble, as it were, uniforms to be worn by the several creatures I am splitting into, uniforms to be worn in certain moods, on certain occasions, and never never never at the same time.

Now, I can smile at the stock quality of these friends, these uniforms, these looking-glasses, these sharers. Each is a character lifted straight from literature and yet, life successfully aping art, they are alive, and fulfil their destinies—or act their parts—flawlessly.

Willie Finch is the clever friend, the bookworm, the abused and cowering, his eyes the most naked I have seen. He can neither veil nor ignite his eyes against the arm-twisters and mockers; he has not my cunning against them, nor the nous to counterfeit indifference—perhaps his martyrdom is his consolation as his tears are their satisfaction. After school, particularly in autumn and winter when the call of the river and the countryside is not tempting to me, I spend hours with him in the Mechanics' Institute Library which does not cater for children. The Reading Room is, however, open and free to the public, to anyone—as a framed set of rules points out in small pica—who is not under the influence of intoxicants, not improperly clad, not smoking, not noisy, not eating food, and not a dog. The Reading Room is furnished with the late-Victorian solidity of a respectable club; there is much cedar; there are deep leather armchairs. Here, two sober, properly dressed, noise-less, miniature old clubmen, Willie Finch and I, live out our friendship. The bond is our rivalry for position in class at school, and our passion for reading or, rather, for reading other things than Deadwood Dicks and comic papers. In the Library we subtract ourselves so thoroughly from the animal activities of living that we can each well be objectified silence itself. I remember, with a clarity nothing can blur, reading in Willie's silent company Paul Bourget, Loti, Ibañez, Herman Melville, Marie Corelli, Maeterlinck's *Blue Bird*, much Dickens, *Anna Karenina*, and Tennyson's Collected Poems—the last from a plump book, gilt-edged, bound like a cushion in padded levant, and having a watered-silk ribbon of a bookmark attached. Since Willie Finch has knock-knees, a bad breath, spectacles with steel rims, bitten finger-nails, and pink hands that look damp, he reads the *Encyclopaedia Britannica*: he is never out of character. His writing is tiny and neat. He has a white mouse he loves, and of which he smells. When the Librarian arouses us at closing time from the anaesthesia of our withdrawal into, say, my Arthurian retreat or Willie's solar system, and we adjust ourselves and our eyes to the facts surrounding us, and walk as carefully as elderly scholars down the stairs, it is Willie who pedantically talks. I am content to quarter-listen politely because he is my friend, although I am not ravished, as he is, by the statistics of the planets and the time-table of the moon. There is certainly some fascination in the landscape of the moon with its Mer du Nectar, Mer des Pluies, Lac des Songes and Marais du Sommeil, with its Golfe des Iris, Longomontanus, Arzachel and Mt. Pico. This is a romantic but, to me, valid fascination. The information Willie has soaked up and can ticker-tape out to me, without fear of being scoffed at or bruised for, is more legendary to my mind than the legends of King Arthur or Orion, more legendary than the Man in the Moon. Willie is impressed that the earth is shaped like a mandarin, and its girth and movements measurable; I prefer the earth flat. He tells me the dull truths in his swift, nervous, scraping voice in which I hear the tones of older and reputedly wiser voices. I listen without conviction but with affection and an insulting compassion, as though I am older and indubitably wiser.

On the other hand, my friend Herbie Bawker can tell me lies which may or may not be lies, and I do not bother to don disbelief because his own mis-statements are more exciting than Willie's borrowed facts. In Herbie's company I feel younger, not in my acted little-boy manner, but as though I am actually Herbie's young brother. He is my Saturday friend of this period, another stock character, with his appropriate smell of ferrets in place of Willie's smell of white mouse. The ferrets, called Jessie and Jim, are almost the only things Herbie owns besides me. He is strong and stocky, with convict-cropped hair, large thick ears stuck on at right angles, a drawling voice, and a grin that so involves the almost visible muscles of his face, one lot setting another lot in action like interlocking gears, that the grin takes a long time to be completed, and an equally long time to undo itself, during which time his small gleaming eyes disappear, and dimples appear above his eyebrows. I walk more miles with him than any person since except my own self with whom I have walked more miles than can be reckoned. We walk the boggy paths of the morass to the stony valleys on the other side, along the river-bank to the weir, into every nook and cranny of the district. It is he who teaches me many of the things I still believe: that all white cats with blue eyes are deaf, that a dog will love you more, and always, if you let it breathe in your breath, that rain is on the way when swifts fly low, or black cockatoos fly northwards, or a cat washes behind its left ear with its left paw. We seem always to be speeding, an inch or so above the surface of the undulating paddocks, speeding but never out of breath through miles of ring-barked gums, down breakneck slopes, along creek-beds filled with stones like potatoes, to reach a certain destination, a certain event, at a certain time. Because his knowledge is so exact we are never late. We find what we have set out to find: yards-wide rings of mushrooms in the pink of perfection, a patch of water-cress still tender and lush, a row of bottle-swallows' nests, a vixen and its litter, a fig tree remaining from the garden of some long-gone pioneer house of which nothing remains except a fire-place filled with boys' dried turds. We arrive at the fig tree in its plenitude a day before birds or other boys, it could reasonably be an hour before, even five minutes, so alert and certain is Herbie.

We learn to smoke. Where do we get the money for cigarettes? He earns it, I think, by being paid for running messages for his mother. I steal it from Mother's kitchen purse, the morocco one whose shabbiness rebukes me as I silently and skilfully open the finger-smoothed steel clasp. Herbie tries to teach me to swear, and to spit. Self-consciousness hamstrings me, albeit safe and credulous in his gentle yet protective company. Of my friends of that period Herbie is the gentlest while also being the toughest in an ape-like way, the least intelligent and the best-informed about the earth and its manifestations, the foulest of mouth and cleanest of mind, the lightest-fingered and most open-handed, the strongest and the weakest. It is not easy to guess which of these qualities, brought into play twelve years later during the Depression, leads him into robbery with violence, and thence into gaol. Why, released from gaol, he is later murdered, I do not know. When I see swifts flying near the earth I almost invariably recall him, and wonder if I am the only human being he ever owned for a little while. Yes, I recall him. We sit smoking behind a hawthorn, attempting smoke-rings. Neither of us is successful until, on the point of giving up, I fluke a perfect one. I am amazed. Herbie is overjoyed, as with Jessie and Jim the ferrets when they excel themselves in rabbit slaughter, as with a dog that has learned a trick.

'Shit, eh, young-un!' drawls Herbie, using his favourite term of flattering praise, and beginning a grin. 'A bloody corker! Shit, eh!'

He pats and kneads my shoulder. His little eyes emit a final gleam of pride, then go under in creases and folds. The dimples appear above his eyebrows. His eyeless grin says: What a clever ferret! What a good dog! What a smart young brother! I find myself smiling as though the smoke-ring really is as impressive a forecasting of . . . of ferret-hood? of doghood? of manhood? . . . as Herbie's continued patting and kneading signify he thinks it is.

Willie is a friend. Herbie is a friend. The word, then, can scarcely be used for Alex Macalister. Lover may be the word. It is not the one to use in the hearing of Mother and

Father—even Father—who like him most and much and, to justify and gratify themselves, talk of him as Laddie's Best Friend. I do not bother to say that, if any, Herbie is my best friend. At least, if it be possible to grade differing sorts of happiness, the happiness I have in Herbie's company is greatest and lasts longest, and lends a corresponding value to him. To my parents, I know, Herbie appears common and half-witted, while Willie appears sickly and namby-pamby. Not that their coldness of feeling for these two is ever put into words or actions, but Herbie's and Willie's antennae of intuition pick up the negative forbearance which turns them wordless and awkward, and ham-strings their already meagre social graces. Alex, on the other hand, turns on charm for Mother and Father. God, such charm! Since they do not know why, he seems charming to them. He has the advantage over Willie and Herbie of also being ornamental. He is slender but firmly rounded, shapely, handsome, with an olive skin and great dark restless eyes which can, when he has a purpose at hand, still themselves to direct so intense a gaze at the victim that it appears the world is being offered. His manners are perfect. He looks, and publicly behaves, like a schoolboy hero incapable of a thought below his navel. Because Mother has questioned me about his scholarship with an offhandedness so baroque it suggests anxiety, and has heard me answer that it is f.a.q. to mediocrity, she is doubly pleased to find him no danger as a rival to my high scholastic place in class. Willie suffers in her eyes by being a rival; Herbie suffers because his apparent oafishness might mar my apparent sensitivity. How people can be gypped by the good-looking! Father's approval of Alex as a fine-looking, healthy, manly boy is trebled, is quadrupled, by the knowledge that he is vice-captain of the High School cricket team. This condones his appearances in school theatrical performances as Nanki Poo and Orsino.

Taken in by his scholastic mediocrity, his decorative appearance, and velvet manners, Mother is more wholly thrilled than I when Alex, who lives in the next block, calls for me every evening after dinner. That whistle in the twilight! It is well for Mother that she cannot see why his eyes are melting, and his boyish wiles on full display, that she cannot guess that he has an anticipatory erection which, his hand through the large hole in his trousers-pocket, he is fondling as if it were an animal other than he himself.

I may be wrong in regarding the sexual experiments Bairnsdale children of my day idly and baldly, albeit secretly, carry out as being harmless—but too many of the boys and girls involved in them are now citizens of the greatest respectability and moral fibre, are mothers, fathers, youngish grandparents, pillars of this and that and the other. The experiments seem inevitable enough for, in an era when adults have not kindly provided us with television crime, horror films, too much pocket-money, too many comic strips and pulp magazines, we are still the sort of children who play our own games, sex being only one of the many, and merely sandwiched between the others.

With Alex Macalister the case is different. He is my first experience of a member of that race which puts a greater value on sex than on anything else: self-discipline, moral convenience, tried-out convention, social unselfishness and the need to make carnal nature walk side by side with reason rather than race ahead without a leash. I learn from him that sex is not a game but something more dangerously exhilarating, more deadly, more victimizing, a disease of the feelings, an itch, a rage, a mania. It is necessary, right here, to confess bluntly that my own nature goads me into using the word mania—that is, for uncontrolled sexual emotion. For me this satisfaction of the flesh is among the least of pleasures that this world affords. The peace it offers is beyond doubt; the price of renewal and renewal and renewal of this peace is its danger. It transforms itself to a drug or a false religion. Some dearth in, or addition to, my constitution inclines me to asceticism. The inclination remains, but I have not always, especially when younger and more polite, when my body was less likely to obey the mind's orders, been able —thank God!—to follow this inclination. My main efforts on asceticism's behalf have been negative. I have not hunted, importuned nor initiated. This selfish indifference, however inborn, however unrealistic, however cultivated, to an exercise performed on behalf of Nature and her (his?) unforeseeable plans seems, ironically, to turn to hunters those one does not hunt. Big Brother (Sister?) Nature is older, longer in the fangs, more selfish and more brutal than I. Much of my appeal for Alex Macalister is, doubtless, due to my indifference and selfishness and Puritanical streak. My refusal, on aesthetic or fastidious grounds, to carry my lust-affair beyond a certain stage, makes my appeal to him stronger. However, we certainly go far enough.

His attentions are flattering, as the attentions of the comely always are: he is fourteen and a half, film-star handsome and popular. I am just over thirteen, not handsome and, while acceptable as a cute little bloke, am decidedly not popular.

I am therefore particularly flattered by the persistence of his attentions and by being the most . . . the most . . . popular? . . . used? . . . of his many victims, perhaps because I live nearest him and am of the age and construction that give him greatest pleasure. I enjoy his fingers moving, evening after evening, with infinitely varying delicacy—*sinister* delicacy, I say to myself, already losing my senses in the gloom under the oaks of the Tannies—up and down my fly, up and down, until, tenderly as a doctor revealing something to be cured, he undoes my fly from top to bottom. With the skill of someone older, or the born amorist, his finger-tips now skim my growing pubic hairs and, becoming subtly stronger and more dangerous, along my organ. I try hard not to quiver as he peels down the prepuce, and more firmly fondles. I am lost, and he knows it with his hand as well as his instincts. With perfect assessment of my state, 'Now?' he says, 'Now?'

'I don't care.' This is my lie.

'Say, "Yes" or "No", 'he says.

'I don't care.'

He knows I will say no more than that. I will not make myself a verbal accomplice, and open to guilt, with, 'Yes.'

I will not deny myself the delight of a gammarouche by 'No.'

'Now?' How honest, and honestly imploring, and natural he is.

'I don't *care*.' Liar!

Next, in a moment of retrospectively moving and too sadly human fever, he takes me in his arms. His breath smells of jam.

This labour of teaching me innocence under the dark trees is neither a secret nor a lie. It is one of the facts of animal development all may not know or want to know. It is a truth of existence I am thankful Alex Macalister affirmed for me.

Later we are boys again, with homework to do. I wipe my hand on the trunk of the oak. We button ourselves. We move from the ancient dark under the trees towards the gas-lamp flickering at the gates.

'Tomorrow night?' he says.

'I don't care.'

We often nearly fight. This, now, indicates to me that our affection is deeper and truer than it seems at the time. What is decidedly valuable about the relationship, which lasts for about a year, is the insight I get into feelings I shall never have the courage, power nor free-wheeling desire to have myself. The experience with Alex teaches me early, and scarcely too early (for which I must always be grateful), to recognize in others the first signs of an emotion getting out of hand, and to escape before it gets out of hand. He introduces me to the sort of conversation I am now skilled enough not to let begin.

'Have you ever done this with anyone else?' His fingers are at the last button of my fly.

'No.' This is almost a lie, but I count it not so since I know what *is* going to happen.

'Really and truly?'

'Don't you believe me?' This means I am lying because, 'really and truly', other boys and girls have been at my fly.

His hand is now on my flesh.

'What about Herbie Bawker?' I move his hand, hoping he will put it back.

'I'm going home.' I am sincerely dismayed that Laddie's Best Friend should defame my best friend with whom I should no more think of messing about like this than I would of smoking with Willie or reading books with Alex.

'I bet you have with Herbie Bawker.' I hit his hand away again.

'I have not.'

'Well, who else with?'

'I told you no one.' I wish he would put his hand back. He knows I wish this. He puts it back.

'Do you like me better than him?'

'You're all right.'

'If you let me do what I'm doing you must like me best, eh?'

'I don't care.'

The conversation, half-jealousy, half a hope to involve everyone equally in his own desire, is, like Alex, a thing from stock. It moves on, if not nipped in the bud, to attempts to arouse me to jealousy by telling me with whom else he has toyed.

Since I find my involvement in lust with him a matter of some pleasure but of no great moment, his involvement with others is of less moment. Incuriosity is the last breeding ground for jealousy.

More than thirty years later, when I have returned to Bairnsdale to be a librarian in the same building where I read the afternoons away with Willie Finch, I meet Alex Macalister in a pub. We get gently half-molo on this and other occasions, talking to each about our older selves in the manner of people talking to themselves. He has four children, his eldest son is of the age, and almost exactly the appearance, that Alex was when we were . . . lovers? As we drink, and say nothing at pleasant length, now and again Alex, the father, the exhausted-looking bank-teller, the golfer and delphinium-grower, the looker down the front of the bar-maid's dress, releases directly at me one of those molten glances that seem to offer the world. His good looks have burnt down to another sort of good looks, weary and disappointed above the drip-dry nylon shirt and leather-patched Crombie sports coat. His wife, he tells me, is a sloppy bitch. I am perversely tempted to recall to him the evenings of 1924, the ground pulsating with crickets as we pulsate with emotion. I am tempted to say, wilfully and to shock, 'Shall we go to the Tannies?' or, more shockingly, 'Does your eldest son go to the Tannies twilight after twilight?' Nothing, of course, is said. Now we are men, nothing is said. Nothing is done. The time for, 'Now?' and, 'I don't care!' is past.

I do not consciously part from Willie, Herbie and Alex. Their necessary departure from me, perhaps, saves me from having to recall that I outgrow them. Circumstance and the school-leaving age of fourteen strike them from the scene: Willie to be a solicitor's office boy, Herbie a butcher's messenger-boy, Alex to spend a year in boarding-school. No good-byes are said. They move away, and habits unravel. I am never again to walk down the library stairs with Willie. Alex is not to stand, hand in pocket, huskily charming Mother in the lamplight spilt on our back veranda while he waits to walk with me into the twilight for a demonstration of desire and fever and jealousy beneath the oak trees. Never again will Herbie and I speed barefooted over the paddocks to the cemetery where, year after year, the martens build and breed under the curled-up eaves of the Chinese oven-altar.

My other particular friends are a group of four boys who satisfy a side of my nature that begins to develop as puberty does, and I pass the age of fourteen; this is the frivolous side, the belonging-to-a-clique side. By the time I am fifteen we five are glued together by our own crazy jargon and private jokes, our matching frivolity, and false conviction that we are the wittiest and most sophisticated boys at Bairnsdale High School. The five of us are merely quicker-witted, more articulate, lah-di-dah, and almost pansyish. We play Mah Jongg and bridge, adore Colleen Moore and Marion Davies, and intensely admire the Artistic Value of the work of D. W. Griffith and Lilian Gish and Richard Barthlemess and Eric von Stroheim. We begin to wear shoes, and file our finger-nails. We all feel that we would like to be Dornford Yates characters, and regard ourselves as arbiters of taste. We commend or denigrate others, adult or children, for accent, manners, clothing and haircuts. We are harmlessly intolerable.

The other four boys have parents rich enough for us all to have the use of such things as horses, a motor-boat, all the paraphernalia of comfortable camping. There are cooks or maid-servants or gardeners to chiack, private tennis courts, and elegant gramophones to play the newest records. As the poorest boy of the group, I find myself, without duplicity, yet consciously enough, attempting to be very charming and terribly witty in a self-debunking way. It is impossible, now, to know whether these socially suspect qualifications earn me my place in the group or whether the group stimulates me to the sort of behaviour I find it difficult to restrain, even now. When one is always happy, it is sometimes hard to restrain oneself from being irritatingly too happy. While utterly happy for hours alone with writing or painting, utterly happy alone with Nature's well-hung sunsets, preposterous cloud-scapes or empty, melodramatic ocean beaches ('Roll *on*,' I yelp at the breakers, 'thou deep and dark blue ocean, *roll*!'), I am happy in the same proportion, then as now, in being a penniless playboy, in laughing and mocking and loving my way towards the grave—the one form of behaviour not to be committed in solitude. One needs not so much an audience as a sounding-board, or, at least, someone to forgive one.

We five are noisily inseparable, the *toujours gais*. In memory a perpetual blazing summer encloses our scampering activities, our hilarity, our puerile witticisms, our almost ladylike ignorance, and our surprising sensitivity in hooking ourselves immediately to nuances in the world of the cinema, painting, writing and the fashionable dross of the moment. We all read and talk far too much. Our accents are *tutti frutti.* It is indicative of the effervescent shallowness of our relations with each other that we never have a deep enough affection even to bicker. We are joined by things, by enamelled ideas and hedonic activities. We swim and row and ride, we gossip and hysterically guess, we giggle our way —without once mentioning what we all know—that one boy's mother is crippled with arthritis, that one boy's father is the town ram, that one boy has webbed toes. We talk sex— no mention from me of Alex, oh, no, indeed—our total information on the subject of man-and-woman contains as many distortions of fact as a mediaeval bestiary.

Mother would, I feel, despite her own feeling for gaiety, be less happy about this frivolous clan I am part of if she had more time. She has no time. When I am fourteen, the sixth child is born, the final baby brother. As with the births of my other brothers and sisters, I notice nothing, absolutely nothing of what for months, and immediately, precedes birth. I am told nothing. If hints be humanly and maternally dropped they drop right past me as I go chattering and singing and skipping on towards necessary pleasure, my little fame, the wider world and old age. Nurse Mawdsley's fur coat hanging on the hallstand is the signal that, once again, Mother is to be wearing a baby as though it were a sublime ornament, and that the weather in the house is to be tempered and tepid, and that, for a while, all family noise is to be pruned so that the unskilful but terribly pointed noises of the new animal can be heard gaining a quality like imperative speech. To me all this is now rather old hat; I have already nursed too many babies too many times, folded too many napkins, held too many bottles at mouths sucking away as furiously as lambs. I perform my minimal duties towards the little creature with a politeness Oriental to the point of cynicism but do not gushingly and forlornly love it as my two sisters immediately appear to do. It is too impermanent. It has none of the immortal quality of poetry. Its talcum powder smell and edible arms will vanish. It will grow rapidly as a weed, will chatter and be nasty, and give itself away outside the family, and grow hairs in its ears, and suffer pain, and die. I am, moreover, somewhat irked, on aesthetic grounds, by the entrance of this latest arrived baby brother. It does not go with my conception of myself which is that I am brilliantly clever, and far too worldly and sophisticated to be the brother of something that cannot utter a word, while I, *I*, am writing:

> *It tossed its weary turrets—old, old;*
> *It tossed them black in the night-grey sky;*
> *It tossed its age-old scents and sweets untold;*
> *It lured me ever on and drew me nigh.*
> *Rusty iron, dew-damp in the moonlight,*
> *Lichen-covered. Lichen-covered stone.*
> *Devils in the blue of moonlight sleeping;*
> *Shattered faces. I am here alone.*

And so on. And so on. *Deserted* is the title. It is one of the numerous poems I am always writing at this period, the sort of adolescent poetry with its recurring references to aloneness that matches the masturbation that now has its place in the lengthening list of things that must be done, because I am, despite being a smart-alec, a poetry-writer and non-cricketer, deeply conventional. Masturbation is what Alex Macalister has taught me to do, and what acquaintances and friends tell me they do, and it is overwhelmingly what Nature orders me to do. Neither Father nor the Church of England nor any grown-up has mentioned the deed to me: it has therefore little of the delicious flavour of guilt one seems always, nowadays, to be reading of in the lives of Europeans. Masturbation seems to me, then, to be no more than a kind of sly and dirty modesty, a form of good manners like not belching publicly or not chewing with one's mouth open. Alex Macalister's revelations of the lunacy behind sex add to the particular value of secrecy, and point up again the fact I had learned with Victor Richmond those years and years ago, that sex is not a game for adults. For adults it is a relentless reality offering, as though at a special and unique bargain price what, indeed, it offers to all—the Darbies and Joans, Héloise and Abelard, Achilles and Patroclus, Nietzsche

163

and his sister, Oscar Wilde and Lord Alfred Douglas—
at a price too often too great to be borne. Knowing, I thought,
so much, how nothing I knew! How long it is to take me,
strolling wide-eyed, year after year, across the minds and in
and out of the bodies of so many people, of differing sexes and
ages and colour of skin, in so many remembered places and
lost years, to find out again what I knew when I first looked
into Victor Richmond's eyes. How long it is still to take me
to learn whatever else is to be learned is guess-work. In 1925,
however, I feel I know all: my constant provings to myself of
my own virility do not, I feel, have their quality enhanced by
the appearance of a baby brother.

I am, however, gradually aroused into a sort of useless,
lopsided and off-again, on-again pity for child-ridden
Mother who seems as happy-go-lucky, busy and noisy as
ever. I observe for the first time that the gold of her wedding-
ring is worn smooth, that the backs of her hands, the texture
of her elbows and the skin at the sides of her neck have all
changed. Mother is older. Older than what, I am not sure,
for she cannot be older then herself (in 1925 she is thirty-six)
and yet that is my impression: older than herself. I sense that
she has become an engagement of forces within herself, that
the 'natural' side of her being, with its demands of being
maternally omnipresent, has to stand with conscious nobility, as though defiantly excusing its workaday splendour
against the sardonic side, the sharp-shooting and self-
ridiculing side. It is her outward expression of this inner
war, the behaviour and utterances of a younger and gayer
person, that make her seem older.

Several things rapidly happen—or seem, at this distance,
to happen rapidly.

The baby is no sooner weaned than Mother has her hair
bobbed. In early 1926, in that country town, fashions drift
slowly into the stream of provincial life, a year or so late and,
having drifted in, take at least another year to rise up from
the younger and more reckless to the older, more wary
women. Not so with Mother. She goes to the barber's, for
there are no beauty parlours in Bairnsdale then, in the same

month as the young women, the flappers and hussies with their knee-high skirts and jazz garters. This is almost shocking, and is certainly defiant of Mother. The operation does not make her look younger, merely impertinent. Once, an eternity ago it seems, most of her aids to beautification disappeared from the elaborate dressing-table, freeing her once-suburban hands to take up the duties and tools of a country mother. Now, without relinquishing any of these tools, seemingly as many-handed as a Hindu goddess, she takes up once more the pots of Pond's Cold Cream and Vanishing Cream, the dry rouge, the tinted face powders: Peach, Rachel, Flesh. Why? And how does she find the time to lacquer her face with egg-white?

Certainly, she is helped about the house by us older children; there is the washerwoman; there is the old Scotchwoman who milks Dolly the Jersey; but a flock of servants would, I *think*, have made little difference to the total of work Mother does. A job taken over by someone else only means that she is somewhere else magicking other work, extra exercises in perfection, out of nowhere. This striving, this positive need for everything to be speckless and decorously tied-off is something I have inherited or imitated from Mother. I can jibe at every scrupulous effort I thus make in Mother's manner, every sally at a faultlessness invisible to most others; I can even compel myself to commit momentary slipshoddinesses. It avails nothing. I must turn back and retie the bow, find *le mot juste*, write the bread-and-butter letter, empty the ash-tray, be absolutely abstemious and sleep eight clear-eyed hours, or drink all night until garnet-eyed drunkenness is perfected. Thus, also, in her fashion, Mother. Now, 1926, the more sordid daily tasks over, she does not merely scrub herself and change into something fresh. She has a bath or a shower; she almost decorates herself. She sits at dinner with the fringe of her bobbed hair gleaming from the brush, wearing her gold brooch with IDA on it, wearing a little rouge, a little scent, wearing too a hostess manner. Sometimes, she comes to table with her fringe caught back under plaited switches of her own hair twisted about her head in the manner of the nicer vamps, Aileen Pringle or Jetta Goudal, her bare forehead illustrating serenity, her ear-rings on.

The point to be made is that she is doing these things against herself. That I clearly see. I smell defiance; there is a faint odour of despair. I do not understand why. At the age of six or eight or ten I would have understood. It is probably the woman nature at her age; it is equally probably an attempt to balance . . . somehow . . . somehow . . . financial dislocation by making a mask of scent and powder and pretty clothes to hide the fact that money is no longer a tamed kitten but a wild cat clawing and gnawing at her children's safety and her own peace of mind. It may be that Father, without actually leaving French-letters under the oaks in the Tannies or the horse-chestnuts along the river bank, is performing mental adulteries observable to her. There is no one to question now; I shall never know. Aware of *some*thing, I record, from time to time, and carelessly, a flicker of pity I do not express, and cannot express, and have no time at all to express, as I rush into and out of the house, for I am selfish fifteen, mad about myself, in knickerbockers of blue twill, my first shoes, my last year at High School, and am wildly concerned with my own whirling little world.

I am now one of the three most senior boys, one of the trinity which controls such matters as the ritual ducking of new boys. One of us three is the school captain, the all-rounder, the Rhodes Scholar kind; one is the brilliant mathematics and science boy; I am the poet of the school magazine, the dasher-off of long flamboyant essays crammed with esoteric fact, obsolete words and five-syllabled adjectives. I am given to chattering in French, and draw flower-pots and garden trowels leaning against watering-cans better than anyone at Bairnsdale High School, 1926. My early skill in mathematical subjects deserts me more and more as my pubic hairs increase; the elementary properties of the parabola are not elementary to me, and require almost more concentration than I can spare for, here I am, growing all over at a fascinating rate, my treble cracking and crackling, my nose getting longer (oh, dear!), and my passion for pleasure of a rackety sort increasing. I wear a clove carnation in my buttonhole. I can do the Charleston. There can have been no more grotesque sight than that of a knickerbockered adolescent, with long golden hair in the conventional brush-back style, Charlestoning across the quadrangle from lesson to lesson. It is what, then, I think of myself as—The Gay One. It may still be what I am, symbolically, that is. Placidity does breed a joyful fecklessness.

Other than the three boys, the senior form contains six girls, all of them several years older than the boys, and many years older in the blunter wisdoms. There are even rumours of sexual misbehaviour by some of the girls, which I do not believe, for they are virtually young women of sixteen, seventeen and eighteen, with breasts under their blue tunics, and seem to me far too old to do what little girls used to do with me when I was a little boy and went in for that sort of thing. These girls, however, during certain unsupervised periods, Study Periods during which we are all 'on our honour' to work diligently, do tell us dirty yarns and, sometimes, do read us dirty yarns from the same sort of typed sheets of paper worn at the folds that I am to be bored by, time and time again, in later life, typed sheets produced from the wallets of commercial travellers from Fremantle to Blackfriars, from Hobart to Manchester, from the wallets of army officers in Japanese Occupation messes, from the wallets of shipboard hearties and ill-met tourists in B.O.A.C. planes at Zurich and Beirut and Djarkata. Where do the girls, who keep these, like their handkerchiefs, in the legs of their bloomers, get the obscene things from? My mind boggles. None of us boys has any. The girls have, as well, a tattered copy of Chic Sale's booklet on rustic lavatories. I have rarely laughed so agonizingly much, the tears streaming, the belly muscles hurting, as when Olwen Connor, the female school captain, reads from this bawdy work. This is not my reason for loving Olwen Connor, but love her I do, and her knowledge of the cruder aspects of life makes no difference to my love for her as something exquisite and untouchably sacred. Everyone at the High School knows of my love for her because I make no bones about it. Everyone also knows that she does not care for me. She drives to school each day in her own jinker: her father is a grazier five miles outside the town. Her grown-up brothers, with expensive masculine names like Dirk and Rex and Rod, are often smashing up long, low, crimson or white open-topped cars as they roar about the country doing pub-crawls from Bairnsdale to Sale, from Ensay to Lakes Entrance, fifty, sixty, seventy miles of drinking in the Australian country fashion. Olwen, if she does not have the passion for me that I have for her, does not dismiss me from her presence; she is a woman, and will not deplete her retinue of followers—I am not the only boy in love with Olwen Connor—by even one poetically soppy member. Since at this moment I am able to think I know, and can state bluntly, that my sexual fervour is less than or at least less unsettling than the fervour of the apparently and reputedly normal, it is not simple to gauge how far below the standard of puppy-love anguish and exaltation mine falls, nevertheless anguish and exaltation of almost intolerable kind I do experience. I draw overlapping hearts, one labelled O.C. and the other H.P., everywhere, deeply pressing into the wood of desks and gate-posts with the pencil, driving the arrow that joins these two hearts with an intensity of day-dreaming and romantic desire that shocks me now. What wasted power!

I bombard her with letters—about unrecallable what!—enclosed in envelopes bearing on their sealed flaps the letters S.W.A.L.K. (Sealed with a loving kiss) or T.O.I.L. (To one I love.) She takes them as secretly as lover ever took letter from lover, with something cat-like in her gestures. She never answers except by a quarter-smile faint as smoke which she lets me catch, behind the backs of the world, when no one is expected to be looking, but when everyone is looking, albeit obliquely and pretending to stare the other way. I should have preferred an answer in writing, an envelope bearing

S.W.A.L.K., but the flitting smile · serves—well, serves enough to stop me from despair. I write poems to her:

In Dreams (to Olwen)

In dreams upon your silver breasts I spread
Blue magic stuffs wherein stars sleep;
Your ears receive sweet jewels that are bled
From silken-lidded roses as they weep;
And for your feet my eager hands have set
The virgin velvet daffodils.

Thereon you walk, among my tears that fret
Your way with silver pearls.
There I worship, and your wonder fills
My trance. O move there always, in its hills,
For of you have I nothing save my dreams.

God knows who the inferior Georgian poet is who serves as model for this piffle and these lies. I certainly never dream of Olwen; I recall only dreams of flying, higher and ecstatically higher above the burning colours and the exquisitely minute detail of a world in which I am able to see both sides of an object, inside and outside a closed box magnificently embossed and decorated, at one and the same time. I write poems of lies which I think I mean, about dreams I do not have, and a desire I have not formulated.

The young, at this stage, do not really exist.

I leave flowers on her desk, Mother's flowers, which I pick like a thief, an outsize pansy with (I say to myself) one tear in its eye, a perfect camellia, a bunch of double violets. She never wears them, never, but, with one of those feminine gestures I now know too well, gives them—not to one of the bigger girls, not just to any girl, but to dirtyish, ragbag little girls in the first form. This gesture of combined delicacy and ruthlessness makes my heart quiver towards breaking. It never breaks. I confound it from breaking, and confound my disappointment too, by lying to myself, 'How kind and gentle Olwen is!'

A curious incident occurs. During 1926 many of the High School girls get their hair bobbed or shingled. Of the six senior girls Olwen Connor alone keeps hers untouched, a single strong curl, brown streaked with gilt, lying between her shoulder-blades, a persisting symbol of my taste: have I not fallen in love with the one girl who will not tamper with her beauty for a mere change in hair-fashions? Although Olwen Connor's beauty does not exalt me as that of the Kensington child in the grey velvet dress to this day does and to the end of life will, it does excite me: I find her beautiful and warm and cruelly untouchable. It is not that I feel I wish to play with her sexually; she is too beautiful to be thus sullied—gentle kisses in a garden, or long strollings hand in hand under the willows and wattles of the river, are something of what I think we want, she and I and her beautiful hair. Then, suddenly, as 1926 nears its end, the school knows that Olwen Connor is to have her hair shingled. An excitement slides across the school's mind like the shallow hem of a wave, sparkling yet icy, limpid yet salty. Oh, you will see that this is not transference of my own feeling to others. I write what is my first love letter begging for what I can only now suppose I call a lock (or tress?) of hair. As ever, she takes this letter, deadpan, as her due or punishment for being beautiful. As ever, behind the all-observant backs of the small universe of detectives, she returns no answer except the wraith of a smile.

The day of mutilation arrives.

After school I watch her, in the strangely empty and silent school-ground, the shadows of the trees getting longer, walk to the horse-paddock at the end of the playing fields. As she harnesses her horse to the jinker I see, for the last time in life, the curl lying down her back. Tears come to my eyes. She drives off. I know she is on her way to Jeremy Confait, the barber who cut off Mother's hair. I hurry in Confait's direction, over the railway crossing, past the ostentatious nineteenth-century bulk of the Grand Terminus Hotel with its vast first storey cast-iron veranda, its hitching-rings on each veranda-post, its livery and baiting stables, its brick-floored yards and roaring bar, into Main Street. Feeling my romantic purpose to illumine me to unconventionality, I walk, I hasten, I almost run, not on the footpath, but through the gardens which occupy the centre of Main Street. I speed along under the elms and starling-haunted palms, between the crescent-shaped beds of municipal roses edged with lobelias, past the Boer War memorial, the bandstand, the drinking-fountain of pink granite, until, far along the street, in the gardens opposite the bicycle shop on the roof of which sits a penny-farthing, I reach the grotto in which is set a fish-pond. Behind this I have decided to lurk, to watch until Olwen appears shorn, to advance and beg the lock of hair I have already begged for. Outside Confait's, tied to one of the barber-pole-striped veranda-posts, the horse and jinker are tied. Outside Confait's, their bicycles leaning against posts and elms, are more than thirty High School students. I pretend not to see them. They pretend not to see me. They murmur together, their faces turned towards Confait's door through the upper glass panel of which they can see, pinned on to the voile curtains, a chart illustrating feminine haircuts: Cherub, Cringle, Claudine and Madonna. Set centrally of these four, in its own oval, is the head showing *Qua Négligé*, A Superior Cut, states the chart, With a Tendency towards *Frou Frou*. Which is Olwen to have?

I could join the group of other watchers which includes other admirers, but prefer to be the solitary and sensitive lover, the one behind the mossy grotto and the romantic fountain. When, after what seems ever, the mob is suddenly so silent for a second that one is aware of the clanging from the blacksmith's, the bitter whining from the sawmill, the gurgling from the fish-pond statue of a noseless boy holding a nameless fish in his fingerless arms, I know Olwen has come out.

"A-a-a-a-a-h!' they all say, from one throat.

I cannot see her.

I have forgotten that I have come to beg.

When she climbs into the jinker, and I can see her, she wears her hat. I do not see the shorn hair—Cringle—until next day. She is still beautiful, yet, for some reason, I write her no more letters or poems, and act the thief no more in Mother's garden. Then, I do not know why my tactics change. I know now. Men will know. Another hour has struck. Women will know why, a month later, on our last day at High School, Olwen Connor hands me, with so whole a smile that it seems, after dearth, many smiles, in front of everyone, in front of the world, an envelope containing a curl of her hair.

'This,' she lies loud and clear, 'is the curl I promised you.'

I do not see Olwen Connor, after this unbelievable moment, for twenty-five years.

Not a long-time keepsake-keeper, I nevertheless carry this curl about with me for longer than I do anything except Mother's last letter to me, much longer than I do the remains of the yellow rose my ex-wife gives me the first night we meet, for longer than other 'locks of hair', and letters in which the words have turned sour, or mocking, or too agonizing to bear. I carry it from one end of the earth to the other for twenty-five years. In 1951, enough blond still in my hair almost to conceal the grey, I see Olwen Connor. I recognize her as instantly as I recognized King Bunyip, Dick Verco; she greets me as offhandedly as he. She is a pretty, little, grey-haired woman vigorously pedalling a bicycle. She is, I later learn, a grandmother. 'Hello, Harold,' she says, speeding by with her sturdy legs. The quality of her voice is a shock to me. Was it not silver-and-golden after all? The feelings with which I burn the worn envelope and the curl, that evening, are too faint to bear the weight of even one word. A sigh—for what?—a sigh, no more. The paper and the creeping flame neatly wrestle and writhe a little; the gilded brown curl from the head of the grey-haired cyclist, the pretty granny with the alloyed voice, emits a faint stench as it bubbles to ash. How foolish of me to have persisted for a quarter of a century in being a sort of sentimental boy when I am really a sort of unsentimental man.

This act of giving the curl in the envelope, in the last hour of the last day of the school year, is the actual finish of my schoolboyhood; with this overwhelming gift in the pocket of my silesia jacket, I walk away towards manhood which I think is just around the next corner in the years, but which is many more corners away, and has little to do with years.

With nine years of formal education behind me, four at State Schools, five at High School, I am ready to earn my living in a world moving inexorably towards Depression. How am I to earn a living? I have given it no thought at all.

Certain school subjects have come, as I lose my early infallibility, to mean little to me except as mental toe-touching; I can touch my toes easily enough to pass examinations. The grossest torture could leave me nowadays as upright and unbending as a ramrod in the matter of cross-questionings mathematical, geographical, historical, chemical or scientific. I have, however, driven by my own inner devil, gone very much further, have ploughed much more deeply than the examination standards require in Art, French and especially English. At fifteen, for example, without guidance, almost against guidance, I have developed an outrageous taste, eclectic to eccentricity, in authors: Dickens, Olive Schreiner, Tchekhov, Katherine Mansfield, Maupassant, Paul Fort, Ibañez, Tolstoi, Gabriele d'Annunzio, Hardy and Barrie. I am so fascinated by Rémy de Gourmont that I translate into an exotic English everything of his I can lay my hands on.

All this, and more, boils down to nothing except that an upstart and word-obsessed adolescent is self-educating himself towards an aim, not to this day accomplished, of stating as incandescently as possible verities not yet fully realized.

I put away my High School cap with its enamel badge in a manner so deliberately and affectedly sad that I neutralize —rather in Mother's self-twitting manner—what may have been the sincere feeling of sadness every human has when doing something, even something hateful, for the last time.

Once again, Mother sterilizes the threepences and sixpences and minute china dolls for the Christmas Pudding of 1926; once again—the baby too—we all stir the pudding with the worn wooden spoon in the large wash-stand ewer decorated with nasturtiums; once again the puddings hang

173

in their cloths from the pantry ceiling with the leg of ham. Paper-chains made from wallpaper, crêpe paper streamers, witch-balls, tinsel and artificial holly are strung across the dining-room ceiling, and looped about the walls. There are conic bottles of Schweppes' lime juice in the ice-chest, short-bread and mince pies in the biscuit barrels. A half-crown is left on the lavatory seat for the dunny-man. The John China-man greengrocer leaves his Christmas gift of a hexagonal green china jar of preserved ginger in a net of oil-on-water-coloured silk; the grocer gives his annual present of a bottle of raspberry vinegar and a large bag of liquorice all-sorts and wine gums. The shop-veranda posts along each side of Main Street are all disguised as Christmas trees by having a euca-lypt sapling tied to each. Christmas stockings of every size from minute to colossal hang in the fruiterers' and confec-tioners' and grocers', each containing the same ritual rubbish they contain when I am a small child in Kensington, and contain still now nearly half-a-century later: the nasty oval over-sweet sweets of nasty green, nasty yellow and nasty pink; the red-and-white striped cardboard trumpet with its wooden mouthpiece; the cylindrical blue-and-white-striped cardboard whistle with its multi-coloured tissue paper mop; the small glass-topped box revealing the grinning face with its pupils of lead-shot to be rolled into the eyeholes, and the inexplicable fluted tin object—patty pan? jelly mould? mud-pie shape? dish for a miniature *Quiche Lorraine*? what?

Once again Christmas is over.

The heat is searing and superb. The paddocks surrounding the town are bleached blond. The distant ring-barked gums, mile after mile, wriggle in the heat-waves, and seem to melt like the bristles of a melting hairbrush. The hills turn powder-blue and gauzy. Mirages resembling pools of mica and shallows of crystal water appear at the far ends of streets and roads. Punctually at eleven every burning morn-ing, the cicadas begin to drill the air, to drill themselves also, ceaselessly and relentlessly, to death in one short day after seven long years underground.

Once again, it is New Year's Eve.

All of us children, eldest to youngest, are let stay up to hear the Old Year out and the New Year in. We sit eating cold Christmas pudding and shortbread and mince pies, and drinking the grocer's gift of raspberry vinegar with small chunks of ice in it, as we do every New Year's Eve. Where is Father? Mother is there in the same, now shabby and darned, wrapper she wore when we played Tit-Tat-Toe. Mother is tired, tired, tired; there are shadows like beautiful bruises under her eyes. The baby is there, and the Richelieu supper cloth, and the Japanese saucer filled with pennies and three-pences for the Salvation Army. Out in the simmering night, on The Common, under Orion and all the stars and planets, the Salvation Army plays and sings. We chew, we drink, we talk softly as though night weighs our tongues. My brothers' and sisters' eyes are glittering as if they have fever. We all quiver—even sophisticated I—in our night-clothes, waiting to hear the front gate click, to hear the exciting footsteps . . . who? . . . who? . . . on the gravel path, on the veranda boards, and the knock—so late and possibly dire. What if it were *not* a Salvation Army collector but Springheel Jack, or Satan, or Jesus himself? It is the Salvation Army collector, radiant and ruddy and smelling of sweat. We . . . even sophisticated I . . . rattle our money into the box. Mother puts in an amazing shilling on the baby's behalf. Where is Father? He is in bed like, he says, all sensible people. The clocks begin to strike; the church bells, the fire bell, the school bells, all the bells in Christendom began to ring swiftly and clearly. We all kiss each other—even sophisticated I. We watch from our door doors everywhere opening, slapping down shafts of light on the gardens, the privet hedges, the picket fences, the grassy footpaths and elm-boles; a chatter-ing roar augmented by turning wheels, motor-car horns, galloping horses and barking dogs, gushes up and up from the town which seems to grow incandescent, up and up to push the sounds of the bells higher, higher and madder.

It is presently 12.5, Saturday, January the First, 1927. On Monday, January the Third, I shall be at work.

Adolescence, it now seems to me, is a period one gesticulates through largely in secret, and for no one, least of all for oneself—that is, one's past self and one's future self. If one be, at this period, noisier than ever before in life, the noise, the guttural rages, the bitter bellowings, the beatings of brows and pounding on tables are as surprising and boring to the executant as boring to the listener. In the fog of this boredom the Present is lost, is under the ether, is joyless and secret. The secrecy, and the boredom making it, occur also if, rather than hullabaloo and cries of fury, one indulges in brooding silences, sulking withdrawals and noiseless typhoons of pique. The adolescent sees nothing of Past and Future because the nothing of the Present obscures them, but he does see himself, does see his physical self, with unnecessary and amazed clearness.

I see myself—visually, that is—with greater clarity than before or since. I occupy my own foreground and, in it, face with distaste many unpredictable situations that I could have predicted and placidly faced when younger. I face also, and too often, the looking-glass. There I am. There is the appalling secret: while, yesterday, I was what I wanted to be and look like, today, I am not what I want to be and look like. My hair is fair: it should be blue-black as a rook and in amaranthine curls. My eyes? Blue. Oh, for eyes of deep green speckled with gold! Daily examining the length of my eyelashes and nose, the colour and shape of my teeth, the quality of a variety of tried-out smiles and head-cockings and melting glances and quizzical ones, I seek for signs of physical beauty for my own pleasure as much as for the pleasure of others, the Olwen Connors of the world, and the passers-by whose hushed voices will float back to me as I delight them in the street, 'Did you see that handsome youth, the one with the blue-black curls and startling green eyes?'

Ah yes, I seek for the one who existed contentedly yesterday and who will exist contentedly tomorrow but who is, today, a secret.

No matter how much hair-oil, in spite of Mother's expressed disapproval of any, I use to paste down my brush-back, I get no nearer a resemblance to Rod la Rocque or William Haines or any of my patent-leather-haired heroes of the films. My nose grows bonier and beakier. Pimples appear. Blackheads appear. Nothing will remove my freckles although I furtively attempt versions of beauty treatments suggested by advisers in the women's columns of newspapers. Slices of cucumber and lemon rubbed on my freckles seem merely to brighten and multiply them.

However, it is not merely as one who cannot now move abroad without a comb and a nail-file in his pocket, and several cloves to sweeten the breath, that I see myself. Adolescence forces me to watch every move and gesture I make physically and socially, to weigh every word, and the accent and intonation of every word I utter. Some new creature is compelling me to make it stronger and sleeker, to get it ready for freedom. All I have spent years learning, and all I appear to know, have become heavy and shabby tools—where are the razor-sharp and exquisitely turned and chased ones I feel I now need for the task in hand? How cruelly and closely, meantime, from behind the fog, the little-boy me, ever astute and clear-cut and calm as a conviction, scrutinizes the side-steppings and almost-blunderings and nearly false-steps of him who is no longer a child, nowhere near manhood, and scarcely anything but a self with a core of nothing but self, and wrapped in layers of self.

On Monday, January the Third, 1927, this creature, not yet sixteen, goes to work as a cadet reporter for *The Bairnsdale Advertiser*. How does he get the job? I think his head-master gets it for him. Is that how it happens? I cannot recall. His parents? Their involvement is doubtful. Father and the headmaster may have flickered their aprons at each other in a special job-getting way behind the doorless façade of the

Masonic Hall, in which sinister building opposite St. John's Church of England, I have heard from Sunday School gossip, there are indelicate and unimaginable rites involving nudity and goats. I reluctantly disbelieve these rumours because I find no practical answer to the questions I ask myself. Why is there no door to the Masonic Hall? What *does* go on there that must not be seen? Why does Father lock his black Masonic satchel away?

In whatever manner he gets the job, and I scarcely think it is by his own machinations, there he goes, on his first money-earning Monday morning, to work. Watch him!

For some reason, for the first time in his life, as he kisses Mother, 'Good-bye!' he says. This is forbidden; Mother has trained the family in the belief that the use of 'Good-bye!' is an invitation to doom; lighter forms of farewell have always been the custom: 'Ta-ta!', 'Bye-bye!' or, 'Be back soon!' Mother, horrified and genuinely upset, demands another kiss, another farewell than 'Good-bye!' Nevertheless it is good-bye. Childhood and Chapter One are over, the man-trap is set, the bucket of icy water is balanced above the door of the next room, there is no, 'Be back soon!' for *that* Hal Porter. When he returns home for luncheon on January the Third, 1927, he will appear the same but already something will be stirring—the Devil in the basement, the Angel in the attic, the two-faced Diplomat in the drawing-room, the Clown in all the corridors—who yet knows?

Watch him go.

He walks, bold as brass, straighter of back than usual, and with longer strides than he needs to take. He is thinking, for the first time, of long trousers and silk socks, but wears the blue twill knickerbocker suit that Mother has cleaned and pressed. It smells, very faintly, of petrol. He has a Cecile Brunner rose in his button-hole. He wears a grey felt hat—his first. Garment by garment, body hair by body hair, sin by sin, he is to be clothed as a man. He carries a pad clearly lettered *Reporter's Note Book* so held that the lettering faces the public, and his hand does not hide it. Clipped into his breast-pocket are two well-sharpened pencils, one cylindrical and H.B., one hexagonal and B.B., each with a piece of india-rubber set in the end.

Displaying thus affectedly, and with cheap pride, that he has severed ties with childhood, as he walks—oh, striding too much, and offensively—under the elms of nine o'clock, to cross to The Common, he receives his punishment. It is doubly a punishment since it rebukes too his own childhood.

The house on the corner opposite The Common, and once occupied by the Adams family, is now occupied by the Macgregors. There seem as many Macgregor children as there once seemed Adams children, smaller and plumper ones with bold pink faces and, inherited from Mrs. Macgregor, violently crossed eyes which the glare on many steel-rimmed spectacles scarcely hides, and which the spectacles them-scarcely correct. Each head is covered with whitish hair like dirty thistledown.

From among the Macgregor roses as packed together, and the delphiniums aspiring as preposterously as calendar flowers—for Mr. Macgregor is a perfervid gardener—the striding youth, the fifteen-year-old growing out of his knickerbockers, hears the saw-toothed voices, the sexlessly cruel voices, the justice-dealing and terrible voices of the country he has left for ever: 'Where dija git that hat? Where dija git that hat?' and, then, 'Silly old Porter! Silly old Porter!'

As Nurse Mawdsley did not turn, and the dunny-man did not turn, nor the dwarf, nor the disintegrating Chinese, nor the skin-and-bone aborigines, so he does not turn. His blood ignites and singes his heart but he does not turn. Once across The Common and around the corner and out of sight of the spectacles glinting among the overfed flowers, he non-chalantly and as though by the most ordinary movement turns the pad towards his body. His fingers cover the proud lettering. He knows, as the Macgregors know, wherein he has sinned. He walks on, rebuked, towards some simple lessons from the primer of disillusion, towards the building which houses some of his future and *The Bairnsdale Advertiser*.

The building is long and narrow, a mere door and a

frosted plate-glass window front the street. One steps directly from the street into a small room. Behind the counter, on which are a file of old newspapers clamped between two strips of pine, a pewter inkwell, and several dried-out clag bottles, Miss Ray sits at her table behind a lofty typewriter. Her bentwood chair with the cretonne cushion is conveniently disposed so as to get the warmth, in colder seasons, from the corner fireplace, and a view, every day and every hour of the day, of what might happen in the street—murder; adulterous notes of assignation passing from hand to hand; fast flappers with jazz-garters lewdly showing; old men creeping along, and dying on their feet of fascinating diseases; unhappy wives; tippling husbands; children who were once premature babies. Miss Ray prefers to catch, less with malice than with pleasure, glimpses of the flighty or the doom-struck. These glimpses enliven her, as glimpses of others' failings and immoralities enliven all women. To be sure of getting as much as she can of what little can take place outside the window, she has scratched two eyeholes in the frosting of the glass under the lettering:

THE BAIRNSDALE ADVERTISER

She seems to me to work, sustained on innumerable cups of treacle-coloured tea, and Marie biscuits, with stolid but mistake-less efficiency, at her numerous duties of typist, office-girl, receptionist, secretary and accountant. Chewing a peppermint, she jangles the keys of the green-painted safe that sits by the fireplace and has a handle shaped like a stove-handle, a clenched brass fist holding a piece of brass dowelling. She climbs on to, and descends from, and rides to and from work, a very ladylike Lady's Bicycle with sprays of roses and convolvulus lacquered on its frame, with a chirruping bell, a glossy pump, a large headlamp containing a wax candle and, enclosing its wheels, a sun-ray effect woven in string. She wears skirts of dim tartans composed of material with the texture of steamer-rugs, and hanging well below her knees. Bum-length cardigans of lacy wool in lilac or nut-brown or heather-mixture are also recallable. The knitted belts of these have furry pompons at each end. Her hair is plaited and wound over each ear like crystal-set receivers. She is of some non-conformist religion, probably Presbyterian. Her religion, her appearance, possessions and habits suddenly interest me intensely because—click!—I realize that for years I have been doing subconscious addition sums of others' appearances, possessions, habits and all that, and arriving at a total which, aided by instinct and *its* adding up of the unrevealed, is the total on which one comes to dislike or bear with, pity or abhor, love or loathe another. It is apparent I am not her cup of tea, as she is scarcely mine. We work in the same place, therefore, in wary amity, dishonestly sheathed in stale politeness. I am fast losing my right to be as truthful and impolite as a child.

Behind Miss Ray's room is the room, no larger than hers, of the editor who seems as old as a beardless Jehovah diminished to fit his working-box. He sits behind a table, littered as a racetrack, and gives the table importance by the fact that he never seems, in memory, to be elsewhere. He is there when I arrive, there when I leave. A glass-fronted cedar bookcase towers behind him; a large pewter inkwell, a verdigrised rack of many steel-nibbed pens, and a blotter with gold-tooled calf corners sits before him in a clearing in the mess. Perhaps because I rarely find much pleasure in looking above his starched butterfly collar, his hands remain most in my mind, hands composed of overlapping dark veins, liver-spotted cold bones, and finger-nails ridged like grey celery. A little Dickensian fire fumes in a little Dickensian grate to the right of this dour god and his table on which the details of mediocre lives are jumbled like rubbish. Far from the fire, back to the editor, in a corner of the room, face to a dirty window curtainless enough to permit a view of gangling burdocks, I sit—the cadet-reporter sits. He works so quickly that he has plenty of time to pretend to be always working when he is really keeping his finger-nails as exquisite as an actress's, and writing poems which now reveal where his mind thinks it is:

In silken flocks, above sleek strings of grass,
Slide on buckled brilliant feet, spruce maids;
Jonquil-painted cheeks among their braids
Glowing golden, sweetly . . . as they pass,
Glowing golden, sweetly . . . as they pass.
Rime-lashed honey eyes flutter,
Bubbles under jade mutter,
May drowns in the jargonelles,
Softly, softly, softly sing the babbling bells.

Wavelings peck the naked bosom-buds,
Long eyes glimmer in the lapping shade;
Silver faces, water-woven, fade,
Swooning sadly on the lily floods,
Swooning sadly on the lily floods.
Feather fins below quiver,
Emeraldine reeds shiver,
May swoops down the whistling skies,
Rubies, rubies, rubies burn the satyr eyes.

I can only imagine now that Norman Lindsay's etchings and water-colours have affected me, and that I have moved one little stage further in the production of masturbation poetry; cock-raising desire, and ill-digested art, and eighteenth-century Hellenic balderdash, causing me to scribble off many such verses. At least, for a while, I am no longer 'alone' in these rhymed ejaculations. It is no wonder that, pretending to do the work I have already done, I find myself with an erection invariably when the editor grunts me to my feet to bring my copy to him.

Behind the editor's room is the rest of the building, a noisy place of machines, to the end of which I never get. Here, his three sons work at their multiple duties on the Linotype machines, and the revolving and slapping machines that print handbills, wedding invitations, tickets for bazaars and cantatas, show programmes, golf-score cards, shire council reports, school magazines rich with nineteenth-century fleurons, and concert programmes executed in as many type faces as the programmes can hold.

It surprises the cadet that, after doing the same sorts of things for years, these adults do not toss off their jobs deftly and flawlessly with a light song on their lips: there are muck-ups, procrastinations, constant last-minute rushes, tangles of temper and unnecessary effort. He has yet to learn that this is the way of the careless, hopeful world. He expects, in those days, from his elevated point of view, and, today, still wants, though without the old hope, men and women to be examples of perfection, to possess a perfection he cannot define fully, but at least a perfection in the minor aspects of living. He is as surprised then, by these slapdash adults, as he is when dancing with his first royal duchess to discover that she breathes garlic, that literary critics breathe ignorance and malice, that Life is life, and everyone has as many of his own imperfections and dishonesties as he has. Most surprising to him is the easily recognizable indifference in others to the flaws they know they have, the absolute lack of any desire to remove these flaws. He is forced to turn the next page in the primer of disillusion, and the next, and the next. The illustrations grow succeedingly less tinted and romantic. The pages are foxed.

Take his first two assignments.

These are interviews which, because of the relative physical positions of interviewed and interviewer, are done at the top of the lungs. I see—and how I should like to warn him!— the adolescent in the deeply dented grey felt hat and the blue twill knickerbockers and the shiny, shiny shoes swaggeringly striding, *remembering* to stride (Death and damnation to Macgregors and bygone boyhood!), Reporter's Notebook in hand (Beware Macgregors!), along and across Main Street to where the Fire Brigade captain, who is also a bricklayer, is working on top of the new wall of the Fire Brigade Hall. The cadet recognizes the Captain's moustache which curves over to hide the mouth. There is his . . . his man? . . . his prey? . . . his first Waterloo in a world now to be composed of moustaches and long trousers? He stands beneath the

Captain among the pretty weeds he once—how long ago?—
sat among to taste an earlier disillusion with *Uncle Tom's
Cabin*. He is circling onwards and yet backwards in time with
the one movement. He unclips the hexagonal B.B. pencil. He
opens the Reporter's Notebook. He is now—it is finally unmistakable—a working man. It needs just one sly clearing of
the old, child's world from his throat, and all will be well.
He has every faith in his power to knit the unravelled
world together again. No more slipshoddiness. Youth is
here.

'Mr. Bunson! Mr. Bunson!' he calls, attempting a depth
of tone impossible to achieve, and a mellifluous briskness.
Crows do better.

Trowel in hand, the moustache, aloft on its rampart, inclines towards him, signifying that it is Mr. Bunson's.

'I am,' shouts the grey felt hat, size six and seven-eighths'
'a reporter.'

'Ah?' says Mr. Bunson. Deaf, eh?

'I am,' he shouts again, now choosiing words that are to be
a banner of alert manhood, 'a reporter. *The* re-por-ter from
The Bairnsdale Advertiser. If you would be so. . . .' Kind?
Gracious? Oh, he is poised! '. . . so gracious, I should like to
have some information about your dead sister.'

He does not yet know the rules. Dead! He cannot guess
that words like *bereavement, loss, passed on, deceased* are not only
desirable but mandatory. He will learn.

'Ah!' says Mr. Bunson. This does not help. Neither does it
hinder.

'May I know her name, please? Her full name.'

He translates Mr. Bunson into B.B. handwriting. He goes
relentlessly and complacently on. And her age? Her address?
When she first came to Bairnsdale? How many children?
Names? How many grandchildren? Names, if you would be
so gracious? And what did she die of?

As he stands shouting, and translating, and writing, a drop
of liquid falls on the page. He looks up. There is not a cloud
in the sky. There are only the trowel, and the moustache, and
Mr. Bunson in the sky, and from Mr. Bunson, in full day-

184

light, Tin Lizzies with running-boards and mica side-curtains shaking busily by, has fallen a tear. With a khaki handkerchief Mr. Bunson is preventing the fall of another or others. The cadet is horrified. He looks down, anywhere but up, down at the page. The tear looks back. He dares not wipe it away, the tear of a moustached bricklayer and Fire Brigade Captain with a dead sister called Annabelle Florrie Tomkins. He is struck mute. He will never look up again. He cannot make the polite and . . . and gracious . . . move-ment of escape. He cannot dissolve in the blazing air. Con-cealed beneath his grey felt brim, he endures imprisonment in dumbness and eternity.

'Hey, sonny,' shouts a voice from the cloudless sky, 'is that all you want, sonny?'

Sonny!

Struck articulate again, back from eternity, 'Thank you very much, Mr. Bunson,' he cries in a cold, an almost angry voice. 'That will be *quite* enough.' He slaps the tear shut in his writing-pad, and off he goes.

'Good-bye, Mr. Bunson!' he says. Good-bye! Would Mother approve of what he is wishing on Mr. Bunson?

Now, hardened, prepared for no more nonsense from hit-and-miss adults, he goes to assignation the second. He passes the water-tower, crosses and turns the corner of the Main Hotel where, twelve years later, he is to spend part of his scandal-making honeymoon. He comes to St. Mary's Presby-tery with its speckless paths, and close-shaven lawns, and cypresses carved to cylinders and pyramids. By the apricot tree he stole from when he was a competent apricot-thief, eight black socks hang on a clothes-line in the alley of sun-light that simmers between the presbytery and the cathedral with its unfinished campanile.

As he reaches the presbytery veranda-steps, Monsignor opens the fly-wire door, and walks out with his squat and ancient spaniel in a gust of what smells like steak and onions. Who cooks, on such a hot day, whatever it is that smells? Who washes the black socks, darns them, pegs them up? Nuns? Monsignor himself?

Monsignor's grey curls have salted down much dandruff on his huge, richly barathea shoulders.

'And what would your name be?' says Monsignor in an authentic brogue, the pores in his face no bigger than the holes in a meat-safe.

The cadet tells his name, or the name he now thinks he has, and by which no one but himself has ever called him.

'Mr. Porter,' says the boy in knickerbockers, holding the book in which a tear is squashed. Monsignor finds it necessary to smile down at the spaniel's back.

'I am a reporter. From *The Bairnsdale Advertiser*. If you would be so gracious. . . .' He cannot forego this. '. . . I should like to have some per-tin-ent information about the paintings being done on the roof . . . the *ceiling* . . . of your church.'

Should he have said *your*? Should he have said *church*?

Here is mystery and Mass and Confession and the Angelus and Hail Marys and *The Awful Disclosures of Maria Monk* and the Blessed Virgin in the antirrhinum of Kensington days, and Mother and Sister Philomena singing years ago in the cab.

'Well now, well now—Mis-ter Por-ter,' says Monsignor to the spaniel, 'you'll come with me, and talk to the man yourself. Come with me.' As they walk, a starling fires itself up and sits on one of the high-up marble statues, on St. Joseph's (or St. Patrick's) crook (or crosier). 'Mis-ter Por-ter,' says Monsignor, secretly finishing a sentence in the direction of the spaniel's back. They walk the unsullied asphalt, around the cathedral, into the cathedral. Whew! Incense, eh! And cool as the inside of an ice-chest.

'Hat *off*!' barks Monsignor, and—horror!—crosses himself with a heavy, thick hand like a labourer's that makes the move one of peasant-like cupidity in the vastness, the loftiness, the subdued and yet post-card gaudiness. The fourteen Stations of the Cross ring them in with plaques of rawly coloured and gilded plaster. A scaffolding is built over the chancel. High up, lying down like Michael Angelo on a platform of planks, is the painter.

'There's your man,' says Monsignor. 'A pea-picker he

was. At Wy Yung. An Italian pea-picker. I found him. But he'll give you the information, Mr. Potter. Come.'

He follows Monsignor down the nave, Monsignor and his smell of old sweat and old spaniel. The painter is now sitting up with flashing teeth.

'Frankie!' says Monsignor, 'here's a Mr. Potter to ask you questions. For a newspaper.'

The teeth flash more, and Monsignor and the spaniel have gone, and the Italian now kneels in his red shirt on the planks, looking darkly down as the cadet hangs his hat on a pew-end, unclips his pencil, opens the Reporter's Notebook and, once again, in shoutings that attempt reverence as well as masculinity, goes on learning to be an adult in an adult's mad universe.

He gets it all, and more.

Name—Francesco Floriani. Born—Nahpolee. Ah, *Naples!* Picka da peas, da beans, picka da pitch, picka da tomate. Alla toime painta, painta, painta. Now painta for Monsignor.

' 'Eaven she'sa finish, see, she'sa finish, by cripes. Purgatorio she'sa not yet finish,' says Francesco Floriani, near his own 'Eaven, half-way through his own Purgatorio. 'She'sa not yet finish. Two munta finish, moi-be t'ree munta finish.'

And hell, Mr. Floriani?

The Italian kindles, reveals that he looks forward to the depiction of Hell. His hands mould in the air what his brush will put on the ceiling.

' 'Ell,' he says, 'Oi make-a gooda 'Ell. Oi make-a *ver*' gooda 'Ell. You see. You come to see-a Frankie's 'Ell?'

And how old is Mr. Floriani, please, if he will be so gracious?

Lives where?

Married?

Not-a married, not-a married.

It is over. The cadet closes the book on which no tear has this time fallen, and reaches for his hat, but there are more than tears to fall from 'Eaven, and it is not over. Interviewed switches to interviewer.

' 'Ow olda you? Fif-a-teen? Seex-a-teen?'

Good gracious me! A Dago, too! It is almost worth a lie of, say, seventeen, but, remembering his knickerbockers in time, 'Fifteen,' he says. 'I'll be sixteen next month.'

'Fif-a-teen gooda year for boy.'

There is no answer to this.

'You gotta girl,' says Mr. Floriani.

'No. Not yet.' He is driven to add, 'I am too busy.'

'Like-a girls?' Although so far-off Mr. Floriani's eyes seem very close and searching.

'Oh, yes. Oh, yes, they're all right.'

'But you like-a girls?' Tiresome, *rude* Mr. Floriani.

'They're all right.' He lifts his hat from the pew. Mr. Floriani does not take the hint and shut up.

'You like-a walk-a river-bank with girl?'

'Yes.' Yes, Olwen—hand in cool hand under the wattles and willows.

'Why you like-a go river-bank with girl?'

There is too much to say, and it is not for Mr. Floriani, so nothing is said. Into the silence before the altar, Mr. Floriani drops the bomb from near 'Eaven. He drops it softly.

'You gotta hairs on your-a belly, eh?'

'Yes.' No one tells a lie to that question, but the truth changes the colour of face and body. He senses that this upsurge of colour weakens, that it is the flesh rising over the mind's head.

'You worka, tonight?' His smile, which has been absent awhile, returns. It is Alex Macalister's smile.

'No.' There is no need any longer to shout in God's gaudy house. Bodies need no words.

'You walka river-bank with Frankie, eh? You gotta lovely goolden-a hair. You walka?'

'Yes.' He means no, no, no; but lies away, surrounded by the fourteen little suffering Christs.

'You meeta Frankie, rowing shed, eight-a clock-a, yes?'

'Yes,' he lies on, before the large crucified bronze Christ, and under the Virgin's stare-stare-monkey-bear eyes of painted plaster.

'Frankie teacha you on the river-bank. Frankie make-a you 'appy. Lovely goolden-a hair. Frankie teacha? You want Frankie teacha?'

He knows the answer to this one. He speaks it.

'I don't care,' he says to Frankie the Dago pea-picker in the red shirt, to Francesco Floriani from Naples who has Hell yet to paint in all the colours and writhings of his own 'Ell.

At eight-thirty that night, the cadet is still in the kitchen at Mitchell Street. He has written what he seems to have learned, in his own thick and blotted handwriting, in his own thick and blotted vocabulary:

SERENADE

> Moon.
> Hydrangea-bosomed twilights burn,
> Slothful as cheetah. Silver sherds
> In willow mosques, whose dewy birds
> Of fierce, green air spirt turquoise aura.
> Moon.
> Moon . . . the mute urn.
> Come.
> Come where its drug flows.
> The calm urn—filigraned—brocaded rose
> Of luscious night drips operose
> In the gallery dim, the void laura
> Under the willow,
> Under the salix.
> Come. . . .

While he writes this, feeling sorry for Francesco Floriani waiting randy in the moonlight by the rowing-shed willow—'the void laura'; feeling proud of his own circumspect nobility and run-of-the-mill decent, clean behaviour; he is irritated by the power he exerts over his sticky-nose body to prevent it rising from the kitchen chair, and hurtling towards the river-bank to watch hidden, 'under the salix', to find out how the Italian may have scoured and dressed and scented himself for the meeting or whether (and I wish I knew right now) Frankie has denied himself, or side-stepped, the demanded tryst. Denying oneself one lesson, one learns another, or many lessons. The constellation of disillusion contains an infinity of planets.

Time passes. February the Sixteenth, 1927, passes, and his sixteenth birthday. He has learned much: to use the telephone, to use the telephone with an especially resonant and cultured accent, to write glibly of drab weddings and piddling accidents and hole-in-corner cricket matches and minute successes and barbaric Shire Council meetings, and church teas, and crazy whist drives, and quail-shooting.

So this is the vastness and wonder and beauty that struck him still and small a decade ago! So this is the Life the poets ignite marvels from—baby scalded by overturned kettle, outbreak of measles in kindergarten, youth accidentally shoots friend, carnal knowledge of young girl, out for a duck, near fatality in bathing enclosure, engagement announced, in a borrowed wedding veil, gave birth to triplets, married sixty years, never travelled in train, narrow escape in fire, loses arm on circular saw, killed by bolting horse, brutal murder, passed away peacefully, executed today, well-attended funeral, vandals in cemetery.

If this be Life, he thinks, and all of Life, what is it I am in such a formless and dispassionate passion about? The other ecstasies he thinks he wants are, of course, nowhere anywhere, and he knows it. He tricks himself into believing that what he wants are more dazzling roads winding across a more mysterious landscape. All he wants to do is to get to the city. Even Nature's trick of compelling him to consider fishing with his own body in the recesses of bodies at the same time human and divine is a trick he sees through. Let his body beware of its ephemeral demands! Fool! All he wants is to escape the nest, and get to the city.

He grows, and keeps on growing towards six feet tall, seems to do no more than that, and time—from this distance —is very much shorter, and more carefree, and filled with experiences of value, than it then seems longer, and tatty, and empty of information.

Mother goes with him to the tailor who measures him for his first long-trousered suits. Upon this, his voice descends to a certain level, and settles there, safe though still with ruffled feathers. He falls in love with ties and silk socks, and is in need of maternal restraint, as an exercise in taste as well as financial prudence. He starts shaving. Now that his legs are long and hidden, he considers he resembles a man. Disguised as such he joins the Mechanics' Institute Library. He buys, week by week, a series of *The World's Great Paintings*, *Stories of the Great Operas* and *Studio*. It dismays me now that he is the only one in Bairnsdale who spends his shillings on such fallals. I am not sure if the dismay be for him or the others. He pours the overflow from the lives of the pointed-at and pointed-out Great into his own home-made and provincial vat; pouring in what he cannot pour out in conversation or elegant behaviour, not in that town, not to anyone he knows, not any more. Today, I admire one thing only about this gangling creature; he does not feel odd-man-out. His conceit is sick-making, but objective. He blames no one but himself, and carries on to no one but himself.

Life in Bairnsdale, in the country town he has hitherto loved so much, begins to drive him out of his serenity with boredom, and to distort his sense of proportion. It is only his lust for information and culture, his intellectual clarity which is fast turning to an intellectual arrogance, that acts as a counterpoise to his desire to cut the painter, and escape the provincial round, and the hell he foresees of endless repetition, to cut the umbilicus and escape from Mother and her children, from Father and the house and all the unmysterious and too familiar objects and sounds.

He takes to long solitary walks, up and down the backstreets, up and down like Satan walking the world, or far out of the town, far along the river, past the hop-kilns and the weir, walking and trying to think himself into a state of distinguished and absolutely unique loneliness, to think God out of existence and to think humanity to death or, at the very least, to debase it to something wicked and mean and disgusting. Circumstances and the accidents of arrival in sequestered places offer him opportunities to manufacture this feeling of fake disgust. He comes upon a man and woman tangled in violent fornication beneath a rug in a thicket of hawthorn, the woman's hat hanging circumspectly on a branch, an oval hole worn in one sole of the man's boots. He pretends to himself that this disgusts him when it is only grotesque and pitiable, giving rise to an inexplicable sadness and to a feeling of lust itself.

He falls, not in love this time, but into a too gay and too garrulous relationship bordering on hysteria, with a young woman of seventeen, a shingled flapper called Bunty whose father is a shoemaker. They appear frequently together, one-stepping, Hesitation-waltzing, fox-trotting and Charleston-ing, at dances for which, as a reporter, he gets free tickets, cricket or football club dances, dances run by Mothers' Clubs or Boy Scout committees, dances with suppers of corned-beef sandwiches and iced queen cakes and coffee made from coffee essence and skimmed milk boiled in kerosene tins, dances at which three-piece orchestras play with wistful incompetence 'Valencia', 'In a little Spanish town', 'Smile a while', 'Moonlight and roses' and 'After the dawn'. In much the same way as his feet tire and ache from sliding on the dance-floors slippery with boracic acid powder or candle scrapings, and the material of his suit becomes dusty, so his heart begins to tire and ache, and the material of his hope becomes dusty. Where are the walls of looking-glass, the chandeliers, the champagne glasses with foot-long stems, the women ethereally beautiful as Corinne Griffith? Bunty is not beautiful nor exquisitely dressed nor brilliantly witty; she is happy and bold and noisy and skinny, with lips painted in a pouting Cupid's bow, with touched-up silver dancing shoes, pink silk stockings, and sale-price dresses of tangerine or flame or reckless green cut well above her triangular knees. He too is neither handsome, nor dressed in tails and court shoes, nor as devilishly witty as he knows he can be. He is happier than he thinks he is but affects a more loud-mouthed happiness than even the young needs display.

Something always seems to go wrong; Life's special purpose seems to be to reveal to him—to me at sixteen—its shoddinesses and imperfections and embarrassments. The vomit of a drunk outside the Picnic Point Dance Hall splashes my shoes; Bunty loses her brooch of iridescent butterfly wings under glass, and weepingly nags and nags as we walk home in the mud and rain, she in bare feet carrying her silver shoes and rolled-up stockings. When I attempt to kiss her calm outside her front gate, she has already begun to smell like a wet fowl; our hard young mouths press with absurd ardency upon each other's as we imitate Rudolph Valentino and Agnes Ayres; our teeth clash together without tenderness or warmth and, more than anything, I am thinking of the fact that I have still to walk home through a mile of puddles and mud in the blackness unbroken by the street-lamps which have gone out at midnight.

I am tired of lights that go out at midnight, of winter and mud, of the family, of the books in the Mechanics' Institute Library, of the frost on the weeds I see through the window from my little rickety table in the corner of the editor's little room with its little fire that spares no warmth; I am tired of Bunty, and dances, and reporting hick football matches and Methodist weddings and the laying of foundation stones for hideous buildings by aitch-dropping councillors; I am tired of writing my falsely witty and dishonestly romantic weekly article: 'Around the Town' by *Rambler*. Around the town! Jesus!

I find myself driving myself to try anything for diversion. I commit self-abuse with a punishing savagery as though committing the most splendid of brutalities and the most engaging of evils by playing masochist to my own sadism. I foster tormenting crushes, for an assortment of the shoddiest and flabbiest reasons, on an assortment of people, some of whom I have never spoken to and shall never speak to. I expect always to be disappointed. I always am.

I develop a passion, never mentioned until this very second, for a draper's daughter who does not know I exist. She looks like Clara Bow, and wears evening dresses gleaming with tiny metallic beads, and walks, I think to myself, like a tigress, a sophisticated tigress. One day as I watch my Clara Bow tigress loping along Main Street, she begins to pick her nose. My love dies in an instant and for all time, to be replaced by an unfair contempt.

I become friendly with the barber's new assistant, Mario Cerretti, an eighteen-year-old Italian who has all the glamour for me of the film-star Antonio Moreno. One morning, after he has come from Mass, we take a Sunday walk along the river-bank. He scratches at a pimple on his jaw; he holds out his barber's pointed finger-nail with its little mess of pus and blood. 'See, 'Ahl,' he says, 'I squasha da bloody pimp.' I change my barber. From then on, when I accidentally pass him, I destroy his vivid smile by a nod of killing coldness, the behaviour of a spoiled bitch.

As I am, one day, hurrying to catch up to my favourite English master of High School days, the man who has helped to shape my literary taste, and has been lavish with the loan of books and advice, a sound breaks from his body, and an unpleasing stink. I do not catch up with him. When, years later, I wish to catch up with him, to thank him for his care and kindness, it is too late: Death has caught up before I am old enough and wise enough to be just to human beings.

I pick my own nose, squash my own pimples, and fart, but covertly, not enchanted by having to—it is, in those days, more and finally disenchanting to have the gods and goddesses I admire for appearing to be above these vulgar actions revealed as being as flawed by ordinariness as I am, then, flawed by a tinpot gentility.

Attempts to escape in solitary walks, in the giddiness of dancing, in odd passions and admirations, in the writing of esoteric poems, and rococo short stories called *Lisel and Aën*, *Albrecht and Trudel* and *Tissinella and the Fat Man*, are all attempts to escape my own over-heated body, and the town wherein the pleasures of barefootedness and tree-climbing and unthinking joy are no longer possible. I cannot escape this body nor its equally over-heated mind. The gods of my boyhood are on the dole, out-of-work for ever. They sit, mildewed with a boring immortality, on the park-benches of my past, and feed on their own tears. Oddly enough, I have none. Burning to free myself, I am lit by a tearless anger I display to no one. I do not even silently accuse and curse anyone, not even myself. Looking back, I am merely being, I see, cunning with myself so that I can be more successfully cunning with others. I am working up to something: I am after that flight to the city; I am planning for that flight to take place with the most apparently simple circumspection.

September and spring, the waves of vanilla pouring in from the fields of Chocolate Lilies, all overwhelm me and my affected procrastinations: I make the decision I have already made, and act on it. Since I have become a baby in the ways of that other part of the forest to which I now belong, or appear to others to belong, it is as a baby I must cry out. Who will give me milk if I do not? It is expressive of a side of my nature as it develops at this period that I cry out with shrewdness and clarity and intense sincerity in the right direction. Milk is given me; arrangements are rapidly made for my escape to Melbourne. Then, and only then, do I announce to myself, to Bunty, to the editor and Miss Ray, to anyone who will listen, to Mother and Father, that I have a desire to go to the city. I want to be on the stage, I say. I want to study drawing and painting. I want to be a *real* author, a poet, writing with the ink of my own heart, not a country town newspaper reporter emasculating and re-arranging the truth in journalese.

Mother and Father make scarcely any comment; Mother's remarks are a little blanched, and resignation lies behind them. Perhaps Father expects no more than eccentric behaviour from the monster he sired; perhaps he and Mother know my strengths and weaknesses, obstinacies and wilinesses, my desires and fancy ambitions, more thoroughly than I suspect.

I have cried out to the headmaster of the High School. He has instantly understood my cry. To my amazement he has suggested that I become a schoolteacher, one of the innumerable professions I should never have considered in a million years. He gets a job for me.

Thus it is, for the last time in my life, my parents provide me with the goods and chattels they think proper—undergarments, brogues, socks, a large leather suitcase, two ebony-backed hairbrushes in a leather container, and two dozen handkerchiefs with a gothic P embroidered in one corner. Letters fly between Mother and Aunt Rosa Bona.

In October 1927, I leave Bairnsdale by the early morning train, alone at last, to advance on Victoria Street, Williamstown, where I am to live with Aunt Rosa Bona and Uncle Martini-Henry while I earn my living as Junior Teacher, Third Class, at State School 1409, Williamstown.

The next eighteen months are among the most crammed and lively and restless of a crammed, lively and restless life. I should not like to live any one month of them over again, despite their exaltations; any one day, despite the ecstasies; indeed, scarcely even one hour. I should, however, like to have restored to me the vitality and enthusiasm, the recklessness and piratical impertinence, the perfect unawareness of pitfalls, which I then have, and which make it no trouble at all, at all, to have many irons in the fire, to burn the candle at both ends, to walk where angels fear to tread, and yet to slip nimbly through certain experiences—that could, and should, have scarred more deeply and very deeply—with no more than scratches faint as scrimshawing. Many of the wrinkles now marking me must have had their birth then as almost imperceivable lines of astonishment, excitement, exhilaration, anger, dismay, happiness and—ultimately—early agony, but it is soothing to imagine, rightly or wrongly, that today my heart remains unwrinkled.

No sooner am I in the train—that is, the moving train, with Mother behind me, and Bairnsdale behind me, and *The Advertiser* behind me—than my several months of gadabout and insincere semi-unhappiness are forgotten, fled away, out of sight.

Looking back, it is easy to see that I never was as unhappy as I pretended I was, merely itchy-footed, flaming with impatience, mad for the city, and as wily as a viper in getting my way.

As the train chatters and roars its way through Gippsland and its sheep plains and hill forests and one-horse villages and provincial towns and cow-peopled shires, in the direction of earliest childhood, towards the towers and spires and never-ending terraces and hemmed-in minute parks that I used to spy on from the balcony edged in cast-iron, I bend down my lips to kiss, am able to bend and kiss with happy tenderness, the *boutonnière* of two Cecile Brunner roses and maiden-hair fern Mother has pinned to my lapel. I have no regret, no tears, no inklings of disaster. It is with rather less tenderness, and a different sort of almost wanton happiness that, as the train roars on complaining contentedly to itself, I make the strange and secretly showy gesture of chucking away into the undergrowth of the Haunted Hills my grey felt hat, so recently the insignia of adulthood. Shocked as I am by the waste, and stricken on behalf of Father's wallet, I am elated by the profligate display of independence. As the train approaches the spot where, a decade before, I explode into my first remembered, angry, angry, useless tears, I am surely smiling, with the stiffness and brazenness of an archaic statue, in anticipation of the years ahead, years decorated with unimaginable delights and the almost unbearable raptures of freedom; as the train approaches the suburban spot where I was once shocked by Father's momentarily not wearing a hat in a public place, I am boldly bare-headed for ever. Bare-headed, bare-faced, barehearted, and bare of any misgivings or mental reservations, I arrive.

On Flinders Street platform Aunt Rosa Bona is immediately visible, like an arpeggio on a sheet of music. Not only is she in a fever of fuss, but she is strikingly dressed in black, even to stockings, gloves and jet brooch. No one is dead.

'Where,' she cries, before she clutches me from the train-step to kiss me an unnecessary number of times, 'is your hat?'

I guard myself from telling the truth, for that will be to arouse outcry and consequent emotional exhaustion. I make up some satisfactory lie putting off the evil day of revealing myself as a hatless nut. She, embarrassed by my nude head, I, by her sable get-up, we travel to Williamstown. Port Phillip Bay still flickers shaggy old man's eyebrows at the end of Victoria Street. The house still smells of mignonette and lemons. I am given a large front bedroom with lead-lighted bow windows, a lead-lighted *oeil-de-boeuf*, and an *art nouveau* electrolier with shades of fluted pink glass. Thinking of my own bedroom, I have a brief spasm of home-sickness, from which I am diverted by the pigeons whose gentle grumbling on the terra-cotta griffins of the gable immediately above the roof of my room I attempt to translate into words.

The next day I begin work as a Junior Teacher.

The Bairnsdale High School headmaster's perception that there is enough of the stuff in me from which schoolmasters can be moulded is an astute one. It would be as tedious to record my minor early mistakes as to record the minor successes: suffice it to say that, in no time, I am a useful teacher, even a good one—dramatic, noisy, happy, over-energetic and a disciplinarian, this last because I will put up with no childish nonsense that interferes with the display of myself or with my conception of what is due to me as an adult. One wears the disguise of manhood seriously at sixteen. The showing-off side of my being; the ability to simulate Lear-like rages I do not feel, as well as the ability to fool myself into being lovingly patient, all serve their purpose. Controlled by the canny and ruthless self-watcher, these qualities are turned into performances that trick the children into obedience. While still sixteen I am put in charge of a class of forty children who are two, three or four years younger than I. I fall in love with them. They are my possession, my material. The love is not for them as individuals but as a mob whose forty minds, under my flashy and domineering control, are to become one, a mind unsullied by errors, unmarked by blots, uncontaminated by misplaced originalities outside the curriculum, and as full of facts as a pomegranate is of seeds.

In Williamstown of 1927 and 1928—and for years later—this sort of educational technique is fashionable: strict discipline, learning 'by heart', legible handwriting, clear punctuation, correct spelling, all these are insisted on or, at least, battled for and strapped for and sincerely hoped for. The ditch between adult and child is still a clear one with little pretence made of using temporary planks across which teacher and pupil run merrily back and forth exchanging anything but information. Happiness, while to be hoped for, is not the final end of educative processes, any more than it is the final end of living processes. Although, then, the Australian Labour Government is beginning to urge the abolition of capital punishment, no crank adult, in the Australia of those days, has spoken loudly enough for record, on behalf of spoiling the rod and sparing the child.

Anyway, outside school, the adult suffers controls as much as the child.

In the matter of sea-bathing, for one example, children suffer rather less, for it is not so defiantly immodest of boys and girls to bathe together in the open sea, as it is for men and women. The Williamstown Bathing Enclosure at the end of its pier is divided by a species of iron prison-grille into two sections, one labelled MALES, one labelled FEMALES. As well, during certain hours of certain days, males only are admitted to the Enclosure. A blue flag flying high indicates this. When a red flag flies, Williamstown knows that the Enclosure is legally a harem only. When the red and the blue flag fly at the one time, both sexes can enter, through separate doors, the waves enclosed by barnacled posts and mussel-footed pickets but, dressed in their neck-to-knee bathing costumes, they can only perform their puffing and blowing breast-stroke or lop-sided trudgeon stroke in the designated section, the salt-gnawed iron bars separating them. In short, the era I have rushed bare-headed into to shock Aunt Rosa Bona, and to shock others into calling out after me in the streets, is the era in which, on November the Twenty-second, 1927, the Mothers' Unions of Australia make a powerful protest against the Evil of Beauty Competitions.

In dozens of suburbs such as Williamstown, similar attempts at moral control persist, preserving a late-Victorian world in which, to be sure, deaths are still caused by bolting cab-horses or by being thrown from a jinker, but which another world is already overlapping: Dame Nellie Melba is heard singing *God save the King* over the wireless at the opening ceremony of the new federal capital, Canberra; Bert Hinkler, Sir Alan Cobham and Ruth Elder are each attempting long-distance aeroplane flights, and there is a great march of the unemployed. I see the word COMMUNIST whitewashed on a brick wall, and do not know what it means. Nor do any of the people I ask. This developing world of which it is often platitudinously said that I and my generation are the heirs does not really cut across my consciousness. I am, as the young are, devoted to myself. I am engrossed with my teaching job as I never was by small-town reporting. I am even more fervently engrossed in so many other activities that it seems today impossible to have been able to do and see all I do and see, and yet have enough time for sleep.

First of all, there is Williamstown itself, an early settlement, so named after King William IV because, with its position at the mouth of the Yarra River, it was contemplated as the port capital. Every part of the town fascinates me, even Aunt Rosa Bona's naice suburban Victoria Street, lined with palms and lawns, and leading, like other naice streets, to the beach, to the Bathing Enclosure with its male or female flags flying, and its clothes-lines of grey-brown towels, and washed-out cotton bathing dresses into the white borders of whose sleevelets the dye has run like weak ink. On the lofty weatherboard sides of the Bathing Enclosure is painted in enormous letters TOWELS AND BATHING DRESSES FOR HIRE and HOT SEA BATHS. Just inside the entrance is a shabby shop where the Enclosure-keeper's wife, Mrs. Pidoto, displays for sale bathing-caps in the shape of mob-caps of oiled silk, seagull-like birds made of mussel-shells, ginger biscuits the size and thickness of novelettes, wafers of gritty home-made ice-cream, and post-cards of fat mothers-in-law in polka-dotted red bathing dresses being nipped on their biggest curves by large crabs. Tamarisks and coprosma hedges stand along the esplanade. There are little wooden shelters on the planks of which are carved hearts and initials and obscene words. There are a bandstand, a roller-skating rink, cast-iron weighing machines, penny-in-the-slot chocolate machines, latticed tea-rooms showing HOT WATER signs, an open-air cinema and, under the pines farther along, shelters made of old cable trams with their slat seats and the enamelled notices saying PLEASE HOLD ON AROUND CURVES. Beyond the pines are the Victoria Gardens where, among palms and pigeons, among beds of bonfire salvia, and granite drinking-fountains with bronze cups attached by chains, are the marble statues of mutton-chop-hairy civic notabilities, and a fountain that no longer plays but stands looking drier than anything in the world. It is all Edwardian-ism running to seed, my childhood drying up, *that* world flaking apart. On the sand of the beach, lilac-grey and fine as caster-sugar, the soldier crabs still wheel, in their season, as they did when Mother and Aunt Rosa Bona paddled and squealed. The women have left no footprints. The gulls imitate their forced feminine hilarity. Tangled in ghosts, the son, the nephew, Laddie the child, strides by in the shape of a lean six-footer with flapping hair, and dares not look behind.

To the west of this seaside suburb lie the outskirts of the town, the acres and acres of the Rifle Ranges, once Grand-father Porter's domain. It is here, when nostalgic for the country and the minuter evidences of seasonal change, I can tramp for mushrooms, smell again the vanilla of Chocolate Lilies, lie spreadeagled (boyishly!) on the capeweed, staring in the direction of a lark's song, or listening to the delirious gargle of magpies. At one corner of this grassy, sea-touching plain are some fishermen's huts, and a rough mole behind which the fishing-boats lie. The huts are surrounded by out-crops of lichened basalt like cows lying down, by oyster shells, wormwood shrubs, sea holly, and sapling racks hung with cocoa-brown nets. I paint these huts and racks and stones often, in washes of water-colour, and with saccharine wist-fulness. There is less pleasure in the deed of painting than in being surrounded by the country scent, and the country sound of grasshoppers and birds.

If I bring my own faint ghosts to beach and Rifle Ranges, there is no need to come thus supplied to the eastern section of the town which has its own ghosts—oh, many.

In the east is the oldest part of the town. Facing across the river-mouth itself, and the pilot lights, in the direction of

Port Melbourne, is The Strand, the originally fashionable section of old William's Town, a curving street of stone or brick houses, lofty, pillared, French-windowed, some of the houses almost follies. They, and their drives and stables and conservatories and gazebos, are all decaying in the shade of great English trees, and under heavy ruggings of jasmine, honeysuckle and ivy. In 1927 and 1928 many of these places are unoccupied, and can be rented, marble chimney-pieces, cedar floors, barn, dairy, servants' quarters, cellar and all, for thirty shillings or less a week, a pointer to the fact that the age of sailing-ship captains, wealthy ship-chandlers, large families and many servants is, here, over; that William's Town is over, and Williamstown down-at-heel, and time a killer. My childhood dislike, child-like and childish, of disintegration, is, here in The Strand, much intensified, for this crumbling and falling and going under in nets of cobweb, in self-dust and wind-chewed stone, is the objectification of loss and wastage. I become particularly fascinated by a house called *Brontë* and, having snapped the rusted catch of a French window, waste more time by standing inside mourning wasted time. I am happy to mourn, as I stare at the soot of long-dead fires, at the circular stain on a marble shelf left by the foot of a wine-glass from which the burgundy has been drunk years before Mother and Father are married, at the words scratched, apparently with a diamond ring, on one pane of glass:

> *Divine sunset:*
> *Captain Taylor. Aunt Annie. Migs.*
> *Rawdon. Jess. Tom.*
> *Oct. 3. 1850.*

In the direction of the disused wharves and piers of more southerly Williamstown, The Strand changes its quality, and changes its name to Nelson Place and The Front. The farther one walks the more of a wasteland the scene becomes: empty taverns and coffee palaces, tumble-down ship-chandlers' and providores', deserted brothels, lanes and courts crowded with fennel bushes as high as sailors. Sailors!

Once there were gander-straddling pig-tailed sailors from every port in the world, and William's Town was a lusty port with its water-police, red-legged soldiers, convicts, nail-can-toppered Peelers, polyglot merchants, crinolined harlots, aborigines, public hangings, dolly-shops and skittle-alleys. Now, in 1927 and 1928, far fewer and mainly smaller ships berth at the unsteady wharves. It is into an almost uninhabited rubbish-heap the men must descend from the decks—the Swedes, Japanese, Lascars, Scots, Mauritius-born Creoles, Norwegians and the unguessable. They go to Madame's Wine Depôt.

As I rove this part of Williamstown, either with my sketch-book or my gaping mind, I walk farther into my own form-less present, further into the blown-out pasts of forgotten others and, one day when the deadly scent of the sea is riding strongly in on a cold and slanting rain, I take my first few steps into one of my own futures.

Cold and soaking, I say to myself, 'A wine will be warming.'

Dickens? Jane Austen? *Wuthering Heights*?

Having as it were condoned thus my own curiosity and rake-helly behaviour, I enter the Wine Depôt.

I should say that, sipping delicately as a chicken at a port wine, aged seventeen years and three months, I have dis-covered nothing except that the rest of the world does not care how one hitch-hikes to the country on the other side of the fence, if I were not aware that Madame has taken a shine to me. In gratitude for not being ordered out, I behave with a circumspection partly composed of ignorance of how much can be drunk, partly to flatter Madame and myself by leav-ing after no more than three or four glasses. I refuse to let any of the seamen buy me drinks. Some shadowy instinct of self-preservation, some sort of scarcely tangible fear makes me as prudent as a maiden. Nor am I yet aware of the wonderful uses of drunkenness, or of any need for self-release. I return again and again to watch the others get drunk, and to hear what men say to each other—lies or truth—when many wines have drowned other truths or lies. I do not fully realize then, nor do I realize until many years after becoming a practised participant in other people's lives, that I am a minor thief rehearsing to be a professional one. I cannot help, then as now, going about stealing the lives of others, or from the lives of others, stealing the untidy fullnessess, the blood-stained defiances, the twisted witticisms, the scrubby secrets, the clumsy displays of love, from all the others I can never be. It helps no one that I faithfully present myself naked to their attention as though protesting too truthfully, 'Look, I've no jemmy! Look, there's nothing up my sleeve!' Nothing is stolen from me in return: no naked man ever loses anything. Having frisked myself first, nothing is left for others. Too aware of their mortality, and not enough of my own, I can cry out, in a voice tinged with their pain and not my own, 'Those who are meeting are parting; to come together is to begin to walk asunder.' They say, 'So what!' They smile, and say, 'There, there, there!' They shrug. I can try weeping in printed words that say, 'It is because you do not weep I weep for you.' They do not read. If they read they do not understand. If they understand they do not weep for me. They laugh, and offer me another heart to play with.

In the nineteen-twenties, I am not, of course, really alive to the fact that heart-holding is a form of my old greed for abundance and information. This heart-holding, which begins there in Madame's high-ceilinged and echoing Wine Depôt, and involves sea-people of all the shades between white-and-gold and black-and-black, persists to this day, and has afforded me salutary and moving glimpses into the beauties and nobilities as well as the uglinesses and pretensions of such people as cockney charladies, London barrow-boys, Japanese prostitutes, petty thieves, no-hopers, Irish confidence-men, Jamaican spivs, alcoholic millionaires, homosexual pickpockets, and wild-eyed saints dirty as a potato. I am not of a nature to side-step the puddles on the way to the firing-squad.

However, Williamstown and its fascinations, State School 1409 and its opportunities for garish demonstration, are two sides only of my multi-faceted life during 1927 and 1928.

I am accepted as a student of drawing at the Melbourne National Gallery under Charles Wheeler, therefore, several nights a week, behold me, with my hair grown longer than even that of the shingled and Eton-cropped women of the day, exaggeratedly striding—my 'thing' of that period—'proudly' cleaving through the milder public, 'head held high', looking neither to left nor right nor at people as I hurtle (God, what unnecessary and ostentatious energy!) down the stairway of Flinders Street Station, across to St. Paul's Cathedral, up Swanston Street, across elegant Collins Street and rowdy Bourke Street, across Little Bourke Street with its shuffling Chinese, its fan tan parlours, its talked-about opium dens, its Kuomintang societies, and shops of ivory back-scratchers and chopsticks, lichee nuts, rice bowls, and packets of jasmine tea; up the slope past the truss-, and bed-pan-, and body-belt-shops of upper Swanston Street; past the wicked end of Little Lonsdale Street where, in winter, the fearless harlots lean outside their open, rosy doors, the clefts between their breasts intensified by the flames of the braziers that stand on the footpath, and by which they warm their flesh as they wait for it to be bought for five shillings. I reach the towering, black-and-gold cast-iron gates of the National Gallery, and race up the steps, between the statues of Joan of Arc and St. George and the Dragon. Once through the revolving plate-glass doors, I turn left. There is a hall containing glass cases filled with instructive tableaux, one only of which is recallable: a sledge of lifelike Eskimos, with Fu Manchu moustaches, being drawn through fake snow (salt? powdered alum? flour? slaked lime?—I can never decide) by stuffed huskies. Beyond this lies the door to the Art Class Studio, the door to what seems Montmartre bohemianism.

Although, busy at their easels, there are several ridiculously antique people of thirty-five or so, 'suburban', 'plebby' people dressed like people, I am satisfied with the much greater supply of young women with harsh, geometrical haircuts, jade-green dresses patterned *à la* Tutankhamen, and smocks and tongues deliberately dirtier than they need be. There is also a supply of young men wearing beards that could be richer. I can get no further in this arty ploy than a yellow moustache based on Ronald Colman's, and a mingy yellow tuft under the middle of my lower lip.

The Studio is as alive with plaster reproductions of famous statues as with unfamous students; its walls are hung with the casts of hands and feet and swags of fruit and sprays of acanthus leaves. The Studio smells of Fixatif, a preparation atomized on to the finished charcoal studies to render them unsmudgeable, and of threepenny Cornish Pasties bought from the pie-shop, diagonally opposite the Gallery, on the corner of Swanston and Little Lonsdale Streets. The shop is run by a skull-faced man wearing a wig of corrugated, ox-blood-coloured hair. The harlots, slapping down always a pound note, buy pies and scented Musk Lollies from him, and all call him Bella. I should like to talk to them but dare not lest they ask for the five shillings I need for so many, many other things.

As for the drawing lessons, I most vividly recall Charles Wheeler's hand—or, rather, the thumb curved back almost in a semi-circle—appearing, without word or warning, on the Michelet paper pinned to the easel at which I am working. The thumb smudges out a faulty shadow. Charles Wheeler makes some soft remark supporting the thumb's action. Or the thumb tick-tocks backwards and forwards *above* the charcoal marks to commend some more successful attempt at chiaroscuro.

'Getting nearer,' says Charles Wheeler, speaking for the thumb. 'Nicer tone. Get-ting near-er.'

As when I was a little child, and the appearance of others was vaporous, so it oddly is with the appearance of Charles Wheeler. There is the curled thumb, there is the soft voice, there is the impression of someone small, delicate, and very *very* gentle. Blue-eyed? He may have been eight feet high with eyes of brimstone. I never really see him. I am, at first, too interested in my efforts to make three dimensions out of the rubbing on and rubbing off of charcoal. I am, later, interested less in the working side of the Studio than in the social side.

Since I am indubitably an ignorant country youth, and impatient (at this time), and am jet-propelling myself through experiences I can scarcely be said to have, since I am still enfevered with my own tiresome adolescence, it never becomes clear to me, at that time, what the purpose of working minutely, night after night, on the cross-grained Michelet with the vine-stem charcoal and a piece of fresh bread as eraser, really is.

I am taken several times to visit Max Meldrum's studio. I see his students at work. The through-a-glass-darkly technique bewilders and irritates me.

In Williamstown, I foist myself on R. W. Sturgess, who lives along The Esplanade and who, like Meldrum, has work hung in the National Gallery. I regard his water-colour work as wishy-washy even though it is the sort of thing I try out myself in my wistful treatments of the fishermen's huts on the edge of the Rifle Ranges.

My arrogance, the arrogance of half-educated youth, towards the work of two mature men who are charming to me, now appals me. These men are fools, I say to my fool self. Line is the thing. Line is *me*. I see myself as Ingres, as Clouét, as Holbein, as Hokusai, although knowing—oh, although knowing well!—that I possess absolutely not one skerrick of the strength and ability to reach within a thousand miles of them. I am too flibbertigibbet, too divided against myself. I discover Aubrey Beardsley and John Austen and, more unfortunately, Harry Clarke, whose macabre illustrations to Perrault's fairy stories and Coleridge's *Rime of the Ancient Mariner* excite me into buying mapping pens and Indian ink and cartridge paper so that I can decadently embroider away, with monstrous detail that keeps me up until three in the morning, and makes Aunt Rosa Bona waspish about electric light bills, at my own set of illustrations to Hans Christian Andersen's *The Red Shoes*.

Considering the National Gallery's Art School *mystique*, it is curious that this same Edgar-Allen-Poe-ish kind of decoration—tilted, staring eyes set in a dust of shadow, pointed chin, jaws at an angle of 135 degrees, intertwined locks of

208

hair clotted with baroque jewellery—should win me the prize for the ticket design for the Artists' Ball, the *Bal Masqué* of 1928. Charles Wheeler is the judge. The prize is a double ticket. I take a long-legged art student, with a nose scarcely less beaky than my own, to the ball which is at the St. Kilda Town Hall. Her name is Wiggy Binder. She wears a *tutu*. Looking back, it seems to me possible that we art students must have given some sort of doll's house performance, which may explain Wiggy's *tutu* and ballet shoes, as it may explain why the hall seems overrun with many striplings dressed as I am: a Wooden Soldier in a red sateen coat, a black papier-mâché busby, red-striped trousers, and with a dead-white painted face on the cheeks of which are two circular crimson splodges. The tune haunting me from my first Artists' Ball and 1928 is 'The Blue Room'; the action illustrating my peculiar and unnecessary, albeit quite un-planned, hypocrisy (of that ball and that year) is the action of piously rejecting invitations to contribute to the students' drink fund. This, though I am already used to discreet tip-pling of wines with Madame's seafarers. More tellingly, I look down my painted nose when magnanimously offered free drinks in the dressing-room behind the stage. This is perhaps a version of not letting the right hand know what the left hand does. More likely it is a conviction that the various activities of my life then are on different pages of the pam-phlet, that the doings on Page Two have little connection with those on Page Three, except in the common factor my-self, who concerns me alone. At least, so I think.

Anyway, I am already the only mourner at one of my own funerals. I perceive that *this* Hal Porter, the one who was, along with the famous writer Porter and the famous actor Porter, to have been the famous artist Porter, is dead. I do perversely try to keep this one alive; but dead he is, and I know it, and mourn him with no tears, even with some amusement. The dead one goes on clowning for another decade, and Fay Compton opens an exhibition at which some of the corpse's work is sold. The dead have their amusements and uses.

I cannot now, slackened down by years and pain and by-gone boredoms and overwhelmed enthusiasms, clearly see how the long-nosed, long-haired, long-finger-nailed—for he has started that too—and un-rattle-able youth does it all. I cannot, either, remember always how he finds his way into so many versions of Another Part of the Forest. I should admire his fearlessness were I certain it was only that, and deplore his insensitivity if certain that he was insensitive. I cannot judge him except to say that, today, I should not like to be him.

He climbs, on what information or instinctive clue I cannot guess, the worn marble staircase of the Bijou Theatre. Everything has the dusty seediness he is beginning to expect to find everywhere. Bronze women with hairless armpits, nipple-less breasts and unsplit pubes hold up triple light-globes lit by low-watt bulbs on the stair-landings; there are acres of looking-glasses with blotched silvering, leathery palms in brass urns embossed with swastikas, roses and cherubs' faces; the carpets are so worn into the boards of the flooring that ruled ridges line them. Beyond all this dilapidated splendour, in a shabby room hidden behind a shabby room hidden behind a shabby room, is Gregan Mc Mahon, the actor-manager. Without warning, invitation or shame, the youth somehow gets through the rooms, and beards the old actor. Whatever Gregan Mc Mahon, pink, bald and smelling of whisky, sees in the earnest intruder, or is yapped into seeing, or pityingly tricks himself into seeing, remains a mystery but, once more—behold the youth, Saturday morning after Saturday morning, in the room behind the room behind the room, mouthing his way through *The Lotus Eaters* or *Morte d'Arthur* or the soliloquies from *Macbeth*, or reciting—with gestures—a more frivolous work that Gregan Mc Mahon has given him to study:

The Ballyshannon *foundered off the coast of Caribou*
(downward gesture),
And down in fathoms many went the Captain (gesture)
and the crew (gesture),

> *Down went the owners* (gesture), *greedy men whom*
> *hope of gain allured,*
> (Gesture) *Oh, dry the starting tear, for they were*
> *heavily insured!*

I can only think of Gregan Mc Mahon today with amazed affection for being so prodigal of his own time, which at his age must have been something rather to hoard, for being so prodigal of his patience and, most of all, of his knowledge and skill, with a young upstart who does not pay a cent, and who possesses not even a good voice, a voice that, even then, must have been showing signs of what it will finish up like, a voice with the quality of some bi-coloured and mangy fur, say a marmalade cat's. To that run-down room with its uncomfortable curly sofas, its ottoman and old' framed theatre programmes, come many of the important enough theatrical people of the day—I recall shaking hands with Beatrice Day and Maurice Moscovitch, with Allan Wilkie, Herbert Mundin, Marie Ney, Ada Reeve, Frank D. Clewlow and Oscar Asche. What makes my smiling at the insufferable young man a little wry is that, while *I* remember with a nostalgic *frisson* these encounters with the famous, *he*, then, is anxious for the celebrities to shove off, to leave him alone again with Gregan Mc Mahon so that he can go on with his gesticulations and what he considers mellifluous shoutings of, 'Aye, Edward will use women honourably . . .' or, 'To be or not to be—that is the question. . . .'

It is through this apparently patient, lovable and kindly man, of whom George Bernard Shaw said that all he knew about Australia was that it produced sheep and Gregan Mc Mahon, that the youth's interest in the theatre, hitherto merely a matter of vainglory, begins to purify itself. Gregan Mc Mahon is lavish with complimentary tickets for his own productions and those of others. It is impressive now to read the list of plays I am enabled to see for nothing in Melbourne during a period of less than eighteen months. It includes *Six Characters in Search of an Author, Alice Sit-by-the-fire, Pygmalion, Outward Bound, Rosmersholm, The Doll's House, Juno and the*

Paycock, *Old English*, *Strife*, *Heartbreak House*, *Lower Depths* and *The Cherry Orchard*. As well, Gregan Mc Mahon gives him the run of a well-stocked theatrical library so that, besides reading plays from Euripides to Tchekov, from Sheridan to Shaw, he can study make-up and stage lighting and the history of the theatre, hear of Stanislavsky, see the settings of Gordon Craig and Benois, the costume designs of Bakst and Lovat and Doris Zinkeisen. He becomes saturated with the lore and follies and deceits and excitements of a world of illusions.

For a middle-aged man to use the word 'objectively' about the era in which he is young is a suspect thing. I therefore suspect myself of avoiding some important fact when I say that, objectively, it seems that, about thirty-five years ago, Melbourne has culturally very much more to offer the avid young than Melbourne has today. There is the quality of the plays presented, as well as their number. Between work and the exploration of Williamstown and Melbourne, between Drawing Classes and drama lessons and free seats in the dress circle, the omnivorous young man—no, not man—the omnivorous young man-shaped being is also able to take his place in a succession of theatre queues. He waits for hours, ham sandwich, apple and cake of chocolate in one hand, florin in the other, while the buskers, street musicians or acrobats perform for pennies. An hour before the curtain goes up, his queue, the queue for the gods, is admitted. He races up the stairs, up and up towards heaven. Arrived at a place on the uncushioned benches of the upper gallery, he must wait, sitting jammed upright on what are no more than the steep risers of a vertigo-inducing staircase, for the long hour, nibbling at his food. It is from these eyries of torture he sees every Gilbert and Sullivan opera, and a selection of other operas: *Rigoletto*, *Il Trovatore*, *La Traviata*, *Don Pasquale* and *L'Amore dei tre Re*. He sees Pavlova dance Dulcinea in *Don Quixote*, *Giselle*, *La Fille mal gardée* and, unforgettably once, *The Dying Swan*. Far, far beneath him where he sits squashed with the other sandwich-eaters and caramel-chewers, he sees the exquisite shape, not human, not bird, exquisitely stirring and quivering in the blue light, exquisitely dying. There is a long silence filled with an ecstasy composed of anguishes defying definition. Then the silence is smashed by the uproar of hundreds of separate human beings transformed into one sound, the sound of hands striking each other with cruel joy, flaying themselves to pain that they might thus express pleasure. It is not until his own hands have punished themselves to a standstill that he finds the lapels of his coat are wet, that his tears have showered down in amazement at an example of disciplined perfection.

It is only fair and necessary to confess here that, despite some intense early experiences such as the Pavlova one, despite being swept often enough off his young mind's and emotions' feet, *some* and *often enough* are disappointingly not *many* and *always*. Without any really sound critical basis, he develops strong likes and stronger dislikes, not only for individual performers but for the form of entertainment itself. Then, as now, he regards opera and ballet with a suspicion they are minor art, that there is an impure and unreasonable distortion, an artfulness. Moreover, he finds, to his horror, that the most esteemed composers—Bach, Beethoven, Mozart and those boys—leave him cold. Lusting to be warmed, to be cultured and all-informed, he spends all the money he can spare, and all the hours possible, waiting in the cheapest queues, climbing precipices of iron-rimmed stairs to the most brutally ascetic seats, sitting death-still on the chirruping chairs of symphony concerts, reading all the treatises and explanations and encyclopaedias he can, less and less happily labouring, as time passes, in the sincerest of efforts to See the Light.

All useless; all utterly useless.

He learns only his own incurable blindnesses; he is forced to accept that there are barren patches in his nature on which no seed will ever take root. He accepts this as one accepting news of a mortal disease but conceals the fact from others. At that period, and for several years after, he is therefore more dishonest than he has ever been before or since. He becomes adept in the jargon of the opera and ballet and music fan. He learns to be ready for the approach of certain lauded moments, and to make a gesture indicating awareness; to lean slightly forward with lit-up eyes and sensitively pouted lips, to cover the eyes with one hand (sensitive), to slump in a simulation of relaxed ecstasy—the tricks are endless and pretty unsubtle. He is too dishonest to admit to anyone but himself that most ballets and operas strike him as affected, boring and bloody silly, and that the music called great means less to him than the sound of the ocean drawing in, and withdrawing, and drawing in again, along the Ninety Mile Beach. He is hopeful enough of one day (This Year? Next Year? Sometime?) springing the truths others so fervently accept, hopeful enough to go on suffering hours of the keenest boredom, enclosed by the meat-pie breaths of galleryites as he gazes fixedly, and with irritation, at some gross soprano shrilling away far below, or at women with legs like timber-cutters' twirling on one toe-point while their arms execute movements that never quite express what he has learned they are intended to express.

He is rather more interested than disappointed when it is more and yet more revealed to him that, far from being the quiveringly sentient and impressible creature adolescence makes him think he is, he is a thick-skinned and flat-footed roughneck in most matters cultural. He continues to conceal this shameful fact from the people he works with and talks with, especially from those in the literary world. He contrives to meet, either through the offices of Father's half-brother, Uncle John Durward Porter, or through his own machinations, such people, then eminent enough, as Louis Lavater, Frank Wilmot, Robin Croll, Basil Burdett and J. S. Macdonald. Uncle John, now and then, no doubt with the amiable idea of letting me meet 'people who will be useful', arranges luncheon parties at a restaurant called Ambassadors. To take part in these dull little gatherings, it is necessary for me to have a day off from school. I take Dutch leave without a moral flicker, brazenly lying that I have some vaguely defined ailment and, though fully aware that the headmaster does not believe me, try to remember, next day, to tone down my noisy vitality as proof of my trumped-up suffering.

As far as the writers themselves are concerned, the over-confident and under-educated young puppy I am then, is, once more, disillusioned: they have neither the appearance nor the manner, the brilliant turns of phrase nor expected striking personalities of men of literature. To the puppy's sincere dismay, which gallops into contempt, they do not know what he is talking about. He lards his table chatter with snippets of esoteric and, often, shock-intending references. I can blush now, and yet feel pity for that dreadfully self-possessed and conspicuous youth holding forth at a table by the Ambassadors' great circular fountain and—there can be no doubt anywhere about this—boring Uncle John and the others as he drags in by the heels his obscure bits of information about the famous. He cannot stop talking. He peppers his conversation with French and Latin. He smokes, in a tortoise-shell holder, pectoral cigarettes, nigger-brown ones with gold tips. Sometimes he smokes Goliath cigarettes twice as long as the normal ones. He is hay-haired and hat-less. He wears a wide black tie. What he is attempting to do by this performance is not now perfectly clear to me. I do recall him bringing his minutely detailed and decadent illustrations of *The Red Shoes* to J. S. Macdonald, and the short story manuscripts of *Hell—for the Archbishop who loved two women* and *Death of the Czar* to Louis Lavater, Frank Wilmot and Robin Croll. Their criticism is as discreet and harmless and useless as unsalted and unsugared porridge. He considers them to be oafs, insensitive and imperceptive. He has the wicked thought that they are jealous of his youth, vitality and ability. Poor young man!

His meal, paid for by Uncle John, is invariably—partly affectation, partly because it sounds a sophisticated meal, partly because he loves it—*Consommé Julienne*, Chicken Mary-land, Lemon Pancakes and, stealing a trick from the past and Nurse Mawdsley, tea with lemon. This last he does not absolutely enjoy but it is as 'different'—deliberately—as a black tie, hatlessness, streaming hair and nigger-brown

215

cigarettes. He whips up a little contempt for the 'suburban' tastes of the others: Tomato Soup, Roast Lamb, Apricot Tart, and black coffee. Really, I think now, what he likes most about these gatherings are the trickling and splashing noises from the fountain, the thick carpets, the frilled and diaphanous aprons of the lavender-clad waitresses, and the orchestra of three women in brown taffeta palpitatingly playing 'La Paloma', 'Rendez-vous' and 'In a monastery garden', melodious muck he thinks he prefers to the Grieg and Handel he conversationally pretends to love and understand.

Just as he is drawn by the off-the-track sections of Williamstown, by that which is opposed to his own youth and bumptiousness—The Strand with its hollow, elderly mansions, and The Front with its Wine Depôt, and gabbling international brawls and bloody foreign noses and brandished knives, so he is fascinated by Melbourne's back streets still reeking of the nineteenth century and overlaid with melancholy shadows, by the little elm- or plane-crowded squares, by the cavernous markets, second-hand book shops, hole-in-corner drinking-fountains, the noseless and handless statues of nameless Seasons and Graces. He slices into genteel slum streets, into cul-de-sacs and narrow alleys, always alone, the better to savour uninterrupted their quality of hoped-for but never-revealed depravity, of suspected but unwitnessed danger.

Shirking the roast lamb, mint sauce, three vegs., apple pie and custard restaurants, he takes to eating and drinking in foreign cafés of which Melbourne, in 1928, has far fewer than today, more authentic places not at all frequented by the general Australian who, in those times, prefers such places as Ambassadors, The Wild Cherry, The Oberon, and The Lattice which is then famous for its enormous wedges of cream-stifled sponge cake and its décor of copper vessels, and piled-up gourds and Turk's Cap pumpkins. He is, indeed, happy to be the one conspicuously blond Australian drinking ouzo or scented Metaxa brandy and eating vine-leaf-wrapped meat-balls at the Greek Club, or shrimps fried in batter at the Japanese *Hoi San Café*. He goes with Max Meldrum and George Bell students to the *Chung Wah Café* in Heffernan Lane, a place not then touristized and, sitting among prostitutes and their Chinese pick-ups, learns to become glib about Chinese menus, adept with chopsticks, and suspiciously knowledgeable about Chinese teas. It needs hardly be stated that his unsuitable choice as favourite is Jasmine Tea. Happy country boy acquiring innocence sip by scented sip!

He tries drinking with the Justus Jorgensen mob at the Mitre Tavern, but their floridities of sincerity are not his, he suspects the slapdash colour of their conversations and convictions. I brutally suppose, now, that he does not know what they are talking about.

Always seeking for what, when he was the little watcher on the cast-iron balcony, he *knew* lay beneath the endless roofs spread before him, some magic place behind the million minute golden panes oiled by the sunset exploding over the ridge of Kensington, he wanders past the florists' shops of the Eastern Market and the shops that sell waiters' white monkey-jackets and chefs' caps and butchers' aprons and the brass pins, hook-and-heart, for grocers' aprons; he wanders Exhibition Street, and comes to the *Café Latin*, and thinks he finds, at the top of the narrow stairs, what he seeks.

At least he is in love again.

He is in love with a café, and for what he can buy—Life—for half a crown. What does he buy that he calls Life? Jazzy frescoes, already dated, even to him. The smell of garlicked salad bowls. Rectangular looking-glasses edged by hat-pegs. A plump and queenly poofter called Flo who sips Strega between the cheap sad tunes he plays on the upright piano from a railed-in platform at the head of the stairs. Vast spotless table-napkins of coarse linen. *Grissini, antipasto, minestrone,* grilled whiting, chicken or lobster *mayonnaise,* Limburger or Gorgonzola, and a bottle-green half-bottle of red or white wine poured from the wickered stoneware jars that line the corridor to the lavatory. Half a crown! Two and six! The waiters, Italian, Basque, French, seem to him deft

217

and perfect. Camillo Triachi, the proprietor, moves, tall and stately and seemingly solid with wisdom, about the room drenched in corny heavenly melody, and vile divine gossip, and the scent of women's best dresses, and garlic, and Coffee Royal, and Turkish cigarettes, and inferior cigars. Life! Camillo drops here a word, there a sentence, from the height of his imperially handsome face. Now and then, on some more fervent Friday or Saturday, Camillo carries with him in one hand a bottle of *Fiori d'Alpini*, in the other a bouquet of liqueur glasses. On some inner judgement of his own, driven by his own charm or foresight or pity, he presents a glass of the scented oil, golden as those long-ago, distant, sunset windows, to this one, to that one, to me, to the watcher in Kensington, the harum-scarum in Bairnsdale, the quester through Williamstown and Melbourne, to *me*. Life! I learn to greet and farewell in Italian; to order *zabaglione*. Life! I meet Toti dal Monte, and hear her sing from Flo's platform. Life! I meet Katherine Susannah Prichard who pours me a glass of claret while I convince her that she should read some of my short story manuscripts. Life!

I never get drunk as I now sometimes get wildly drunk, but rise often like a bubble to planes of exhilaration in which I seem to myself to cut like flying scissors through streets filled with sage and lovely and beautifully ugly and ineffably happy people as I 'stride' under my streaming golden hair and streaming golden thoughts for the last electric train to suburbia, to Williamstown, to a childlike sleep. As I submerge, Flo's music plays on in my mind: there is the fume of Mocha coffee and Camillo's free *Fiori d'Alpini*; I feel a smile winding itself about my lips, engraving itself circumspectly there to remain night-long. Life and Life and Life!

Yes.

Nevertheless, circumstance háving permitted me to find out these simple silly pleasures and to taste them with unspoiled tongue, it is time for me to be taught other things, to be admonished, even to be punished for, really, I have not yet—late 1928—been punished. It has all been too easy. I have not been splashed by another's pain, let alone my own.

If not yet proud, I am not yet humble; if not yet gilded, not yet dirtied; if not completely undisillusioned, not yet completely disillusioned; if far from ripe, ripe enough for the plucking of coarser fingers. I have danced too long by myself. Nature abhors the solitary, and is strongly charged with the forces to strike it down. Human beings, affecting to abhor solitariness, will snatch at the contented lonely one to rob him of aloneness and content.

The avalanche starts.

There I am, one moment, throwing my felt hat into the Haunted Hills, sipping Camillo's *Flowers of the Alps*, slipping sharp-eyed as a ferret through back streets and the old avenues of public gardens, chattering lies of culture at Ambassadors' luncheons, performing an earnest and loud-mouthed slavery for my beloved forty pupils, watching Charles Wheeler's thumb or Gregan Mc Mahon's bald head or Pavlova's arms, mooning along before the Blake water-colours or Japanese colour prints of the National Gallery, scribbling away recklessly, blind with words; there I am, one moment, on my swift and burning and recklessly unabashed ascent to my own heavenly nowhere. Avalanche! The next moment I am on the way down to someone else's shocking somewhere, a somewhere not Life but life.

There is, first of all, Miss Lucy Hart. She arrives as a temporary teacher at the school. Her clothes are immediately seen to be possibly expensive, and certainly un-Australian. Her *cloche* hats pierced by *diamanté* arrows, her Garbo-ish coats with collars of deep unknown furs, her one-strap lizard-skin shoes, her handbags, her necklaces, all seem to be of colours and materials and outlines subtly different, imperceivably slicker and sharper and harder and more brazen. Miss Hart—and I never call her other than that despite what happens between us—seems always to be in her Sunday best, and a fashion-plate Sunday best at that. To me she seems immeasurably old. She seems also to be composed of two personalities, one dangerously hard, one dangerously soggy. She has not long returned from a trip to America.

There, say the half-a-dozen young female junior teachers to whom I attempt to show off, she has had her hair dyed. There, they say, soaking ginger-nuts in their playtime tea, she has had her face lifted. Without being sure, I can nevertheless almost believe them. Miss Hart's face has an unlimber pink and white blandness, and her hair crowds down in inflexible undulations on forehead and temples, hair the colour of flower-pots, and of that one colour only with no gradations of it. Her pale blue eyes, like doll's eyes, do not ever seem to move sideways.

I perceive that she likes me, and think it is because my line is playing the wordy jester. She smiles at me, as it were wholly for me and secretly, in the middle of staff conferences when everyone else is looking at their own toecaps or the creases and caught threads of their own or others' skirts and trousers. She's a bold one, I think, smiling back in a way I consider charming, trying out a lop-sided one practised in my shaving-mirror. I do not like her, nor the rigid intensity of her smile, a sustained grimace, but am flattered that she projects this at me rather than at the most handsome of the male junior teachers, an almost-larrikin in pink Oxford bags and cracked black patent leather shoes.

Because she lives at the Rifle Club Hotel, once Grandfather Porter's haunt, which is just through the railway gates from school, at the shopping end of Victoria Street and on my way home to Aunt Rosa Bona and Uncle Martini-Henry, and because she seems always to be leaving just as I leave, we fall into the pattern of leaving school together and —how patiently and skilfully older women make young fools tick over—into making me seem to have inspired in her an affection for the parts of Williamstown that most entrance me. See us walking to the time-ball tower and loose-planked jetties built by the convicts, to the graves of convict-murdered guards and warders, to the bluestone taverns and ramshackle markets of The Front and the empty follies of The Strand. It never enters my head to suspect this honest huntress, this patient huntress, when she refuses my invitations to afternoon tea with Aunt Rosa Bona who would, I now know, have read her like a book. How many miles she must walk in her black-and-white shoes, her ears rattling with my romantic enthusiasms, her muscular legs quivering with ennui, to get what she wants! The Devil knows how many hints she drops of what she wants. Perhaps none, perhaps none at all, but, if any, I miss them all. She buys me rolls of Michelet paper, an autograph album with suède covers, and pages of pastel pinks and mauves and lemons, a box of handkerchiefs, a pair of goldish-brown silk socks the niggardly pattern of which I remember to this day. Delighted and grateful, I continue to miss the point. I give her a water-colour of the cemetery fountain about which I have painted delphiniums, antirrhinums and lavender bushes in place of the actual docks. Yet, recalling my sincere obtuseness, I recall also that I most carefully say nothing to Aunt Bona or anyone at school of Miss Hart's largesse, not a word. Why? Who has warned whom? In my weekly Sunday letter to Mother, however, I do, at least in the beginning, mention these gifts. Mother writes back to say that young men do not, and should never, accept presents from women. She repeats this in several letters, with underlinings by the obviously well-licked indelible pencil Mother uses. I take it to mean that I am making, not errors of discretion, merely errors in taste; that I am being ungentlemanly and Bohemian. Neither does she, so far as I know, write to Aunt Bona. Why? Because she knows that women, anyway, with their magnificently small aims, almost always get what they want and, with it, what they scarcely deserve but certainly earn?

Miss Hart, finally, bored to madness by crumbling stone and weedy lanes and cracked tombstones, gets what she wants: the use of my untrained, unsympathetic but nature-geared young body. She pays for it. At this moment, I am still uncertain whether to feel compassion or serves-you-right for Miss Hart. I am not sure if the score be settled or if one of us owes the other.

In what may well be a last desperate throw for the horn of an imperceptive idiot, she makes me think I want to learn to play Bridge, and offers to teach me, eight o'clock, Tuesday night, Room 12, Rifle Club Hotel.

I still do not know if these sorts of doors are really the sorts of doors for seventeen-year-olds to knock on: for other Miss Harts and other Hal Porters, maybe, maybe. Had her perspicacity been greater she needs not have learned what she learned from me; what I had to learn I already knew of myself and did not wish to know.

Punctual as always, at eight o'clock exactly, combing his hair, he walks the carpeted corridor smelling of the hotel's Mulligatawny Soup. His shoes are newly polished, he is freshly showered, his finger-nails are particularly speckless so that he may learn Bridge without shame. His underpants are innocently—tattered—there is no other word. He reaches Room 12. He knocks.

'Who's there?' says Miss Hart.

'It is I,' he says, nominative after all parts of the verb *to be*.

'Oh,' says Miss Hart, 'I'm not quite ready. Is it eight o'clock yet? Not quite ready, but. . . .' She pauses. The pause, the position and nature of the pause, that does it. Too late now he realizes the sex-stained colour of her voice: Alex Macalister's colour, the colour of Francesco Floriani's voice lassooing down from his own incomplete and painted Purgatory.

'Not quite ready, but. . . .' *Pause*. '. . . come in,' says Alex, says the Dago, says Miss Hart turning the key of the door of Room 12. In his torn underpants the erection begins. The door opens. The door closes. The key is turned.

Just as a mother, perpetually anxious for her children's safety, can never make herself independent, so women like Miss Hart, perpetually anxious for their lust's safety can never make themselves independent. Miss Hart has therefore lost her head and, after several weeks of doubtless scarifying patience, has gone too far. Beneath a Japanese kimono patterned with wistaria, white on black, she is, he thinks, palpably naked. Palpably, he thinks, palpably.

Self-possession overcomes him. His eyes strike straight at hers.

Her eyes are slightly skew-whiff, a cant he is often enough, later in life, to observe in the eyes of women on heat. It is as though they look somewhere to fear of refusal, somewhere for a bitter weapon to strike at him who refuses, somewhere with modest surprise into the recesses of their own nerve-ridden bodies, somewhere in pitiless pity for the stern flesh they are driven to chew to nothing, mostly—witchlike and unrelenting—in the direction of their desire, to assess him and compel him.

She could instantly drag him to the bed but goes on with horrifying conversation, horrifying because its tone is conventional, and her squashed and corn-set toes are nude and tragic: 'You see, I'm not quite ready.'

Quite!

'I was changing after dinner. You know. Freshening up. I know *you* won't mind, dear boy.'

'I don't mind, Miss Hart,' he says, ruthless now that the avalanche is upon him. And more ruthless: 'Shall I wait outside?'

'No need. Unless you'd rather. But I thought you wouldn't be shocked if I dressed in front of you.'

He knows that answer.

'I don't care,' he says, and feels her eyes flash like an X-ray to the front of his trousers. Palpable, he thinks, a palpable horn.

Miss Hart has certainly lost her head. She drops her kimono which hides her toes while revealing other mysteries. She is not palpably naked. She is merely as naked as life and pain and stupidity except for pink celanese bloomers, like Aunt Rosa Bona's, like Mother's, like those of any Summer Sale, and those on any backyard clothes-line. There are smeared dashes of talcum powder on her painful flushed bulges and floppings. It is a ludicrous and pathetic nudity, older and squatter than the nakedness of nymphs of marble, than of the lamp-holding women on the staircase of the Bijou Theatre, than of Greuze's *La Source*, than of the cream-curd Griffenhagen bucolic he bought at thirteen with his first prize money. It has none of the taunting beauty of art, of marble, of paint, of what he has been trying to teach himself is beauty and truth. It is a lie seamed by the marks of stays, and padded with an age of flesh. It is a body older than Mother's, maybe older than Aunt Rosa Bona's. It is an unfair gift, uncompromising, unleashed, unrefusable. Madame Bovary, he thinks, Anna Karenina, Tess of the d'Urbervilles. He feels like crying. His erection agonizingly persists.

I do not know what other simpletons of seventeen, thus seduced by women two-and-a-half times their own age, do after they have been used, or what they think, or remember. I remember that he walks the beach, under a moon, backwards and forwards at the water's final edge, up and down, not striding but bowed into rumination by an experience as necessary as unnecessary, bowed like an older man, like an old youth, like a dead boy, and saying to the water's final edge, 'I've done it. My fingers smell of woman. Was she a woman? I'm no longer a virgin. I'm a man. Am I a man?' I can smile—a little—at him in the moonlight whispering that. Is he a man? What is a man?

Walking in the moonlight, he feels that the wistaria pattern of the kimono has somehow been imprinted on his body from hers; that this pattern is smudged on the backs of his thighs where her legs, to his surprise, have hooked and gripped. His mouth still feels plugged by her unexpected tongue, and the amazement of its rape of his mouth, its slime and power. He spits on the iridescent sand where he played before the time for playing was over. He sees the wad of stiff greying hairs, not the colour of flower-pots at all, forced up towards what she wants from him, or life, forced up by the pillow she has dragged under herself. He sees in many directions at the one time: the orange-coloured roof of her mouth of false teeth, his shameful ragged underpants lying on the kimono on the bedside mat, the deck of cards set like a centuries-old lie on the fake oak dressing-table, his own bare legs in shoes and fallen-down socks, his crumpled shirt-tail, he hears some other he moaning and shocked and enraged and exultant, uprooted from his designed self and buried in the wet muscles of woman, of the woman—of Miss Hart.

Having moved, the avalanche keeps on moving, inexorably, with speed, admonishing and punishing, and edging him not only to the other world beyond his desired one but to his own other world beyond the one he thought was his alone.

Within two weeks he borrows fifteen pounds from Miss Hart. I am a prostitute, he says to himself, but I'm working hard for it. Or does he say gigolo? I cannot recall if gigolo were an Australian word in 1928. Prostitute then. Why? He has not the slightest intention of paying back the fifteen pounds: that is all Miss Hart learns from him apart from the disposition of Williamstown's older buildings and headstones. He never walks home from school with her again. He taps on Room 12 wearing new underpants. With the fifteen pounds he buys dancing pumps; and is measured for a black suit at Buckley and Nunn's where Father bought the black silk poplin tie, and the mourning band that helped prove Grandfather Porter's death.

Black, as Mother has said, breeds black.

I do not believe this, have never really believed Mother's enchanting and nerve-chilling superstitions. I buy the black suit to make entrances—blond hair, black suit—at the *Café Latin*, at the Tennis Dances I am wanting to go to with one of the pretty junior teachers, at anywhere. But black does breed black, and the avalanche will keep on moving, and will push me farther and farther to the very heart of blackness. The stages are graded with a nicety that, for several years, at this time, leaves me uncertain of the value of goodness, the value of evil. It is fortunately an uncertainty that is dazzled out of existence by more enriching certainties.

Avalanche on the move, Stage Two.

One of my pupils, Wock . . . Wock Somebody, and two boys from another school, find or steal, I forget which, some detonators and, accidentally, blow themselves up. I think everyone else must be shocked. They say so. I am to learn that shock does not mean to them what it means to me. I am certainly shocked, and not only because this is the first time that someone dear to my vanity, and part of my pride, has been erased from my little scene. When Grandfather Porter, until then my only known and remembered dead one, disappears from the scene, I have no feelings except disappointment that Father and Mother let me down in the matter of what books have displayed to me as the correct behaviour for the bereaved, no cries of, 'Vex not his ghost! Oh, let him pass, you who would upon the rack of this cruel world stretch him out longer!'

When Wock is destroyed, my pupil—*mine*—I am lacerated doubly. He is a grubby boy with warty hands, and a voice of angelic transparency as he sings 'Strawberry Fair' or my old haunter 'Row, brothers, row' during singing lessons, a boy whose handwriting and spelling I have compelled him to improve, labouring perfervidly for the future he is not to have. I have convinced myself that he seems happier for this improvement as I am both selfishly and selflessly happier. He grins at my praise and grows younger, as at my rantings he grows frowning and wrinkled and older. Sometimes I wink at him in class, and he winks back, the return wink meaning, I hope, 'Oi don' moind you bein' crabby, sir, and sometoimes strappin' me. Oi understand it's all for moi benefit.'

It may mean, of course, 'Oo the bloody hell you think you are? Just you wait. Just you wait.'

On the day he is blown up, after school is over, I have strapped him. Lacerated doubly, indeed, is the energetic junior teacher. Wock can improve his spelling no further, will never accomplish *embarrass* and *harass*, *symmetry* and *cemetery*, not in words. No copperplate for Wock. I have wasted my time and his. He can never wink his lidded-down or blown-out or smashed-in eye at me to forgive, or appear to forgive, the blow of the leather strap on his grime-lined palm, now as tattered as my virgin's underpants or as positively incapable, rain or shine forever, of holding itself horizontal at my command.

For his death, as for the death of my younger and wiser self between the powerful embrace of Miss Hart's thick legs, I drift along the beach at night, whimpering and whispering, 'I'm sorry. I'm sorry. I'm sorry. Please God, let Wock Somebody hear that I'm sorry.' Sorry that he can learn to write no more legibly; sorry that time has wasted him; sorry because, forgiving or polite or trapped into response, he can no longer wink.

After my death (and I am to have many deaths after, and many yet, many deaths of un-innocence) in Miss Hart's anxiously volted body, comes my resurrection as a money-grubbing prostitute, a stinking Lazarus doomed, thank Life, as all the resurrected are, to a better and final death. After Wock's death I am to be shocked into a death-like trance from which there can never be a full resurrection, the realization that people are merely what they are and not what I fervently, at this hopeful-hopeless very moment, desire they will be.

Listen.

On the morning after the explosion, the newspapers already black with headlines, the school is invaded by press photographers. Comedies take place. These comedies are fascinating and nauseating to me. In fleeing from the world of *The Bairnsdale Advertiser* where I earned money by writing of some dollop grotesquely over-dressed that 'the bride looked charming in et cetera' or of some local, well-disliked skinflint that 'the deceased, who was a well-known and respected et cetera', I am not expecting to be, just because of Wock's death, brought face to face with a version of my own

227

small-town, boyishly raw cadet-reporter's lies exaggerated into a brisk and faultless nightmare. The Headmaster, as though bringing in Socrates, brings in a photographer to my classroom, a man whose face is lean and lined like the face of a handsome dissipated hound, with over-wise sunken eyes, lens-like and too dark, all pupil. This, I think to myself, is from photographing, as much by the mechanism of his own body as by his camera, such things as the Old Age Pensioner ejected from his bed-sitter, the steeplechase spill, the train smash, the spot marked X, the accused entering the Criminal Court, the no-armed artist who paints with his brush in his mouth, the murdered child's parents, Wock's desk—*The Desk of the Dead Boy*. But the photographer in his crumpled cocoa-brown suit does not photograph Wock's desk, which is near the front of the room. He decides on a desk more centrally placed, more suitably disposed to illustrate *Wock's Classmates Mourn Him*. He rearranges the pupils in the surrounding desks. As I watch—'with horror and contempt', I tell myself—but really with scandalized curiosity, I see what he is about. I can almost enthusiastically commend his choice: this pretty, fair-haired girl wearing a pale dress in the desk behind the empty one, this dark boy with the neat tie in the desk beside hers, this curly-headed one here, that good-looking one there. There, a little to the right, you! And, you there, with white jumper, move just a teeny fraction *that* way! His pictorial falsehood arranged, 'Now, bow your heads,' says the liar with the camera. The actors and actresses bow their heads.

Next day, the funeral. The school reeks of wreaths. The funeral is to move along past the school. The children, the hundreds of them, are to line the roadway on both sides. Since the photographer's performance of the day before my mind has badly played shuttlecock and battledore with itself:

It's all lies. The photograph was a lie. It wasn't Wock's desk. The children weren't mourning.

All right, it was lies, You yourself tell polite lies. They were lies for the father and mother, who will be comforted and proud.

Why should they be?

They're simple, ordinary human beings who will snatch at any comfort.

A photograph in a newspaper?

A photograph in a newspaper.

God! How do you know?

I don't know. Even if it were a true photograph it wouldn't comfort me. But people of that sort. . . .

Which sort?

Simple, normal, ordinary. . . .

How do you know they're simple, normal, ordinary?

I don't know. It's what newspapers and books say they are. It's what they imagine they are. I don't believe anyone is.

If they no longer have Wock, at least they'll have the cut-out references of his notoriety, prettied-up photographs, prettied-up lies.

You're cheap and hard.

No.

Sentimental and hard, then.

Oh, no, no, no.

You don't really know what life's about.

I didn't say I did. I'm merely alive. And I'm learning what others say life is, what others act life as. I'll learn, I'll learn, I'll learn.

I ask one of the girls to gather together such of Wock's books as are kept in the classroom cupboard. They have all been corrected except one. It is the only one I open. Leave the others closed, as Wock closed them on his smudgings and waverings and blottings: his mother will open them and blot them more. I open his essay book, and correct the last of his essays, the uncorrected one on the topic, 'Look before you leap.' There are four mistakes only in spelling; in the essay before there are nine. *Steadily Improving* I write in red ink, shutting down my face to zero, and shutting the book, and that is nearly the last of Wock for me, for the workaday me who must go on living as he must go on being not alive. *Steadily Improving*: nearly the last of Wock. Nearly the last of an old me?

Midsummer mid-afternoon: the school is lined up on the

drain-edges. A hundred wreaths, florist or back-garden, have gone to the funeral parlour. The school band, with the drum enshrouded in two of the caretaker's black Italian cloth aprons, has gone to the funeral parlour two blocks away. It is ice-cream weather, swimming weather, a hot hot day. Across the road, with her class, Miss Hart stands under a grey silk umbrella. I know, I *know* her stays are cutting ridges into her flesh. I know where. The children swing their towels and bathers.

Suddenly, far-off it seems, either in the remotest depths of heaven or the last echoing cavern of one's own heart, the drum is heard. The funeral is on the move. Everyone becomes, fleetingly, still and silent; a veil of embarrassment drops smartly across faces, and instantly up to reveal faces more alert and different. The newspaper photographers, aloft in the trees, stir like apes and drop their cigarettes. The perambulator-wheeling women stop. The Scotswoman comes from the tuck-shop wiping her fat hands on her girlish hips. Five men, one holding a pot of beer, come from the Bristol Hotel opposite. There is a change in the tone of the thudding of the drum: a corner has been turned, and Wock is on his way.

'S-s-straighten up,' hiss the teachers, discreetly. 'Heads-s-s down. S-s-silence. Heads-s-s. S-s-silence. It's-s-s coming.'

The men from the hotel take off their hats with slow-motion gestures; the one with the pot of beer drains deep, and conceals the empty pot beneath his empty hat.

Ravished and torn, tough and sentimental, harsh and sensitive dope, I bow my head; I close my eyes; I press my palms on them as I used to in Kensington. Through the dark swamped with phosphenes, Wock's hand, outstretched for the fall of the strap, pokes itself into the core of my mind.

There is laughter.

Yes, I hear laughter, the laughter of hundreds of children. It is stifled, it is hands-over-mouths laughter, but it is laughter enough to be heard through the thudding and ever nearing thudding, the tell-tale heart thudding of the drum.

I open my eyes.

In front of the mourners' cars, in front of the cars of wreaths, in front of the flower-covered coffins in one of which are the nasty remains of *Steadily Improving* Wock (Coffin One? Coffin Two? Coffin Three?), in front of the school band marching out of step, in front of the drum swathed in the caretaker's aprons, trots a little fox terrier. He is in some sort of step, three or four trots to one drum-thud. That is all I see before I close my eyes again on the laughter-congested faces.

Avalanche.

Miss Hart.

Wock.

In a flash that seems to mean everything, as though I have been electrocuted into another person, as though all the lights have been turned on in another dimension, I appear to see and understand that Romeo and Juliet, Troilus and Cressida, Dr. Crippen and Ethel le Neve, Miss Hart and sex, are terribly amusing, that Isadora Duncan and the scarf, Rimbaud and his cancer, Wock and death, are terribly amusing, that sex is hilarious, and death too screamingly funny for words. Yet, at this discovery from nowhere, this vision that all others can laugh and laugh and laugh, tears crowd into my eyes, for I have no sense of humour at all. I remove these tears, two or four only, behind the backs of the convulsed children as the grinning dog, with the alert perkiness of a racecourse tout, leads the way to the cemetery and its fountain edged by docks (delphiniums? antirrhinums? lavender?), leads the way to some sort of verity.

I have been warned.

I have not yet been completely punished.

I do not much heed the warnings.

I go on writing poetry opalescent and baroque. I run up the Friday stairs of the *Café Latin*—'*Come sta, Camillo?*' I walk, bold and slick as a Colette gigolo, along the carpeted corridor smelling of soup of the evening, bee-eaut-i-ful soup, to Room 12. I smuggle my black suit smelling of new black stitching into Aunt Rosa Bona's house, and hide it, in its box, in the bottom of my wardrobe. The school year ends. Leaving

Williamstown, and Miss Hart, and Gregan Mc Mahon, and Charles Wheeler's thumb, and Wiggy Binder in her *tutu*—oh, leaving everything and much of myself—I climb into the train for Gippsland at Flinders Street station. As the train starts I silently sing Mother's song: 'Good-bye, Melbourne Town! Melbourne Town, good-bye!' I do not consider bursting into tears. I am smoking a cigarette, a Goliath, in a holder. I am hatless—this is bold and dangerous of me still. I am hatless and, I tell myself, heartless.

Oh, you fool, you fool, you fool!

My first impression of Gippsland and Bairnsdale, a dozen years before, was of infinity and light; one felt oneself the speck in the core of an illimitable globe of crystal.

In December 1928, returning hatless, and chastened to what I call heartlessness ('I am world-weary! What is Life? What is Truth?'), with my supply of romantic hopes already diminished, and many of my story-book illusions and gim-crack ideals mauled by myself and others, it is uplifting to be bowled over again by the same impression of space and dazzle. This was no heaven to nose-dive from like one's own self-appointed Lucifer. It maybe that, adolescently chasing the dreams and fantastic lanterns of others through alleys and cafés and studios and dishonesties and pretensions and ageing flesh, I am only chasing what I have run away from, that I am much more homesick, much more a bungling, simple country boy than I admit or act. It maybe merely no more than that the weather persists perfect, day after day, and that the months of December 1928 and January 1929 are so diamond-bright, and saturated in such a purity of heat, that they are, in memory, two of the most delicious months of my life, months cleansing and electrifying and sensual. I tear through the flashing streets presenting a city-burnished self at the back doors of my acquaintances. I find everything about them beautiful. How wide their streets! How wise and recognizable their gestures! How uncultured and fearless their voices! How strong as ambrosia their cups of tea!

I remarry, as it were, my four frivolous friends of High School Days. We swim hour after hour after hour in the green water under the willows by the Rowing Club under which I never did stroll hand in hand with Olwen Connor, and under which Francesco Floriani from Purgatory and Napoli either waited or did not wait for me. We five gallop horses up into the hill-billy, derelict gold-mining towns to

233

steal walnuts and limes from orchards belonging to no one. We row on the glittering river, or travel by steamer down it, past hop-kilns and peach-orchards and maize-crops and pumpkin-paddocks, under the cliffs of Eagle Point, between the silt jetties, through the lakes crowded with black swans, to the Ninety Mile Beach, where we are thrown about in the green champagne waves of the ocean, and then lie, hour after sensuous grilling hour, powdered with sand and salt on the three-hundred-yards-wide beach, or in the valleys of the dunes, murmuring funny filth and wild scandal and inanities. We dashingly wear Palm Beach bathers which are just in, and be-bobbled sombreros, and spectacles of blue glass set in wire that cuts the bridges of our sun-raw noses. About us, reading novels by Elinor Glyn under Japanese sunshades, sit women, their faces glossy with cold cream, in wide-legged beach pyjamas: the first, but hardly—alas!—the last, women I am to see in trousers.

Breasts are not fashionable. Nevertheless, I find myself, covertly, from under the Mexican brim and behind the blue glass, spying on those fuller breasts that defy fashion.

Bunty becomes reformed, in my opinion, to someone else tempting and exciting. I conceive her to take on a resemblance to Lila Lee the film star. Pressing more closely to her than in the old days, I dance with her in the Fire Brigade Hall, in the Mechanics' Institute, in the Picnic Point Hall, whirling giddily around in the Valeta and The Pride of Erin and the Gipsy Tap, even attempting the Varsity Drag. After the dances, I fervently wrestle with her under the overhanging shadows of garden cassias on the way home, or, under the stars, at her front gate, sophisticatedly nibbling at her earrings, fondling her little flat breasts, licking the nape of her shingled neck and introducing my tongue into her mouth, but never succeeding—she is not Miss Hart—in getting my hands near where they have decided they would like to get. These struggles with Bunty exhilarate me much more than Miss Hart's struggles with me: I have several seminal accidents. For the first time in life my face is slapped. This is, for some atavastic reason, a shocking and humiliating experience, almost an emasculating one. It is particularly so for a green city slicker who is less interested in getting what he does not get than in displaying the few technicalities he has acquired on and in a body bulkier than Nigger's used to be, more shameless and shameful and unreal than Bunty's which, like mine, has bones that are near the surface, angular lithenesses, a waist, and the acid freshness of immaturity.

As much as I am in love again with my old Circe Bairnsdale, so I am in love again with home. This love makes me drift, giddy with affection, my hand outstretched to touch and stroke, among objects familiar from the first: the Renardi, the red design on the Rockingham plates, the silver with its sharp edges, and incised and incisive crests, blurred by years of Saturday morning polishing, the fading gold on the reeds and cranes of the Japanese screen, the iron boilers large enough to stew a warthog in, the battered copper saucepan in which eggs are always boiled and the Christmas Pudding money, the apple-corer, my own wooden egg-cup and tooth-marked silver spoon. I can stand, dizzy with sun, and the burring of bees, and the flicker-flicker of skippers, savouring that recaptured sense of abundance, among Mother's cucumber vines, the rows of butter beans and red beet and celery and shallots, the loganberry canes, the loaded plum trees, the taller bushes from which I stole camellias for Olwen Connor—always the perfect one that Mother had been gloating on, and missed, and had to be told lies about. I am interested—objectively, I make clear to me—to discover that, whatever I *think* of the family, however much I curl this or that affected, seventeen-year-old lip, however much they irritate or bore—my brothers and sisters, Father, Mother—I love them with an animal blindness, a nerve-shot conviction more powerful than duty. This is an intensification and refinement of the feelings I used to have in the tumultuous Sale days when, in a riot of child cousins and bubbling babies and squealing aunts and swearing uncles, I knew it would be no trouble at all to grow on the spot a beard and a German-Swiss accent, and stomp about crying, 'Cut 'em! Slash 'em!' to the still existing past.

It is now the present. Mother's last baby is a boy of six who has already cut off the top of one finger with the axe, even though he is not to go to school until next year. I wonder if Mother will walk to school with him on his first day. She is now a different mother. All that early intensity is bygone. Or is it? Are her needs, and the needs of youngest sons different? I do not know; I do not know.

I have hidden my cigarettes, washed my mouth, and chewed a clove, well before the train gets to Bairnsdale. I see Mother before she sees me, and am upset at what I think the light of the almost vertical sun is doing to undo her powdered and discreetly painted face, to make her appear thinner and drawn of face and agonized-looking. Her eyes seem raking the carriages with a distraught forlornness as though I might not be there, or as though something she does not wish to meet has come riding in and now hides its taunting smile behind one of the closed jalousies. Then she sees me, and all that illusion is over. The cruel sun, no more than the cruel sun! She is smiling and alight, and not ravaged at all, and is foolishly running. She is as young, as girlishly silly, as unembarrassedly noisy as ever.

From the moment I see her, and the moment I set foot— Mother hanging on to my arm like a hussy—on the divine gravel, on the divinely weedy gravel, outside the station, I am struck silent and cut down to size again, I am miraculously, passionately and immediately in love with Bairnsdale again. Poor yokel from the *Café Latin* and the *Bal Masqué* and the corridor of the Rifle Club Hotel!

Since I am, for the first week, also home-dazzled, and cock-o'-the-walk, and out-and-about displaying myself and my hatlessness and my city ties and cultural platitudes like a sandwich-board, it takes a while for me to become uneasily aware that, despite Mother's prattle and singing and domestic oaths, she is up to something, that it is not the cruel sun that lends her face that look of fear when she thinks no one has an eye on her. It is fear itself. Why? And what has she to say, for something to say she has?

I am imperceptive enough and guilty enough, the hypocrite protecting Mother from indefinable corruption, to mistranslate Mother's haltings and suddenly fraught glances into pauses on the brink of a question, I fear, answerable by a lie Mother will not believe. I have not prepared a lie. Idiot-like, I never do. I await to side-step, by whatever leaps to mind, the questions I conceitedly think Mother is too nice to ask: 'Do you smoke, Laddie?' or, 'Do you drink intoxicating beverages?' or, 'Will you explain to me exactly why that woman at your school gives you autograph albums and silk socks from Henry Buck's? Henry Buck's isn't cheap, you know.' To save myself the trouble of grave and patent lies, I bibble-babble on, like a bar-room *raconteur*, of my art lessons, of the fancy people I have met in Gregan Mc Mahon's room upstairs at the Bijou; I gurgle along, not taking a breath, about those touched-up aspects of life I deem suitable for her to hear. She is easy to side-track from her intention, whatever it may be, by accounts of the luncheons at Ambassadors Restaurant: Uncle John, *Consommé Julienne*, Louis Lavater; Uncle John, Chicken Maryland, Frank Wilmot; Uncle John, Lemon Pancakes, J. S. Macdonald.

The device of talking fast and shallow, and with the pinch of mockery I have inherited or imitated from Mother herself, pays off. The fear runs like rain from her face. She becomes flushed, and skittish, and dim-witted with happiness for her self-extolled Life-of-the-Party son. Ignoble skulduggery and varnished half-truths lull Mother's astuteness.

Looking back, it is easy to know what she needs so much to pour out to her eldest son, and to know with a sickness of horror that he has used trumpery guile to switch her from sharing a terrible secret of fear, that he has so white-anted her confidence that she denies herself this relief of sharing lest one tear of blood fall on the page of his comfort and importance.

As she has done every year, she sterilizes the Christmas Pudding threepences and gewgaws; bakes the ham in its thick jacket of dough; roasts several fowls. I observe that the ham is smaller, that there are fewer threepences, and not one sixpence, in the little copper saucepan. I observe, but say nothing. Nothing is gained by telling one's parents what they themselves have already learned—that they are poorer than they should be. I observe that Mother, tilting the brandy bottle to examine how much there is for the Christmas Pudding flames, says of the little remaining, 'That will have to do, this year.' I hate to be not able not to observe signs of poverty all about: the turned and patched sheets, the darned damask of the table-napkins, the rubber spout covering the broken spout of the everyday china teapot, the kitchen-chair cushions covered with the cretonne of old curtains, the electroplate on biscuit-barrel lids wearing thin enough to reveal the goldish metal beneath, the tines of the kitchen forks worn sideways. When the Christmas decorations are brought out, and the family is rounded-up into tacking them up, I recall that once these now shabby frivolities were crisp and glittering.

On Christmas Eve, I help Mother—where is Father?—fill the toes of the younger children's hung-up socks with the customary bits and pieces: the sixpence, the handful of Jordan almonds, the blood orange, the pieces of crystallized ginger. I am selfishly and Big-Man glad that I have been unselfish enough to buy, partly with the remains of Miss Hart's fee, partly from my own junior teacher earnings, some frivolous city toys because, I observe—struck with one sort of pity for the children, and another more disconcerting sort of undeserved pity for Father and Mother—that the presents she is putting in the pillow-cases that hang by the socks are presents of a largely practical kind: shoes, belts, singlets, ties, school stockings. I flush with yet another sort of angry pity when, after Mother and I have tiptoed back to the kitchen, and are having midnight lime-juice and shortbread, she says, she standing with the glass jug, I sitting like a Cavalier lord, 'You're a good boy, Laddie, a good boy.'

A good boy!

'We really couldn't afford many toys this Christmas.'

Shall I say, 'You shouldn't have had so many children. It's both your faults. Lower middle-class carelessness. Why didn't you and Father realize that. . . .' Et cetera, et cetera?

Of course I say nothing; but my face must be marked by the colours and flickerings of the emotions I cannot put into words, and these must appear to be the marks of embarrassed modesty to Mother. She puts down the jug. She puts the palms of her hands on each side of my face. She bends to kiss me on the forehead for the fourth last time in life.

Quickly—oh, instantly—she sees she must get out of this too prettily sentimental scene. She tips me a wink wide as self-denial, and then, opening her eyes babyishly circular, pouts in the bee-stung manner of Mae Murray, and sings in a squeaky boop-a-doop voice:

> '*You made me love you,*
> *I didn't want to do it, I didn't want to do it. . . .*'

Even though I begin to giggle I am aware that, behind her expression of idiot fatuousness, there remains still that other expression of the searcher, the pleader on the point of pleading and interrogating.

As ever misreading, engaged with keeping unquestioned my own imitation of an honest, clean-living, sexless and abstemious son, I throw a red herring, I escape to my bedroom to get Mother her present, a handbag that, roughly pricing, has cost me two sessions in Room 12 and Miss Hart. Mother acts joy, delves in the recesses of the bag with feminine noises, looks in the little mirror and says, 'Hell and Tommy! It's time I was in bed!' but stays on, pouring more lime-juice, and chattering away. She is, she says, going to sell the Renardi.

Unseen in the luminosity, the avalanche has not stopped moving. This is Mother's last Christmas Eve; she has three more kisses only to give me; she has three months only, almost to the very day, to live.

Christmas passes.

Day by day, and night by night, slides back into the past. Each night when I return, the last one home, from dancing with Bunty, from chattering with friends, from a moonlight steamer trip, from a supper of Banana Sundae and Lemon Squash Spider at Russo's, from this and that and the other, I am conscious of completing a design. There we all are under one roof, the one family, the one tiny entanglement of humans, our breaths and snores and sighs mingling in the dark we own no matter how far, and in what exquisite landscape we do not own, we wander in our own separate dreams.

The New Year passes. We spend New Year's Eve as we have always spent it: the grocer's gift of raspberry vinegar, the cold Christmas Pudding, the Salvation Army playing on The Common. As 1929 comes in, there are, the newspapers report, many children begging in the streets of the Melbourne I wheedled my way to in search of romance and knowledge and Life.

On January the Fifteenth, 1929, Marshal Foch dies in Paris.

Shoplifting in Melbourne is found to have enormously increased, and to be increasing.

On January the Twenty-second, the Ex-Kaiser, Kaiser Bill, who killed knock-kneed Uncle Arthur Abernethy, who was an orphan, who was Grandfather Ruff's farm-boy, who gave me the Teddy Bear before he died at Gallipoli, this Kaiser Bill enjoys his seventieth birthday at Doorn although his wife has chicken-pox.

Vesuvius erupts.

Soup kitchens are set up in Melbourne.

On the day before I am to return to Williamstown and work, Mother gets a letter from Aunt Rosa Bona. This letter is more terrifying to me than child beggars, multiplied shoplifters, Vesuvius in eruption, or soup kitchens.

She was, writes Aunt Bona, getting Laddie's bedroom ready for his return, giving it a thorough doing-over. To her amazement, in the bottom of the wardrobe, *obviously* hidden under a rug, she found a Buckley and Nunn's box containing a black suit. What has Laddie been up to? She does not want to interfere, but did Mother know about the black suit?

As I come striding home from the Rowing Club, the damp towel slung over my shoulder, wishing I were not too old to wear bare feet and paddle again the snowy dust of the path trenched deep through the silvery hay of The Common, I see, between the elm-boles, Mother standing at the gate reading the letter she must just have taken from the post-box,

I wave like an Anyone-for-tennis? character, and call out,

'Anything for me?' but the question rings away past Mother without touching her, away to the late afternoon mountains, to the dying sun and the cooling sky and nowhere. She lifts her head. I have never seen so terrified a face, its lines of control askew, its colour having no name.

'What's wrong?' I say, myself also terrified. 'What on earth's wrong?' feeling that my vitality, and Red Indian suntan, and noise, and bleached and crackling hair, are all offences.

'This,' says Mother, 'could be for you.' She extends the agitated sheet of paper in my direction. Her hands, which I have never seen shaking, are shaking violently, are suffering with her. I watch them clamp on to the gate-post as I read.

Never having been caught out in my life, I am felled, I am struck stupid and mindless. Where is my vitality? My impertinence? My noise and poise? My sharp wits? My cunning? Where are there lies? Here comes one, the only possible one.

'I earned the money.'

Although too true, my intention not to tell the whole truth makes the words falsely fall, suddenly clipped and classy accent notwithstanding.

Mother says nothing. Mother is hanging on to the post, and looking through me.

'Really and truly, I earned it. Some extra work. Sort of art work. I was keeping the suit as a surprise. It only arrived the day I was coming home. I was already packed. So I thought. . . .'

As I gibber clearly on, using the most faultless sounds I can, ready to go on lying and lying and lying, it is borne in on me that Mother is not listening at all. I could be singing 'The Ball of Kirriemuir'. I run down.

Then, Mother, the old young woman, says to no one except fate and all the hidden writhing forces, 'Black breeds black.'

Ah!

She is not wondering how I paid for the suit. This may be a point for later, but not now. She may cross-examine me later. She never does. Payment is not the point. Suits are not the point. Secrecy is not the point. Blackness is. I have traded with the Devil. I have strolled fearlessly in the dark, dark room in the dark, dark house, in the dark, dark lane. Her eldest son has sold his mother, broken the bond of years, slashed the umbilicus. I am the foreigner in league with whatever stands behind the portals of midnight.

Then, because she knows that, however evil I am, however strange and on the Devil's side, I am also a silly male, a blundering boy too smart-alec to be ever wise, because she is a mother, and I am flesh from her own flesh, she forces her hands to reject the post, and be as still as the hands of the brave. She compels her face to be a woman's and a mother's. She presents her smile in which is the tooth with the minute semi-circular piece chipped from it.

'Don't worry, Laddie,' she says. 'It was a shock, that's all. Bona always was a fuss-pot. It's just that I've got a growth inside, and am going into hospital for an operation in March.'

Since I am quite unable to faint, or scream, or make really bestial noises of horror, even if I were not in the street, and since no one has taught me what sons say to mothers in such circumstances, I do not faint, scream, cry, 'Horrible, most horrible!' or say a word.

The next day, seeing me off at the Bairnsdale station, Mother gives me the second last kiss. There is a ridiculous scene. About five minutes before departure time, just as Mother is saying, 'I've written to your aunt to say that it's all right about the black suit. But you're not to wear it until I come out of hospital,' the train is shunted backwards a little. My carriage, being near the rear of the train, is shunted beyond the platform. I am beyond Mother's touching. With distress and shame I hear Mother, the charming and tastefully dressed woman in the grey and white *cloche*, screech out like a Macbeth witch, shrill out like an actress in tattered robes, 'Laddie! *Laddie!* I haven't kissed you! I'll never see you again!'

People look at her, and look away.

I wish I could.

Her face is distorted in the classic manner, and hideous, the mouth square.

Almost immediately, the train moves back to its original position. When the station-master's bell rings, and the train really begins slowly to leave, we kiss. Because I am ashamed for Mother, I hang out of the window waving and waving long after she and her eau-de-Cologne-scented handkerchief and white gloves are out of sight, and I am in country she is never to see again.

An hour or so later the train passes through Sale. Across the paddocks I can see the house she was born in and married in, and the towers and trees and dormitory windows of *Notre Dame de Sion* where, as a little girl, she learned to play the piano badly, and to sing, 'Through forest boles' while Sister Philomena beat time.

There I am, back in Melbourne which seems dirtier, and Williamstown which seems duller. I see my first talking picture, 'The Doctor's Secret', in the State Theatre, with the fake clouds sweeping across its fake starry sky, with its columns and 'antiqued' statues and stuffed doves in imitation cypresses, and Rudolph Valentino's *Blood and Sand* cloak pinned to the foyer wall. I become eighteen.

Although eighteen, I have never gambled, never been to a horse race, a dog race, a yacht race, a car race, a musical comedy, a political meeting, a tennis tournament, a boxing or wrestling or football match, a fan tan school or a two-up school, a brothel or a military tattoo; I have never visited another country or another God; I have never been, in any position of importance, to a funeral.

That is soon to be arranged for me; one has to start somewhere.

Avalanche on the move, Stage Three.

Scarcely ten minutes after Mother dies, Father and I are out in the new world: he into this world to perform simple wickednesses for another twenty-eight years; I into this same world to have simple wickednesses performed on me, thirty-four years of them already.

It begins almost immediately.

My sobs well past, my long-enough-dormant intuitions reawakened and wide-eyed, Father's sobs just out of sight, we walk, Father and I, smelling metallically of exhaustion, our arms about each other's waists, across the road from the death-room to the rectory. We are on our way to tell the over-handsome young minister that Mother is irrevocably dead. This is either for something to do first in the new world, or a politeness to the minister who, a mere several hours before, has kindly fanned Mother with a heart-shaped woven fan, a Fijian object and, one guesses, a missionary relic. He is also responsible for directing Mother to gabble out some farewell prayers and admissions of frailty. As Father and son, entwined, cross the road, I notice that I am taller than Father.

The minister opens the rectory door. It is eight o'clock in the morning. He wears a brocaded silk dressing-down and sandals. Fijian? His legs are white and shiny below the too-short silk. Forgive him, he says, he was just about to have a shower. Forgive us, we say, she is dead.

He takes us inside. His daily woman does not come until ten, he says. He makes tea. The cups and saucers do not match. The biscuits are broken. The sugar in the bowl contains tea-yellowed lumpinesses, bigger than, but the same colour as, the crystals that used to sit in the eyelashes of the Adams tribe. The minister talks to Father, but looks at me. Later, in the looking-glass, seeking marks of suffering, I see that I am momentarily good-looking in an 'interesting' way —thinner cheeks, distended pupils, black shadows under my eyes. The telephone is, says the minister, at Father's disposal. Father makes decisions. He will go to the funeral parlour, which is just along the street, and see Fred, the director, himself. It is easy to see that Fred is a cobber, is a golfer or a cricketer or a Mason, perhaps the whole bloody lot. I am to stay and telephone. *Ida passed away this morning. Harry.*

Do I understand? Do I know the addresses of all the aunts and uncles, and such old school friends as Mother has kept up with?

I understand. I know the addresses.

Father gulps down his tea, and goes, bowed, diminished, pitilessly practical as he must be, and not on the ball at all.

I sense a relaxing to relief in the minister. He pours me a third cup. As we sit and sip I wonder if tea is the replacement for my lavish tears in the hospital. Where do tears really come from? Could one cry if dying of thirst?

The minister moves over into my preoccupation, and sits close beside me on the worn leatherette, telling me with dreamy zeal a number of violent religious lies I seem to have heard before; his arm encircles my shoulders; now and again, with perfect conviction, it wooingly presses in some hemstitched platitude of consolation. He, too, says the minister, is a mother's boy.

Too?

He understands.

Understands what?

He thinks it will be a good idea if I have a shower. After the long journey, after the long night by Mother's bed, a shower will clear my head for the telephoning. Should I like a shower?

Bereft of tears, a Sahara, shocked far beyond any other shocking, no longer in any world but the world of my raw instincts, but retaining the passwords I learned in the other world I thought I was getting to know, there is nothing to say except, automatically, deadened and deadly, 'I don't care.'

This means, 'Go on, Life, show me all your faces! Show me the attics of Hell! Bring on your tame devils!'

He has his shower while I undress in a spare bedroom so sparsely furnished that my mind aches. Poor minister, I think. The dressing-gown he has given me is a winter one of rough grey flannel with skimpy frogging and a frayed cord. It smells of naphthalene. Poor handsome minister waving fans and prayers half the night over delirious women he doesn't know; poor minister with his broken sleep and broken biscuits and broken lusts.

'Ready, Laddie?' he calls at the spare room door in a brighter voice than the bereaved should have to hear.

Ready, aye, ready!

I have been under the shower a minute or two before he has the strength to defy a prayer for himself (not for me, he will not have thought of a prayer for me), and the courage not to knock and thus tempt refusal, but merely to open the door.

'Everything all right?'

'Yes, thank you.'

'A good idea?'

'Yes, a good idea.'

Pause.

'You're pretty brown. In fact, very brown.'

'I did a lot of swimming last summer holidays.'

There is again a pause. I am soaping my armpits.

'You're very white where you aren't brown.'

'Yes.'

'Your bee-tee-em is very white.'

'Well, I *am* fairly fair.'

'You are rather. Yes. Very fair hair.'

God, God, God, I think, these pauses! Fair hair where? Fair hairs where? Don't be as arch as buggery, and bright as a fucking button! Don't be a mug, mug. Get it over, poor man with the cheap carbolic soap and the spoiled sugar and the frayed dressing-gown cords and the immaculate loneliness.

'Would you like me to scrub your back?'

'I don't care.'

He scrubs my back, only my back, and perhaps scrubbing my back or someone's back is all he needs, although one hand cannot prevent itself from resting itself, apparently necessarily, on one of my white (very) hips. He watches me drying myself on a thin towel, closely, as if to learn the secrets of drying bodies. I do not let my eyes watch him at all. His are the eyes that want to see, between the lattices of prayer and hymn. Let them see.

When Father comes back, the minister is dressed, I am dressed, the telegrams have been sent, I have rung the Scotswoman who milks Dolly the Jersey to tell her that

Mother is dead, that Dolly the wife of Curly, is dead, and will she tell Dolly's children?

When Father offers to pay for all this, I feel on the point of protesting, 'But I've already paid!' I think of the broken biscuits, and keep my mouth closed.

Father and I get back to the house in Mitchell Street. My fourteen-year-old sister, as though accepting what Father is to do to her, has already become house-keeper: although her eyes are swollen, the kettle is boiling.

Mother's kitchen—*the* kitchen is a shambles of lunatic kindness; neighbour women have come weeping with scones and brawn and saucepans of soup.

The children's eyes are round, and empty with darkness and perfectly unmoving like stopped clocks.

What is left of Mother is brought to the house she once called hers, and which is now crowded with uncles in black ties, and black-clothed aunts. The coffin is put on trestles in the middle of the living-room, at right angles to the Renardi she talked of selling. The coffin-lid arrives screwed down. Nobody says so but I presume that this is because what caused her death also causes quick decay. Fred, the funeral director, has scattered white tablets, like aspros, about the room. Are they to absorb whatever stink should seep from the coffin?

The younger children do not weep, at least not in front of the aunts who all weep again each time a late-arrived aunt enters to weep and re-inaugurate weeping. The children watch, as through watching with sombre interest, a festival strictly for adults. They are already sold down the river. I know that they know this. If my heart could have broken, it would have been then. Hearts have no intention of breaking. The thought that mine could is the nearest to any anguish I can get on their behalf. We should all, I feel, defying every-thing, rush together, all we children, twine and knot our-selves together, strain our throats heavenwards, and give a concerted silent baying from our marble mouths. That is for groups in statues. We do nothing. Mother has made us well-behaved. The children watch, eat distastefully at neighbour women's tomato sandwiches, and are blankly politer and quieter than I have ever seen them. Where is their father?

I find myself counting, in the mind's eye concealed behind my stiff face, what remains of Mother—the chiffon hat in the hat-box, the drawers of clothes, the dresses in the wardrobe, the switches of hair hanging on the dressing-table, the ugly white china rose, the sliver of Castile soap in the dish decorated with moss roses, the stone jars of pickled onions in the pantry, the patched sheets in the linen press, the pumpkins she has already picked and stacked on the tankstand, the crochet-edged pillow-shams, the lines of thrift and thyme along the paths, the cuttings of guelder rose and pelargonium in the cuttings-bed. Which was the last plant she planted? Which was the last biscuit she cut?

This sentimental game ultimately sickens me of myself. What is over cannot be anything other than over. Bury the dead. I grope under my shirts, and find the hidden packet of cigarettes, and smoke one, and then another. Who is now about to regard it as wicked? Bury the dead.

Nevertheless, it is very hard for me to prevent myself from absurd revelations of distress the next day when the coffin is carried through the garden to the hearse. I fight down what deprivation eggs me noisily to commit by making myself remember that this thing being taken from the house is not Mother. Mother was the one who was driven off in a buggy to the hospital ten days ago; Mother left the house then, walking towards the buggy on her own feet with the corn on each little toe.

Father and I and Uncle Martini-Henry sit in the orchestra stalls, the first mourning coach. They wear navy-blue suits, black arm-bands and black ties, Father wearing the ones Mother made him buy for Grandfather Porter's death. Aunt Rosa Bona has brought from Williamstown my black suit, tissue paper and free coat-hanger and all, sin in a box. Mother, dying, has taken the trouble to say she forgives this sin which was manufactured to make appearances at Tennis Dances and the *Café Latin*. It was not made for funerals. I wear my grey Harris Tweed, no arm-band, and a green tie. I know I have shocked Father who does not care that he is shocked, just as he could be shocking me, who abhors being shocked, but is momentarily beyond all that, by holding my hand, brutally and desperately, hurting, holding with both his hands in a kind of golfing grip.

It is necessary for me to support this middle-aged, virile, athletic man from the car to the grave, and to keep my arm tightly around him.

When the first shovel of clay is slid down on to the coffin-lid, he emits guttural moans, and tries to step down into the grave. Hamlet, eh? I hold him tight, this human and wicked mortal who is moaning, and striving like a child against my heart, weeping perhaps in the awareness that, now, Mother gone, Mother disposed of like rubbish in a flowery rubbish-heap, he is free to begin destruction, to live on in a comfort of inferior sensuality, free to destroy some of his children with indifference.

The telegram saying that Mother's 'condition' is 'grave' arrives, by chance, at the same time as a venomous but justifiable letter from Miss Hart who is transferred now to another school. The letter threatens 'legal action' if I do not pay back the money. I am in the train to Bairnsdale before I have time to read the letter. Uncaring, unmoved, I screw it up, and drop it into the twilight the train is imprinting with its own din and gold and gushes of spark-shot smoke. I travel mute, an animal waiting the rabbit-killer, frightened for the first time in my life, frightened by the thought of Mother's unimaginable pain and more imaginable fear, frightened that I am to be punished for my own placidity and happy, happy little evils. At Stratford (on Avon), at ten o'clock, I am half-away with sleep and fears when a voice comes calling my name along the carriage-corridor. Aroused to defensive action, locking mind and heart, all my inner and outer doors, I go calm, and await the assault. It is not the assault I expect. It is someone to drive me the rest of the way by motor-car. As whoever drives and I roar through the bush —my first ride in a motor-car—the headlights call into being, and distort to something else, and discard in a gush, a tunnelled and nightmare treescape such as I have never seen. It pours by me, visible and terrible as wasteful time.

> *Row, brothers, row,* my nerves sing, *the*
> *stream runs fast,*
> *The rapids are near, and the daylight's past.*

In Bairnsdale, the car stops outside what is, to me, the Deaconess Miss Rodda's Church of England Girls' Hostel, now a private hospital. I descend, and thank, and comb my hair before I open the gate. As I walk, for the second time in my life, up the wide, terra-cotta-tiled path, and skirt the oval of conspicuously well-behaved plants in front of the ascent of slate steps, I perceive that everything is in apple-pie order. I am met at the door by a swift shadow smelling of ether.

This shadow, this nurse, takes me, as the Deaconess once did, into the front room.

On the white, white bed, in the place where I sat in the asthmatic arm-chair holding my Panama hat and the bruised and speckled apple, lies a woman.

This is she, this is Mother.

This fowl-like creature with the sharp nose and the diminished cheeks and the damp hair and the glittering eyes is Mother. On one side of her stands the Matron, her spectacles filled with electric light. On the other side, willowy and fresh, mildly agitating a Fijian fan, stands a shirt-collar advertisement handsome minister with lips too red and soft for peace. Where is Father?

Stirring weakly against the air as against great cobwebs, writhing like something in a chrysalis, the being on the bed calls out, 'I waited, Laddie. I waited. I wouldn't let them let me die until you came.'

Oh, God, the wreckage of bones on the bed is frightened! It is frightened, and in the arena fighting with itself. I stumble blindly towards the fight. Yes, this is Mother. She kisses me. That, *that*, is the last of her supply of kisses. It is a dry kiss, light as the touch of a passing flame. She, the woman smelling of too much eau-de-Cologne, of champagne, and some sly undercurrent of sourness, is my mother giving me her last kiss.

'This is my eldest son,' says Mother, momentarily calling up her social manner. The surfaces of her lips move strangely and slowly, never quite meeting, so that her teeth glint like dog's between them. 'From Melbourne. I waited for him. I waited.'

The social manner slips.

'There was I,' sings Mother blurrily, 'waiting at the church, waiting at the. . . .'

Her eyes close.

They open. She has closed them to think up another voice which she now uses, an abraded version of her 'charming' voice. She has controlled her eyes too, *just*. They look sly.

'I should like to be left alone with my son for a while. Do you mind, Matron? *Dear?* It may be the last opportunity.'

'Now, now, *now*, deah,' says Matron. 'Theah'll be plenty of taime, deah. Many yeahs. But we'll pop out. . . .' She looks at the minister. '. . . and hev a cup of tea whaile you hev a little chat.'

They go, the minister handing me the fan with a deep, weak gaze nothing to do with dying women or fans. His fingers which touch and press mine (sympathetically?) are damp; the handle of the fan is tepid and damp.

'Shahmpeen, whenever she wants it,' says Matron, touching the bottle as she goes.

'She's the cat's mother,' says Mother. 'Give me some champagne. From that thing with the spout.'

I pour. I feed the unsteady mouth, as though feeding a pot-plant, from the white spouted vessel.

> '*Shahmpeen Chawlie is m' name,*
> *Shahmpeen-drinkin' is m' game,*'

sings Mother.

I make little noises. I begin to cry. I am forced by myself to bend to kiss this silly frightened face.

'Don't kiss me,' the face says sharply, twisting itself aside from my face which is dripping like a hung-out sock. 'And stop that crying. Don't cry, Laddie. Don't cry. I'll be home to cook your next Christmas dinner.'

Her eyes, however, must leave us. The woman and her fear argue with each other.

'Next Christmas. Of course I will.'

'No, I won't. I said good-bye to the children this afternoon.'

'I'll be there cooking the mince pies.'

'Johnny's only six. I'll never see him again.'

'Next Christmas. . . .'

That is enough. It is not too painful to tell. Nothing is. It is too boring, too hopelessly silly. It is unrehearsed. It contains no message. It proves nothing. It goes on and on for hours. The frightened mind struggling with its poisoned cells, strives now to present this, now that, of its suffering and defiance and confusion and imprisonment. Its past with all its love and absurdity, all its nobility and frailty, splashes over into the untrappable present with its fears and uselessnesses.

'Don't worry about the black suit,' she says. 'I forgive you.'

'Look after your father,' she says.

'Be a good boy always,' she says.

'Comb your hair,' she says.

'I owe Mr. Dahlensberg twenty-five pounds. Pay him,' she says. 'Don't tell your father.'

'Don't worry about the black suit.'

'Be a good boy, a good boy.'

'Sell the Renardi. . . .'

'Your hair. . . .'

Soon enough after long enough, she leaves the littered and dirty shore, she is off and away, adrift in her rudderless skiff on the weedy shallows of delirium, singing, speaking of and to people I have not heard of, tacking here and there in other years and a dimension I know nothing of. Obediently, in a torment of obedience, I clamp down on my tears.

I am not the only watcher. The minister performs his last duties, and departs. There are Father, the Matron, a nurse, shadows that stand or come and go. I am not the only watcher until, out of the whisperings, I hear my mother say:

> '*Tit-tat-toe, my first go!*
> *Three jolly butcher-boys all in a row. . . .*'

Now, I am the only watcher. I am alone. Mother and I are alone, alone, alone, alone, alone. Her bedtime plait hangs over her shoulder; its end, tied with tape, lies on the furry tablecloth. The Kensington lamp breathes like a warm golden animal. It purrs and stutters. The fire is crumbling apart like incandescent cake, like a world in dissolution.

> *Stick one up! Stick one down!*
> *Stick one in the dead man's ground!*

Alone.

I have been punished at last, at long long last.

As my defences of happiness crack within me, they and I begin to make sounds I did not think I could, hard and harsh, bestial and elemental sounds. When I have pillaged my reservoir of tears. when I have finished my first bout of agony at the marble chimney-piece, when I have done what all humans must do, Matron is saying, 'Ai'm affreed she's gone,' and is wiping with a piece of cotton-wool a disgusting and pathetic occurrence of foam from Mother's lips so that Father and I may kiss what no longer needs kisses.

It is from this thing on the bed I must now flee.

Oh, God, the watcher on the cast-iron balcony screams out within me, Oh, God, put me back on the balcony! One scream within, and one only. There is no one to hear.

God is dead.

Father, undaunted, takes the rings from the fingers, and puts them in his wallet. It is his turn now for agony. I wait until his gruntings and sobbings subside, meantime straightening my tie, combing my hair, and setting my face at nix-nought-nothing.

At that moment I am sure that God is dead, that any love I must have for the world I must make for myself—beginning, at last, after years of happy nothing, at nothing. It has become simple. Mother is dead, God is dead, love is dead, all that I was is dead. So, I think, waiting for Father to make himself publicly possible, waiting to begin watching again those who are watching what they think is me, the dead one.

I do not know that, not only have I not started to die, I have not started to live.

I have not even helped Father across the road to the rectory.

Hedley, Victoria, Australia.
22 Hogarth Road, Earl's Court, London.
March-September, 1962.